The Guide to FamilySearch Online

By James L. Tanner

Published by Bookmark Graphics

The Guide to FamilySearch Online

James L. Tanner
Bookmark Graphics
625 E. University
Mesa, Arizona 85203
genealogyarizona@gmail.com

ISBN 978-1-61166-015-9

Printed and bound in the United States of America

This Guide is dedicated to the memory of Allison Bowers

Table of Contents

Preface

What Is FamilySearch?

FamilySearch is a website, a tunnel in the mountains, a library, an indexing program, a scanning project and many more things besides. Overall it is a corporation owned by The Church of Jesus Christ of Latter-day Saints (the Church) with several functions relating to family history and genealogy. The purpose of this Guide is to provide a comprehensive guide to one aspect of FamilySearch: its websites. In order to understand where all of the resources on those websites come from, it is important to discover a little of the history and philosophy and religious background of the organization.

The involvement of the Church in the field of genealogy cannot be understood without examining its doctrine and teachings. As stated by Joseph Fielding Smith, a former President, "Salvation for the dead is the system whereunder those who would have accepted the gospel in this life, had they been permitted to hear it, will have the chance to accept it in the spirit world, and will then be entitled to all the blessings which passed them by in mortality" (*DS* 2:100-196). Provisions have been made, therefore, for the living to provide, vicariously, ordinances of salvation for their deceased family forebears and friends. This cannot be done without information about the dead."

At the April General Conference of the Church in 1894, President Wilford Woodruff announced that he had received a revelation and admonished the members saying, "We want the Latter day Saints from this time to trace their genealogies as far as they can, and to be sealed to their fathers and mothers. Have children sealed to their parents, and run this chain through as far as you can get it…. This is the will of the Lord to this people." Later that year, the First Presidency of the Church authorized the formation of the Genealogical Society of Utah. Franklin D. Richards was selected as its first president. Archibald F. Bennett, later an executive secretary, gave the following historical summary: "It was to be benevolent, educational, and religious in purpose-benevolent in gathering together into a library books that would help the people trace their ancestry; educational in teaching the people how to trace their ancestry…; religious in that they would do all in their power to encourage the people to perform in the temples all the necessary ordinances."[1]

One of the founders of the Genealogical Society of Utah, Nephi Anderson made the following statement in January of 1912:

"I see the records of the dead and their histories gathered from every nation under heaven to one great central library in Zion — the largest and best equipped in the nations, but in Zion will be the records of the last resort and authority. Trained genealogists will find constant work in all nations having unpublished records, searching among the archives for families and family connections. Then, as temples multiply, and the work enlarges to its ultimate proportions, this Society, or some organization growing out of this Society, will have in its care some elaborate, but perfect system of exact registration and checking, so that the work in the temples may be conducted without confusion or duplication. And so throughout the years, reaching into the Millennium of peace, this work of salvation will go on, until every worthy soul that can be found from early records will have been searched out and officiated for; and then the unseen world will come to our aid, the broken links will be joined, the tangled threads will be placed in order, and the purposes of God in placing salvation within the reach of all will have been consummated." [2]

This religious mandate explains, only in part, the vast effort the Church and its members have expended in creating one of the largest record repositories for genealogical information in the world. It is truly amazing to contemplate the extensive genealogical organization of the Church.

Through the years the Church's genealogical interests have been conducted under a variety of names and organizations. Beginning in 1894 the Church sponsored the Genealogical Society of Utah and despite the name changes in 1944 to The Genealogical Society of The Church of Jesus Christ of Latter-day Saints, then in 1975 to The Genealogical Department, later in 1987, and another name change to The Family History Department, the Church kept using the name and titles of the Genealogical Society of Utah. In 2000 the Church consolidated the Family History and Historical departments into the Family and Church History Department. Today FamilySearch is used as the tradename for the Utah Genealogical Society, even though FamilySearch, International is also a separate corporation.

FamilySearch, the Larger View

FamilySearch provides a broad spectrum of support for all aspects of the genealogical research cycle and for all levels of expertise. Many of the original source records are uniquely available from FamilySearch. There are several areas of content; original source records, compiled records and indexes, instructional material, forms, administrative materials, finding aids, personal information and family trees. With such a wide range of content and, considering the fact that changes are being constantly made, the reader is encouraged to explore the websites frequently to find additional information and features.

Why You Need This Guide

If you are interested in finding your ancestors, as millions of people around the world are, then you need this guide. In the rapidly changing world of technology as it applies to genealogy, there are relatively few people who realize the vast scope of the FamilySearch online resources. So much attention is paid to commercial online subscription websites through the media, popular TV shows and advertising, that the low-key, almost background image of FamilySearch is lost in the hype. This Guide provides detailed instructions to the content and organizations of all of the current FamilySearch websites. You will likely be surprised not only with the extent of the lesser known sites, but also with features in more popular and better known sites.

During the past few years, more and more genealogical resources have been finding their way online and the FamilySearch websites provide the most extensive free genealogical resources available on the Internet. Recently, these online resources have grown to the point that you cannot ignore these resources and be thorough in your genealogical research. This is especially true with almost daily online addition of digitized source documents and indexes from the extensive collection of microfilms acquired since 1938 when filming began. During calendar year 2010, continuing into 2011 and on into the future, FamilySearch added and will continue to add, hundreds of millions of original source records including both indexes and digitized images. In addition, FamilySearch is in the process of developing a huge family tree collection, now referred to as New FamilySearch. These combined records include well over a billion individuals in a pedigree-like structure. This Guide is your guide to these incredibly large and complex databases.

If you are a long time user of FamilySearch websites, you will find insights into features and information you likely did not know existed. But if you are relatively new to FamilySearch, you will find a wealth of instruction that will open windows of opportunity to enriching your genealogical experience.

What Is and Is Not Included In This Guide

Genealogy is an involved and challenging pursuit. This Guide will not teach you how to do genealogy, but the FamilySearch websites can and will help you to learn. This Guide will not help you with the myriad skills needed to research old records and build a credible pedigree but, again, the FamilySearch websites will help you learn the necessary skills. Neither will this Guide go into the details of how to contribute information to New FamilySearch or to the FamilySearch Research Wiki or do FamilySearch Indexing. All of those websites have built in instructions and tutorials and in the case of Indexing and New FamilySearch extensive manuals.

This Guide will help you navigate through the huge and complex online world created by FamilySearch. You will learn, in depth, how the websites are organized and what resources are available. During your study of the websites, if you run across a problem or question, be sure and read further, you will likely find that your difficulty or question was anticipated. I will shortly introduce the extensive Help

Center and other help links available in different parts of the websites. Pay particular attention to the help screens: there are huge resources that will support, not just your online activities, but also all of your genealogical research.

How This Guide Is Organized

If you were going to explore in a jungle, you would probably take along a compass or the current electronic equivalent. This Guide is the guide or compass to FamilySearch and its vast jungle-like web of resources. Sometimes the entryways, or portals, into this web jungle do not give you any idea about the resources hidden within. This Guide takes each of the FamilySearch entryways and leads you through the links with explanations of how to find your way to information about your family you may have otherwise missed.

Each section of this Guide looks at one of the main entryways into the FamilySearch collection of websites and then explores all of the links, giving both an overview of the information available and specific instructions on how to locate the objects of your search. Because some of the websites have significant sub-site resources, like the Research Wiki and TechTips that are part of FamilySearch.org, the sections are further broken down into subsections where appropriate.

Section One covers the major FamilySearch.org website. It begins with a backward look at the old site that was replaced in December, 2010. Each of the following subsections cover a particular portion of the website that works semi-autonomously. There are sections for the Historical Record Collections, the Family History Library Catalog, and other links from the startup page. There are additional sections on the Research Wiki, the Forums, TechTips and other resources on this huge and complex website.

Section Two is devoted to the FamilySearch Indexing program, a huge multi-national volunteer effort to index the scanned images from the FamilySearch Historical Record Collections. The Indexing program has its own online 90 page Guide. Although the Indexing website is linked to FamilySearch it is a separate website and is very heavily used. Current figures for Indexing show that the volunteers are adding about 1.5 million records a day.

Section Three looks at the New FamilySearch program. New FamilySearch has two online guides of over 200 pages in PDF format located in the Help Center. One guide is for members of the Church, the other is designed for those who are not members. It is not the goal of this Guide to reproduce this extensive manual in a different format. For this reason, the discussion of the New FamilySearch program will be more in the nature of an overview with an emphasis on the help resources available and with references to the manual as necessary. The first subsection is an overview of the entire program. Each of the succeeding subsections deal with aspects of the program, such as searching, combining records, entering sources, discussions and so forth.

Section Four presents a look at other FamilySearch websites with resources that have yet to be incorporated into the main FamilySearch.org site. The sites covered include several lesser-known sites, some of which are more related to the FamilySearch organization than to genealogical research.

In discussing the FamilySearch.org websites, an overview will be followed with a detailed analysis of each of the links, both internal and external to the program. In making references to the FamilySearch websites, I have tried to be consistent with the terminology and capitalization as viewed on the websites, which are not always consistent, so please be patient with the text.

What You Need to Have, Besides a Computer, to Use This Guide

This Guide is a reference to an online website. In order to use the information, you will need a computer with a connection to the Internet and a browser such as Internet Explorer, Firefox, Safari or Chrome. The way the information is displayed may vary from browser to browser, but generally websites like those from Family-Search are sophisticated enough to display properly no matter what browser is used. However, if you are experiencing difficulty in viewing a website, you may wish to change to a different browser.

A web browser is a software program that runs on your computer for retrieving, presenting and exploring the World Wide Web. There is a measure of confusion between what is meant by the "Internet" and what is called the "World Wide Web" or simply the Web. The Internet is the hardware, the computers, the connectors, and the memory storage devices. The Web is the system of software applications that include all of the information running on the Internet. A website is a specific location on the Web that can be as simple as a single page of a Blog post or as complicated as the Google search engine. Please see the Glossary at the end of this booi

In order to understand this, or any other Guide about the Internet, you will need to be familiar with the terms used in describing websites, as well as the basic terminology about the Internet and the World Wide Web. There are hundreds of introductory books on the subject of the Internet. Most public libraries will have several books for loan. It probably would not be a good idea for me to suggest looking on the Web for books on learning about the Web. If you can do a book search on the Web, you probably don't need an introductory book.

Much of the communication between FamilySearch and the users of its websites is conducted by email. Although it is possible to register for an LDS Account or a FamilySearch Account without an email address, many of the functions of the different FamilySearch website presuppose that you, the user, have an active email address. There are several ways to sign up for free email on the Web such as Google Mail (gmail) or Yahoo mail. I strongly suggest you have an active email account and check it regularly if you are going to pursue involvement with the FamilySearch websites. If you feel uncomfortable about using your "family" or "personal" email account for FamilySearch, then sign up for an alternative account to be used for your public online presence.

Just a note. Anytime you find a word you do not know. If you do know how to look at the Google.com website. Just type in the word "define:" with the colon, followed by the word you do not know and you will get a list of definitions.

* * * * * * * * * *

A Note on Change and New Editions to this Guide

An active website is ever changing. The basic structure of the site will be conservative, but the content will change as FamilySearch continues to add records from its huge collection of digitized microfilm. There is no way this Guide, or any other static print media, could completely reflect the content of the site, so it is not the intention of this guide to provide current lists of content, but to provide a guide to the structure of the websites. If there are changes in the sites which are not reflected in this guide, it will be covered in future revisions. Even though it is inevitable that the sites will change, it was my intention to provide a starting point for understanding the scope of the sites. Future consolidations may eliminate some sites entirely so I apologize in advance for any seeming omissions caused by unforeseen changes. Please feel free to contact me about any inconsistencies or omissions you may find at my current email address for this Guide listed on the copyright page.

An additional note, many parts of the FamilySearch.org website could be considered to be "under construction." Links may not work as expected or at all. You may end up outside of the site with no convenient return link. Do not panic. Simply return to your browser's home page, point your browser to FamilySearch.org and start all over again on the FamilySearch.org startup page.

If there are going to be so many changes to the websites, how can a printed Guide keep up with all those changes? The answer is print-on-demand. As changes are made to the websites, those changes can be incorporated into subsequent printings of this manual. Since only enough copies are printed to satisfy immediate demand, when you purchase the

Guide, you will always be getting the latest edition. New versions of the book will reflect the changes to the FamilySearch websites as they occur.

• • • • • • • • • •

The FamilySearch Help Center

The Help Center is easily one of the most extensive and useful program or website help centers on the Internet. This may seem like hyperbole until you get in and use the product. I will be going into more detail later in the Guide, but look for the links to the Help Center on almost every page. This valuable resource provides answers to questions about all of the FamilySearch products and services. In each topic in this Guide, you will find further references to both the main Help Center and to the various other help resources integrated into the websites. Occasionally, there will be this icon:

This icon is to remind you to look in the Help Center or other help menus for more general information about the websites or to answer specific questions.

More about Genealogy and The Church of Jesus Christ of Latter-day Saints

Members of the Church of Jesus Christ of Latter-day Saints (LDS) believe in the eternal nature of families. For a more extensive discussion of this topic please refer to the Church's website LDS.org or its companion site, Mormon.org. Because of our beliefs concerning the eternal nature of families, members of the Church, perform proxy ordinances for their deceased family members who did not have the opportunity to hear the Gospel of Jesus Christ during their lifetimes or have the ordinances performed, for example baptisms and marriage sealings. This sacred work is done in the Church Temples scattered throughout the world.

Because FamilySearch.org and all of the associated sites are Church sponsored, of a necessity, there will be numerous references to the fact that these websites are used by Church members to not only search out their deceased ancestors, but also to record the dates of the Temple ordinances. At the time of the writing of this Guide, the New.FamilySearch.org website is available only to members of the Church and to a select number of those outside the membership. During the next year or so, the site will become more accessible until it is completely available to the general public.

* * * * * * * * * *

A Note about Formatting in this Guide

As you read this Guide, you may note instances where you would expect initial capital letters or other types of formatting and do not find them. As much as possible, I have tried to use the exact same format as the websites, including the use of initial capital letters even though it may appear to be a mistake. I did not want to call attention to the differences, so I have not marked them in any way. If my text differs from that on the website, then the mistake or inconsistency is mine.

You have probably noticed that I have inserted comments about topics not strictly related to the Guide or even in some cases, to FamilySearch. These asides are identified by the preceeding and the following row of dots.

* * * * * * * * * *

Section One: FamilySearch.org

The Origins of the FamilySearch.org Website

Beginning in 1998, FamilySearch began the development of a website. On May 24, 1999, the website went online for the first time[3] and almost immediately crashed because of the overload of use.[4] As of the date of this writing, FamilySearch.org, the website, receives roughly 250,000 hits a day.[5] Since its introduction on the Web in early September 2010, the newer Beta.FamilySearch.org website has climbed to over 150,000 hits per day. With the changeover from the Beta.FamilySearch.org site in December of 2010, all of the existing traffic was consolidated onto Family-Search.org. As of the date of the writing of this Guide, the older FamilySearch.org website was also available online, but is scheduled to be removed at an unspecified time in the future, possibly at the end of calendar year 2011. Measuring Web traffic depends on data gathered from both the source, that is, the website being measured, and from linking sites and is only a rough estimate in many cases. The owner of a website can obtain much more accurate information, but any information about Internet traffic should be viewed as estimates.

* * * * * * * * *

A Note about Website Organization

Websites can be organized in almost any possible fashion, but the organizations usually fall into two general categories, web-like or linear. A linear website is dominated by pull-down menus. Clicking on or holding your mouse curser over a pull-down menu gives you a list of options to choose from. You move to the option by either holding down your mouse button or simply moving your cursor down the list to highlight your selection. Once you click on your selection, the website changes to your selection. One way the sites are maintained is to keep all of the pull-down menu items selections available on every page. In a sense, you never leave the home page. The older FamilySearch.org website was very much a classical linear site.

As websites have changed over the years, newer sites use a web-like approach to their organization. The updated FamilySearch.org website uses a more web-like approach. There are no pull-down menus. If you click on a link, you are taken to that area of the site and hopefully, clicking on the logo will take you back to the beginning. The more you use the Internet, the more comfortable you are with the weblike approach to organization. Less experienced users do have a tendency to forget how to navigate a weblike site. If you find yourself having difficulty navigating the updated FamilySearch.org website, just remember to click on the logo. If that fails to take you back to the start-up page, then just re-start the website from your browser.

• • • • • • • • • •

The Historical or Classic FamilySearch.org Website

At the time of the change over to the new website design in December, 2010 this is what the old, historical site looked like:

Figure 1.1

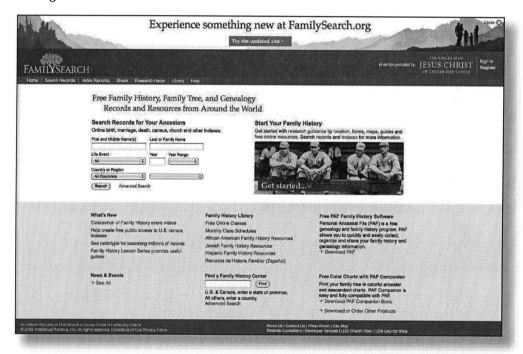

In order to understand the new site and to understand the interrelationship between the various FamilySearch websites, it is important to review some of the resources of the original site. Here is a list of those resources:

- FamilySearch/Family History Library Catalog located under the Library tab.
- Ancestral File
- International Genealogical Index

- Pedigree Resource File
- Social Security Death Index
- Vital Records Index
- Record Search Pilot
- Historical Archives Collection

One of the major concerns expressed by users at the time of the changeover was the disposition of all of the old resources. Whenever you use an Internet resource for genealogy, you need to understand the resource's origin to determine the reliability of the data contained in the resource. The following, is a short discussion of each of the major resources originally available in the old FamilySearch.org website. It is helpful to review the origin of these various resources in order to understand the migration of these resources to the newer websites.[6] Information for this section was obtained, in part, from James B. Allen, et. al., *Hearts Turned to the Father*, a special issue of *BYU Studies* 34:2 (1994-95), pp. 303-337.

FamilySearch/Family History Library Catalog

Often described as the largest genealogical collection in the United States, the Family History Library contains over 2.4 million roles of microfilmed genealogical records; 727,000 microfiche; 356,000 books, serials, and other formats; 4500 periodicals; and 3725 electronic databases. These records contain the names of more than 2 billion deceased persons. All of these resources are extensively catalogued in the Family History Library Catalog. Currently, the Catalog is being expanded to include digitized materials as well as books and other materials from the worldwide Family History Centers. The Catalog was updated with the release of the updated FamilySearch.org website in December 2010.

The Ancestral File

The Ancestral File (AF) is a compilation of more than 36 million names on user submitted records from previous Church efforts in 1966 and following years, asking the members of the Church to submit their four and five generation Family Group Records. Because of duplications and errors in the original submissions, in 1979 another effort was made to have the members produce an accurate set of records. These newer records were the basis of the Ancestral File.[7] Programming for The Ancestral File began in 1984 and the first prototype was released in 1987. The file became publicly available at the Family History Library in April, 1988.

The names in the Ancestral File are organized into family groups and pedigrees and are therefore considered to be lineage-linked records. Individuals who submitted their records to the Ancestral File may no longer be living and the contact information may be out of date. The submissions to the Ancestral File do not contain the date of the submission, nor do they usually contain source material detailing where the information was obtained.

At the time the Ancestral File records were computerized, the database was closed and no further additions or corrections to the file can be made. No attempt has been made to verify the data in the Ancestral File and the information should only be used for beginning research.

Each of the records in the Ancestral File has a unique number referred to as the Ancestral File Number (AFN). Many computer genealogical database programs can display the Ancestral File Number including the Personal Ancestral File program.

International Genealogical Index

The International Genealogical Index (IGI) is a database that contains several hundred million names of deceased persons from throughout the world. As part of the index, the IGI also contains information about a single event for each of the deceased persons. If there were multiple events, such as birth, baptism, sealing, etc. then a record was created for each event. Each entry is a standalone record and is not linked to any other records even within the same family or even pertaining to the same person. The majority of the information in the index reflects collections of vital records from the early 1500s to 1885. These records are often referred to as "extracted" records because volunteers copied the records from original sources.

The IGI was first published on microfiche in 1975 as the Computer File Index (CFI) and went through various editions. The original CFI included names extracted (copied) by members of the Church and other names submitted by Church members since 1970. The name of the file was changed in 1981 to the International Genealogical Index. The IGI grew by about 9 million names each year, expanding from 34 million names in 1975, to 81 million names in 1981, 108 million in 1984, 147 million in 1988 and finally 187 million names in 1992.

In 1988, the IGI was issued on compact disk; with the rise of online resources, the entire file was finally put onto the FamilySearch.org website. The IGI continued to expand until presently, it contains approximately 600 million names, with an addendum containing an additional 125 million names.

Pedigree Resource File

The Pedigree Resource File (PRF) is a user-contributed file of millions of lineage-linked individuals and families submitted in the GEDCOM format. In addition to an online index, the original submitted files are available on a series of CDs and DVDs from the Church Distribution Services (http://www.ldscatalog.com). The latest set of disks as of the date of publication of this Guide was Set 42 containing disc 142 and an Index. No merges, corrections or additions were made to the files submitted to FamilySearch.

Social Security Death Index

The Social Security Death Index (SSDI) is prepared and updated by the U.S. Government. The file is available only on the Internet and contains records of deaths of those persons who had social security numbers and whose death was reported to the Social Security Administration. Some of the records in the SSDI date back to 1942, but most of the records start in 1962.

The Vital Records Index

This online index originally contained records from Mexico and Scandinavia only. However, other indexes were available in compact disk format for Australia, the British Isles, Middle America, North America and Western Europe. Most of these sources have been discontinued and only the compact disks for Australian and Mexico Vital Records indexes are currently available. The other records have been merged into the Historical Record Collections.

Record Search Pilot

The predecessor to the present Historical Record Collections was the Record Search Pilot launched in 2010 and available from the pull-down tab called Search Records. With the development of the updated site, additions to the Record Search Pilot were discontinued later in 2010. The number of collections in Record Search Pilot was frozen at 378 collections. Beginning in December of 2010, all of the new records were added to the updated FamilySearch.org Historical Record Collections including the 378 collections on Record Search Pilot. Just so there is no misunderstanding, the Record Search Pilot collections are all incorporated into the updated FamilySearch.org website.

Historical Books/Family History Archive

Also available on the old FamilySearch.org website under the Search Records pull-down menu or tab was the Historical Books collection, entitled the Family History Archive or Archives (There are both singular and plural references). This program at Brigham Young University digitizes published genealogy and family history books from participating libraries. The libraries at the time of this Guide's publication included: the FamilySearch Family History Library, the Allen County Public Library, the Houston Public Library – Clayton Library Center for Genealogical Research, the Mid-Continent Public Library – Midwest Genealogy Center, the BYU Harold B. Lee Library, the BYU-Hawaii Joseph F. Smith Library, and the Church of Jesus Christ of Latter-day Saints Church History Library.

The books from the FamilySearch Family History Library also include volumes from the various Family History Centers around the world.

As books are scanned, links to the books are included in the Family History Library Catalog. There will be more explanation of these links in following sections.

Analysis of the Old Databases

The information in all of these databases was preserved in some form or another, either completely or partially, in the updated websites. Except for the Social Security Death Index, none of these records could be considered to be original or primary source records. The Ancestral File, the IGI and the PRF were all derived from other pre-existing records either through records extraction as in the IGI or through users submitting the records to FamilySearch as in the Pedigree Resource File. In the discussion below concerning the updated FamilySearch.org website, I will explain where and how these original records were absorbed into the new databases. Most of the records went into the New.FamilySearch.org program but a few, such as the Vital Records Indexes were included in the Historical Record Collections. The choice to include records in the new databases, for the most part, seems to depend on an evaluation of how the records fit into the newer collections. All of the information concerning Church Temple ordinances was included in New.FamilySearch.org

● ● ● ● ● ● ● ● ●

A Note About Screen Shots and FamilySearch URLs

Throughout this Guide, I use a variety of screen shots, or images of the various screens online from the websites. To get the most out of this Guide, it would be good idea to follow the links and see the screens on your own computer as you go through the Guide. That way, you will be able to experience the interaction of the websites. If there is something new on the page, you can explore the new features on your own. In my experience, I find many people who are upset when a website changes. Websites are by their very nature dynamic and not static. In the course of discussing the FamilySearch websites, I will make this point quite a few times to remind you that the changes are not bad, just different.

Speaking of changes, at the time this Guide was written, FamilySearch was in the process of converting all of its web addresses (URLs) to a

consistent format. For example, Wiki.FamilySearch.org becomes Family-
Search.org/wiki. You will see both types of address in this Guide. The
older form of address will still work for some time.

● ● ● ● ● ● ● ● ●

The Updated FamilySearch.org Website

FamilySearch is constantly in the process of updating and redesigning their
websites. Some of the elements of the site are designed to be updated such as press
releases, Blogs and update announcements, but other elements of the sites change
from time to time. Here is a sample of the main startup page for the FamilySearch.
org website:

Figure 1.2

Overview

Despite its deceptively simple interface, the FamilySearch.org website contains hugely important genealogical resources; the Historical Record Collections, the Family History Library Catalog, the Research Wiki, instructional videos and almost all of the resources from the older site. The Historical Record Collections are the online images the FamilySearch project to scan the 2.4 million rolls of microfilm stored in the Granite Mountain Records Vault near Salt Lake City, Utah. The Collection also contains indexes obtained through FamilySearch partnerships with other entities.[8] The Research Wiki went online in about 2007 and contains tens of thousands of articles concerning genealogical research and records sources. Both the Historical Record Collections and the FamilySearch Research Wiki are continuing to grow at a phenomenal rate, with records being added almost daily. With the exception of the records incorporated from the previous website, the material in the updated site is almost all entirely new to the Internet. Although the initiation of the projects that created the Research Wiki and the Historical Record Collections predate the introduction of the updated website, it was only after the website was introduced that these records began growing at a phenomenal rate.

The Family History Library Catalog has also expanded its scope to contain references to digitize family and local histories. Although, the introduction of the links from the Family History Library Catalog to the digitized materials was begun before the website was updated, the redesign of the way that the material is presented by a catalog search assists the users to identify the readily available digitized material.

In addition, to the huge databases of resource material, the website also contains links to many instructional videos and other resource materials. Some of these materials were previously available, but because of the new design of the website, the resources are now more readily accessible.

Where do the records come from? — The Granite Mountain Records Vault

Beginning in 1938, the Church began a systematic program of microfilming original records in repositories around the world. By 1954 the collection had exceeded 100,000 microfilm rolls. Plans were developed to excavate a vast storage vault in Little Cottonwood Canyon, east of Salt Lake City, Utah. The rocks in that area are a solid mass of quartz monzonite which provides an optimal environment for storing and preserving all types of historical records, particularly the millions of rolls of microfilm. Blasting and drilling began in 1960 and by 1966 the tunnel into the mountain was dedicated and named the Granite Mountain Records Vault. By 1998, the first digital images began to be made of the archive records and by 2004 a program was underway to convert the microfilm images to digital format for publication online. The first images were put online on FamilySearch.org in 2007.[9]

The entire acquisition process and storage of the records is accomplished under the direction of FamilySearch. Beginning the record acquisition process, FamilySearch committees prioritize where and when the records will be obtained. Representatives of FamilySearch negotiate with each archive or repository to digitize the records for preservation. Online access to the records is offered as an incentive to allow access to the records. The records are then scheduled for digitizing. Presently nearly all records are captured with high-resolution digital cameras. The originals are sent to FamilySearch in Salt Lake City for auditing so that the images will work in the system. Each of the record collections is then described and cataloged. Index points called "waypoints" are added to each collection of records to facilitate browsing. The information added to the records includes the arrangement or order of the records, places, dates and record types.

Once the records are waypointed, they are ready to go online. FamilySearch also has an ongoing program to index all of the records. Hundreds of thousands of volunteers worldwide donate their time and expertise to compile names, dates and places into online indexes. The records are standardized with names and places, making the images easier to search, and are then published online.[10]

* * * * * * * * * *

A Note about the Social Security Death Index (SSDI)

Although I referred to the Social Security Death Index (SSDI) as an original source, it also contains derived or copied information. There is a small but significant error rate in the social security numbers themselves, since it was not until 1972 when applicants were asked if they had already been issued a number, or were asked for proof of identity. The fact that a source is primary or original does not necessarily mean that it is either accurate or reliable. Every source record has to be evaluated on its own merits, including the SSDI. When possible, information should be compared to other sources.

* * * * * * * * * *

Links on the Startup Page

Figure 1.3

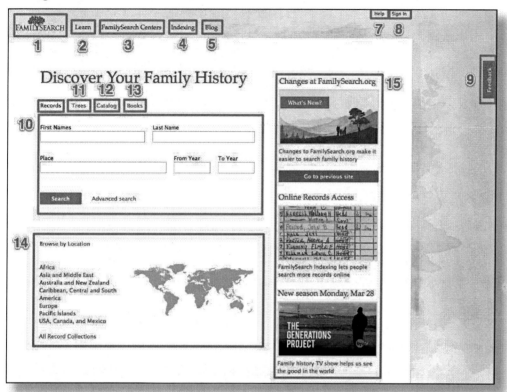

Here is a screen shot of the top part of the startup page. For convenience, I call the first page of the websites, the startup page rather than the older term "home page." A home page implies that it is someplace to come back to in order to reach other parts of the website. Today's websites do not rely so much on the concept of ordered pages. There really is no first or second sequence to using the FamilySearch.org website. Most of the resources are either independent of each other or linked in some way because of interaction. Don't worry about this right now. As you work through the various options you will see that the site is really a loosely linked series of almost independent websites.

Each of the links has each been identified with a number. Each number corresponds to a description below identifying the link in more detail. For example, if you want to know about the logo, marked Number 1 on the screen shot, you can go to #1: Logo below and find out what happens when you click on this link. By finding the screen that corresponds to where you are in the website you can find your way around and through the site with ease.

This is probably a good time to remind you again that FamilySearch.org is a website and websites can change from day to day and even from minute to minute. As you look at the screen shots used as examples, you may find that items have changed over time. In the screen shot above, those links marked #15 are very likely to change because they are used for announcements and news about the website. If a new link appears on a page, just be brave and click on it to see where it goes. You may find a whole new FamilySearch website has been added.

Just another note, on the old website, and commonly on other websites, there are a number of tabs with pull-down menus to add to the selection of items from the Home Page. Here, none of these links have pull-down menus; all of the links take you directly to another page in the website. This may seem confusing at first, but as you will see, the very first link will usually take you back to the startup page. I say "usually" because not all of the logos throughout the website, at the time this Guide is being written, have been linked back to the first startup page.

Now, here we go with the list of the links on the top part of the startup page:

#1: Logo
#2: Learn
#3: FamilySearch Centers
#4: Indexing
#5: Blog
#6 Settings (Not on the screen until you sign in, see Figure 1.4 below)
#7: Help
#8: Sign in
#9: Feedback
#10: Records
#11: Trees
#12: Catalog
#13: Books
#14: Historical Record Collections
#15: Variable Links

#1: Logo

As I mentioned above, the logo is not just for decoration. Clicking on the logo will usually take you back to the Startup Page. The challenge here is that the whole website is really a loosely linked group of semi-independent websites. For example, when I started writing this Guide, clicking on the logo when searching in the Research Wiki portion of the site, took you back to the Startup Page of the Research Wiki but not back to the Startup Page of the whole website. As I expected, issues like that were eliminated. Now the links for the FamilySearch.org startup page appear on every Wiki page. As the site matures, nearly all of these inconsistencies will be eliminated.

Figure 1.4

• • • • • • • • • •

A Note about Logos

It is becoming more common among website developers to use the site logo as a way to return to the startup page of the website. Most of the larger websites have used this as a convention for years, but it is now being implemented almost universally. If you use the popular Google search site for example, you will soon find out that clicking on the Google logo takes you to the startup page. The convention of using the Logo to return to the startup page is being implemented on all of the FamilySearch websites, but may still not work yet on some of the screens.

• • • • • • • • • •

#2: Learn

The "Learn" link on the startup page is located in the upper portion of the screen and clicking on the link takes you to multiple links including the FamilySearch Research Wiki startup page. The Learn Page also contains links to a long list of Research Courses and a link entitled "Getting Started" that is still under some development. I will come back to the Learn link a little later in the text. But for right now, here is a screen shot showing the Learn link:

Figure 1.5

Clicking on this link takes you to this page, which will be discussed more fully later on in the book.

Figure 1.6

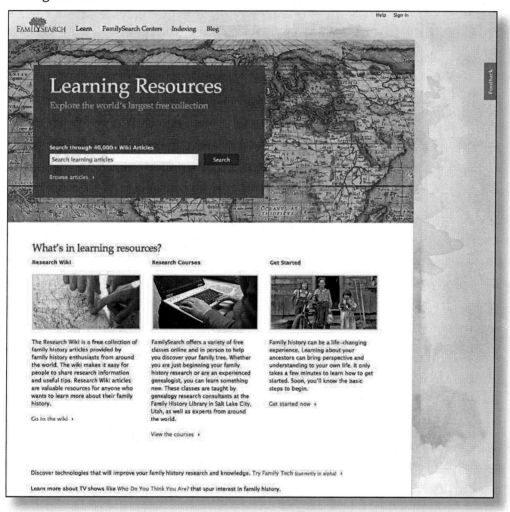

This Learn page seems to change regularly. Note the two links at the bottom of the page. These are new items which may become more integrated into the website in the near future or may be renamed or replaced at some future date. The first of these is the TechTips.FamilySearch.org website introduced at the first RootsTech Conference in 2011. The TechTips website is essentially a blogging site with individual contributors who are not necessarily connected to FamilySearch. The second link takes you to a page that discusses current and past TV programs about genealogy and family history. The link to the page is https://learning.familysearch.org/who-do-you-think-you-are-and-family-history

#3 FamilySearch Centers

Figure 1.7

FamilySearch has over 4500 Family History Centers worldwide. The larger FamilySearch centers have classroom facilities and offer training on genealogical research and the FamilySearch products. Staffed by volunteers, the Centers can offer help understanding and using their available resources. Classes and services are offered for free although there may be charges for copies, supplies and other materials.

Microfilms ordered from the Salt Lake Family History Library are viewed at the Family History Centers through the use of free microfilm readers.

Clicking on the link to the FamilySearch Centers will bring up the following page:

Figure 1.8

If you enter in a zip code or city and state, the search will give you a listing on FamilySearch Centers nearest to your location. Here is an example of a search showing the map with FamilySearch Centers indicated:

Figure 1.9

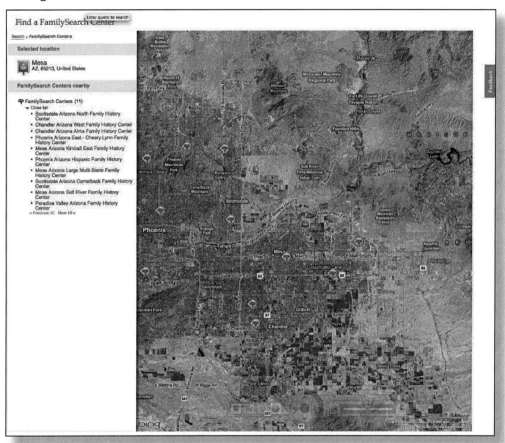

Historically the FamilySearch Centers have been referred to as Family History Centers. The large library in Salt Lake City, Utah is still called the Family History Library. Some of the newer centers, such as the one in Riverton, Utah are now called Family Search Libraries. It is possible that the names of the Centers will change over the next few years as signs are updated. As far as the FamilySearch.org website is concerned they are all called Family Search Centers.

There are several other resources that are available from the FamilySearch Centers' page. There are two links to a list of FamilySearch Online Research Courses. As you will see as we go along, because this website is constructed as web-like, there may be multiple links to the various pages. There are two links on this page to free online classes:

Figure 1.10

Clicking on the either of the two links to the free classes takes you to the following page:

Figure 1.11

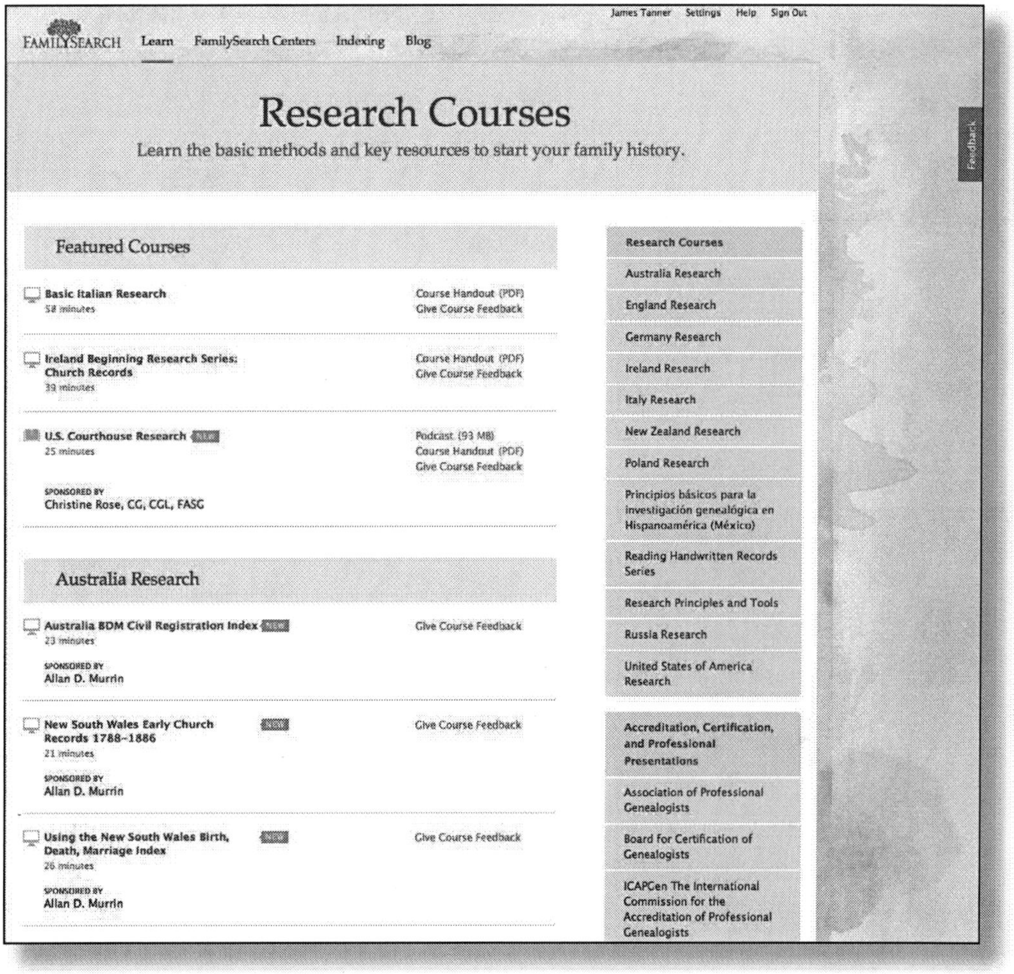

The screen shot only shows the first part of the list. There are well over 120 online courses. Some of the courses have online video presentations with a live instructor; others have online presentations with audio and on screen images. Some are text-based courses.

The range of these courses is noteworthy. There are some very basic courses, while others may be at a professional level. Classes continue to be added and the number and types of offerings will increase.

The Family History Library in Salt Lake City, Utah

Going back to the FamilySearch page, the bottom of the page has a link to the Family History Library in Salt Lake City, Utah. Here is a screen shot of the bottom of the FamilySearch Centers page:

Figure 1.12

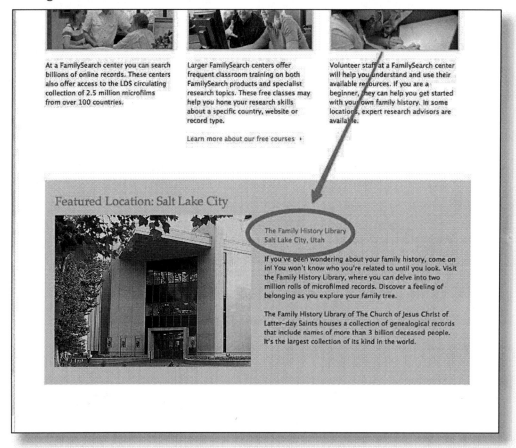

Clicking on the link to the Family History Library takes you to the following informational page. Only a portion of the page is shown, but the page contains up-to-date information on the Family History Library.

Figure 1.13

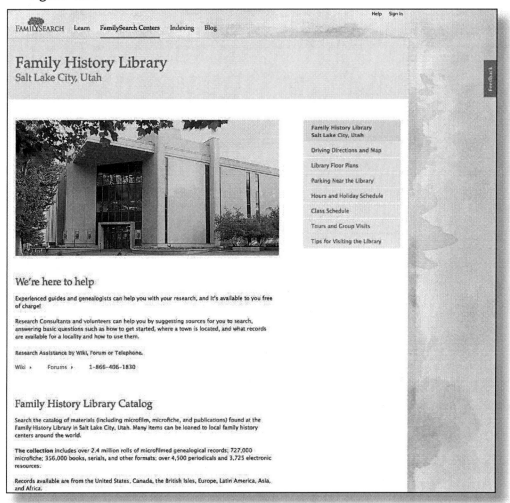

Please note the list of pages linked on the right side of the screen shot. Each of those pages shows specific information about the Family History Library including Driving Directions and Map, the Library Floor Plans, Parking Near the Library, Hours and Holiday Schedule, Class Schedule, Tours, and Group Visits and Tips for Visiting the Library. This page also has links to the FamilySearch Research Wiki and to the FamilySearch Forums that will be covered later on in this Guide. There are also links in the text of the page to the same pages linked in the upper right of the page.

Here are screen shots of some of the links on the page excluding those that will be discussed later in this Guide.

Driving Directions:

Figure 1.13.1

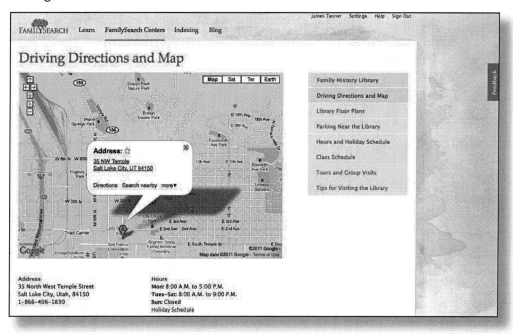

Library Floor Plans:

The Library Floor Plans show the layout of each of the floors of the Family History Library. There are links to each of the maps on the left hand side of the screen. The following is a screen shot of the Main Floor plan. I did not include a screen shot of each of the floors in this Guide as they are all very similar.

Figure 1.13.2

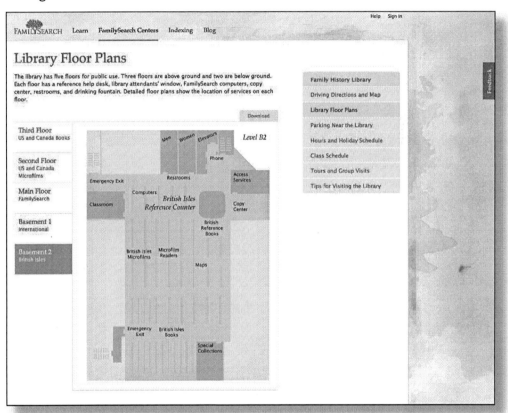

As you can see from this screen shot, the links to the other floor layouts are on the left hand side of the screen. There is also a link to download a PDF copy of each floor plan.

Parking Near the Library:

During the past few years there has been a lot of construction in the down-town area of Salt Lake City. Parking is at a premium and most of the parking has a daily charge. One alternative is to take the TRAX or light rail train that runs every few minutes and stops less than half a block from the Family History Library. Unless you are staying in one of the hotels close by the Library, you will need to consider both the cost and time involved in finding parking. Just one caution, Salt Lake City blocks are very large and the distance from West Temple Street where the entrance to the Library is located, to 200 West is either very close or very far depending on your physical condition. You might also remember that Salt Lake City is high in the mountains and you should be aware of the weather conditions and the altitude if you have any difficulties walking or breathing.

Figure 1.13.3

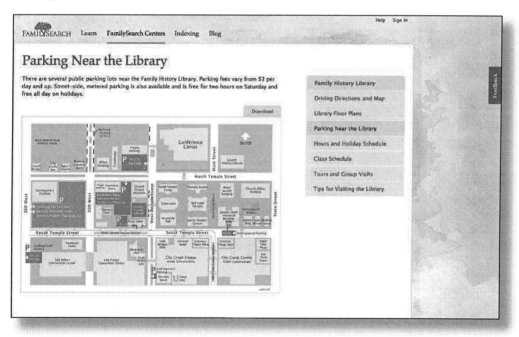

Hours and Holiday Schedule:

This schedule changes from time to time. If you are planning a trip to Salt Lake City to visit the Family History Library, I would suggest you verify the hours the Library is open when you plan to be there. Although the hours don't change much, there are days when the Library is closed that are not commonly observed outside of Utah, such as the 24th of July, which celebrates the entrance of the pioneers into the Salt Lake Valley. Here is a screen shot of the Hours and Holiday Schedule page:

Figure 1.13.4

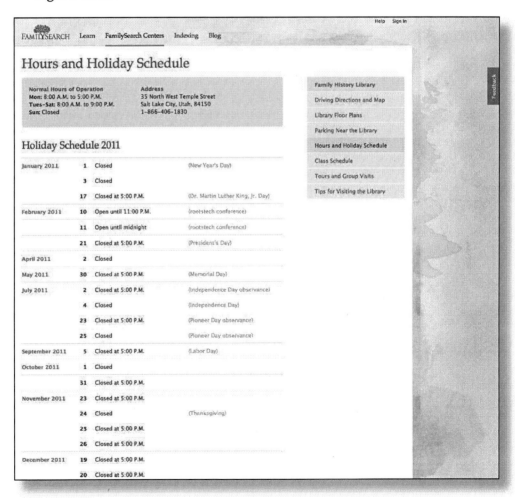

Family History Library Class Schedule:

The Class Schedule will also change frequently. Some classes have limited seating so you may wish to ask about getting to the class early. Also some classes require registration. The calendar on the left side of the screen scrolls through the months for future planning as shown by the arrow on the screen shot of an older version of the page:

Figure 1.13.5

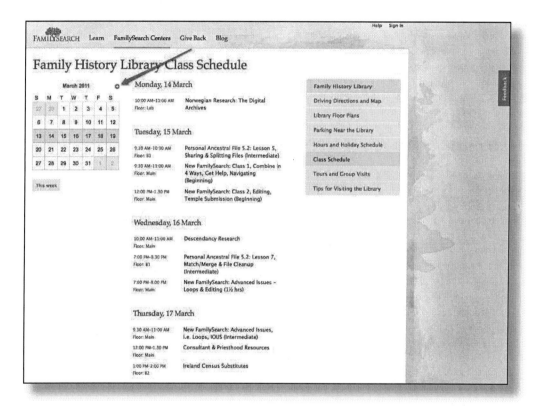

Tours and Group Visits:

This page provides information and a registration form for Tours or Group visits. The following is a screen shot of part of the page:

Figure 1.13.6

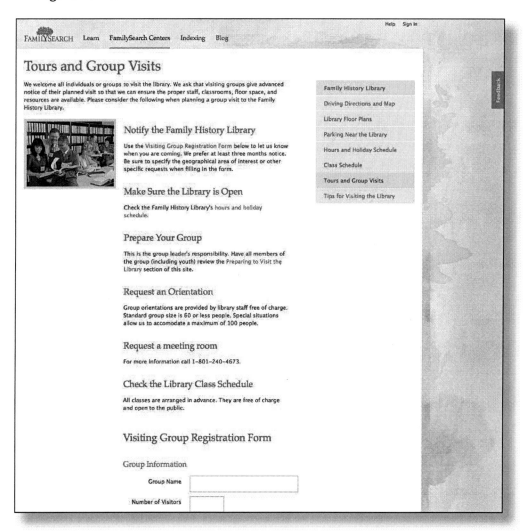

Tips for Visiting the Library:

Although this page is entitled "Tips," it is very important information to make a productive visit to the Family History Library. Anytime you go to a library, especially the Family History Library, you want to have clear research objectives in mind or written down. Your first visit to the Library can be overwhelming and you may spend more time than you expected learning how the Library functions and how to use the resources. It also surprising how busy the Library can be. Do not hesitate to ask questions; there are always a lot of people there to help. Here is a portion of the Tips for Visiting the Library page for reference:

Figure 1.13.7

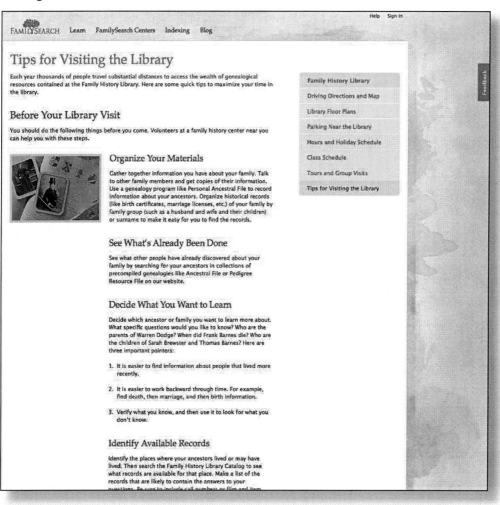

Back to the Startup Page

By this point, you may have forgotten the startup page of the entire website. You can return to the startup page by clicking on the logo in the upper left hand corner of the screen. At this point I am going back to the startup page for the entire website. For reference, here is the same screen shot we had previously with the numbers to refresh your memory: (Note: Number 6 is missing and is not on the screen until you sign in).

Figure 1.3 *(Repeated)*

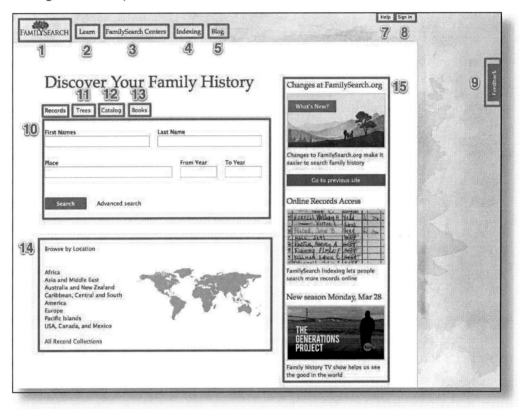

Now I will continue with the explanation of each of the numbered links.

#4 Indexing

Figure 1.14

There are a lot of ways you can contribute time and resources back to the system. Indexing is one of the major ways you can help and participate in providing a valuable service to the genealogical community. I will go into the Indexing link later in another section of the Guide.

 FamilySearch Indexing is a huge cooperative enterprise where volunteers from all over the world are helping to index the Historical Record Collections (See #10 below). The Help Center has a specific area for Indexing that contains a 90 page User's Guide to FamilySearch Indexing (September 2010)

Skipping ahead a little, there is another small link among twenty-one others, on the bottom of the startup page entitled "Give Back." I will be discussing all of these links later on in the Guide, but here is a screen shot showing the Give Back link:

Figure 1.14.1

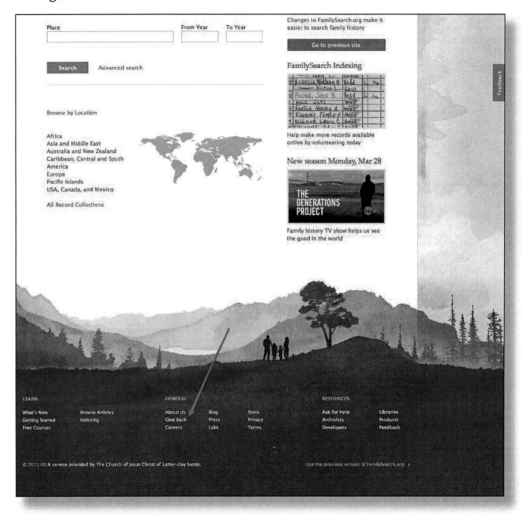

The Give Back link goes to a page explaining three major ways of contributing; volunteering to help with FamilySearch Indexing, adding articles to the FamilySearch Research Wiki and evaluating the programs and websites for FamilySearch. Each of these three is outlined on the Giving Back page: (shown in two screen shots)

Figure 1.15

The bottom part of the screen has the other two options, contributing to the Wiki and evaluating programs and websites:

Figure 1.16

Research Articles
Help others with your insights

Your gift of knowledge helps people around the globe with their family history research. The knowledge you share may include first-hand knowledge of changes in your home town or what you have learned through the process of searching for your own ancestors. Whenever you learn something new, you have an opportunity to share what you have learned with others, help them to learn along with you.

You can also help edit and refine what others have shared to make their information more complete and accurate. There's no need to be an expert genealogist. You just need to be willing to share what you know so that it might benefit others.

Contribute an article today ›

FamilySearch Evaluation
Evaluate new and future FamilySearch concepts

Your gift of insight will help FamilySearch design, develop, and launch new FamilySearch products and services. By simply completing a brief survey you can join the evaluation pool and make your voice heard. Everyone is welcome.

You could be invited to participate in a virtual one-on-one evaluation session using the Internet. It only takes about one hour.

Sign up to participate ›

#5 Blog

The word "Blog" comes from a contraction of Web + Log. Originally, blogs were commonly very personal online diaries. Now they are usually short, very small websites, featuring a periodic post. The writings posted to the Blog became known as "posts." There are now millions of blogs on the Internet, some of which are sponsored commercial websites with millions of viewers. Some blogs remain personal and journal-like. One factor that has made the number of blogs explode is that major web companies have allowed people to create a Blog and host it online on a commercial website for free. In the forefront of blog hosting is the huge Internet giant, Google with its Blogger or Google Blogs program. In just a few minutes, anyone can create a

blog and begin posting online to the world. Commercial enterprises have been quick
to realize the publicity value of blog posts and have either hired bloggers or employed
their own company personnel to write blogs. Celebrities, political figures and profes-
sionals of all kinds are actively using blogs to promote themselves or their businesses.

FamilySearch has also been quick to recognize the value of having blogs and
posting information on a regular basis. They have a number of blogs, one of which is
represented by a link on the startup page:

Figure 1.17

Clicking on the link to the FamilySearch blog takes you to the list of the
most recent posts. This page changes very frequently as FamilySearch contributors
add blog posts. Here is a screen shot on 29 April 2011:

Figure 1.18

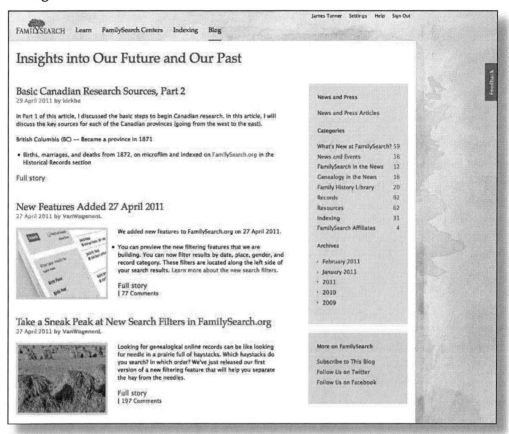

If you compare this screen shot with the blog at the time you read this Guide, you will see the progression of the contributions.

At the bottom right of the page, you can see three links; "Subscribe to This Blog", "Follow Us on Twitter," and "Follow Us on Facebook." There is an explanation of following FamilySearch on the Facebook social networking program later in this Guide. Following a website, like this Blog, with either a subscription or on Twitter presupposes that you have a "reader" account, like Google Reader, and/or a Twitter account. These options are offered more to the person who already has these accounts as there is no explanation of how to subscribe or follow on Twitter. Setting up a "reader" is as easy as clicking on the "More" menu on the Google search page. Instructions on how to set up a Twitter account are on the Twitter.com website.

#6 Settings

Here is a screen shot showing the Settings link:

Figure 1.18.1

Clicking on the Settings link takes you to your personal account information with a link to edit your LDS or FamilySearch Account. I will not show a screen shot because the information is user specific.

#7 Help

As I mentioned near the beginning of the Guide, the Help link is one of the real treasures of the FamilySearch.org website. Here is a screen shot showing the link which appears on every page of the website:

Figure 1.19

The following page is the search page of one of the most extensive help systems available for any program or website on the Web. I have never found anything comparable to the depth and breadth of the information contained in this ever-growing Help Center.

Figure 1.20

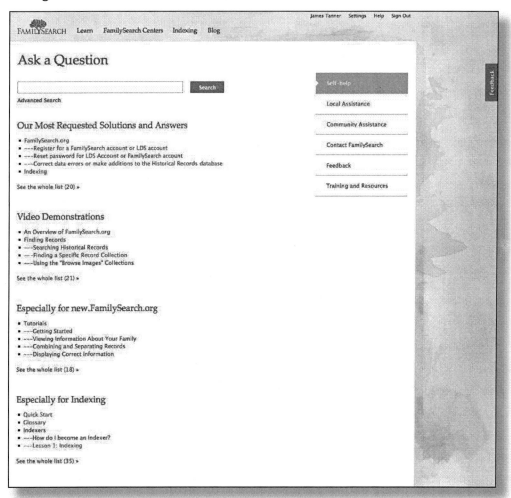

Most of the items on the page are self-explanatory. The blank space for asking questions is just that: a space to type in a question. The search capabilities of the Help Center will find articles pertaining to the words in your question. I will go through each of the functions of the Help page with illustrations of the results of clicking on each item.

The first screen shot shows what you get when you click on the Advanced Search link.

Figure 1.21

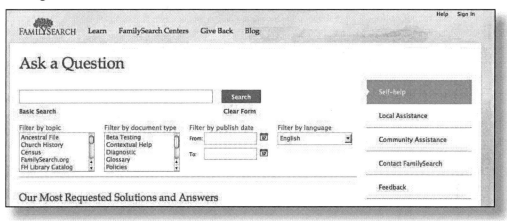

In an advanced search, you can filter the results by topic. The topics are:

- Ancestral File
- Church History
- Census
- FamilySearch.org
- FH Library Catalog
- Forums
- FamilySearch 2.27
- FamilySearch Classic
- HelpCenter
- IGI
- Indexing
- Mormon Immigration
- New FamilySearch
- PAF Personal AncestralFile
- PAF Companion
- Pedigree Resource File
- Historical Records
- Resource File Viewer
- SourceGuide
- Temple
- UDE
- Vital Records

You can also filter your search results by document type. The choices are:

- Beta Testing
- Contextual Help
- Diagnostic
- Glossary
- Policies
- Answers
- Temple
- Training

Another valuable filter is by date. This is a way to find the most recent statements on the programs and products. Clicking on the tiny calendar page will bring up an actual calendar where you can select the beginning and ending date range of your search.

Figure 1.22

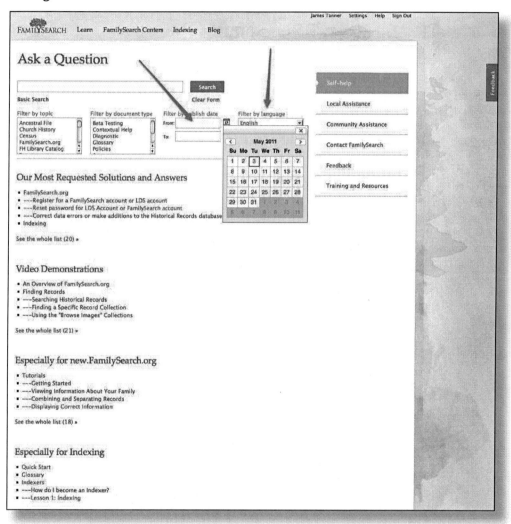

The Results is a list of articles that correspond to the search parameters you have entered into the program. By clicking on the heading of any article, you can read the full explanation which usually contains further links to related articles.

An Introduction to Searching

Before going too much further into FamilySearch.org, it is important to explain some of the basics of searching on a computer. When faced with a blank search box, many people have no idea how to start a search or what to put in the box. There are two opposite poles in the searching world; starting your search with all the information you know and starting your search with a minimum of information. Almost all search engines (programs that have a search function) operate the same way. They do what is called a "string search." That is, the search engine looks for matching characters. For example, if you were searching for death records in Arkansas, you might search for "Arkansas death records." In this case, the search engine will look for all the instances of the word "Arkansas," all of the instances of the word "death," and all of the instances of the word "records." Usually, but not always, the search engine will also look for combinations of words, such as "Arkansas death," "Arkansas records," "death records," and so forth. Depending on the search engine used by the particular program, you will get different results from your search from different word orders. So, "Arkansas death records" might produce a different result than a search using "death records Arkansas."

Which method do you use? Do you put in everything you know or a just a minimum of information. Some search engines will try to match all of the search terms you use. So, if you enter "Arkansas death records" unless all of those terms appear somewhere in the database, the search engine will return only those records with all of the terms. Some very sophisticated search engines, like Google's, for example, let you choose which words you want to include and which words you want to exclude. I suggest you avoid the tendency to try and fill up all of the search fields. Usually there is no reason to do so.

FamilySearch has a reasonably good search engine. I have found over the years that the best strategy is to start with a minimum of search terms, especially when searching for individuals by name and other information. If the first search does not produce any results, then try adding one search item or term at a time. Searching is a way to find what you want from computer programs, and searching online databases takes time and effort. Searching effectively has to be learned and learning comes from practice. Try every term and every combination of terms you can think of. If you still cannot find what you want, then start over and do the search again. Only after spending a reasonable time searching should you give up and conclude what you are looking for is not in the database.

In searching for genealogical information, there are a few things to remember:

1. There is no one "correct" way to spell a name. In searching for names you need to understand that names may not be written consistently, even a person's own

name. Those who recorded names, like census workers, church officials, and state or county workers, may have written down what they heard, which may not have been correct. Over the years, my own name has been spelled a dozen different ways. When you are searching, try different spellings. Do not automatically rule out a person being the same one you are looking for just because the name is spelled differently than you expected or different from some information you already found.

2. Place names change over time. Some areas have been conquered or otherwise changed jurisdictions, many times in various wars and the ruling country may have changed all the place names. Eastern Europe is a good example of changing place names. Some towns have had names in Polish, German and Russian at different times. If you are searching for places, remember that the names change.

3. Not only do place names change, the jurisdictions also change over time. Every state in the U.S. has had county boundaries change over time. A town that was in one county at one time may be in an entirely different county and even a different state at a later date. Remember to search in adjoining states and adjoining counties if there has been a boundary change.

4. If you are searching for a common name, try searching for someone else in the family with a more distinctive name. We all think our name is unique until we start doing genealogy. There are very few really unique names. Most searches, especially in large databases, will produce many results for a more common name. In these cases it might be easier to switch to looking for a different family member with a more unusual or less common name.

If I were starting a search for my great-grandfather, I would start by putting in his name and perhaps a date or place. If I got no results I would slowly add what information I had to see if adding information got any better results until I had all of the information available in the search. Then for good measure, I might try searching for a member of his immediate family. Take your time and think about what you are really searching for.

Searching in FamilySearch.org

The Help Center is a good place to learn how to search on the FamilySearch.org website. There are several other places on the site where you can search. You can search the Family History Library Catalog, the Research Wiki, the Forums, the Historical Record Collections, and several other databases. As I focus on each one of these databases, I will highlight some of the search procedures that are needed for that database. But, first, I will go over some search issues that apply to all of the various searches.

FamilySearch.org is all about finding and using information about your family history. The name "FamilySearch" gives you the message that the websites are all about searching, so it is understandable that there would be many places to search. The main FamilySearch.org website is made up of a number of related websites under one umbrella site and a number of huge databases, that is, collections of information.

Although the general rule is to start with a few terms and add terms as needed, I will illustrate using a search in the Historical Records which is the main search on the startup page. It covers many different types of records.

I start by entering a place, "arizona" in the Place field. I am going to look for my great-grandfather Henry Martin Tanner. But first, I am going to start with a general search to see what I find.

Figure 1.23

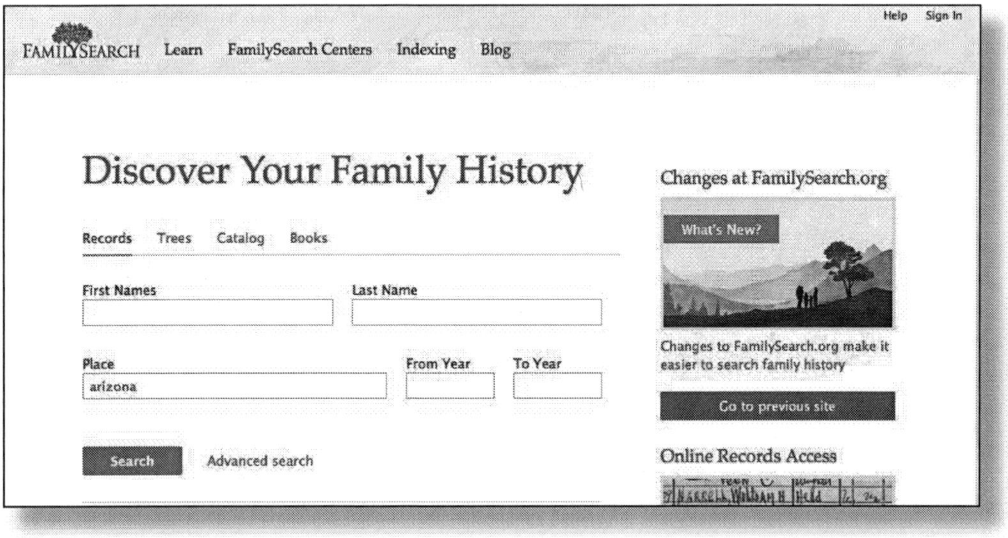

You will note that "arizona" is not capitalized. In FamilySearch.org whether or not you use capitals does not matter for searches.

When I click the search button, this is what I get:

Figure 1.24

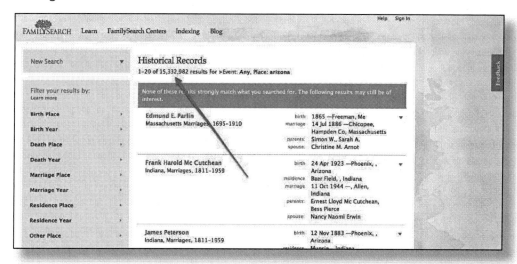

Obviously this response is not too useful with over 15 million results. So let's add a name. I can do this on the left side of the return page in the blank fields provided and then click on the Search link or just hit "enter" on the keyboard.

Figure 1.25

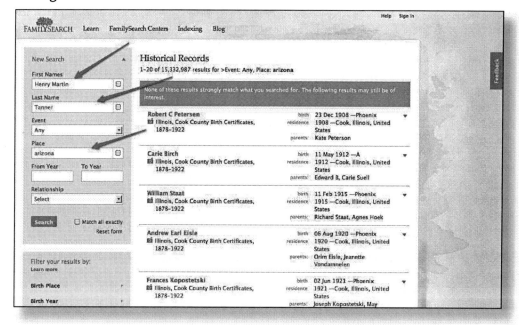

Here are the results of adding a little bit more information:

Figure 1.26

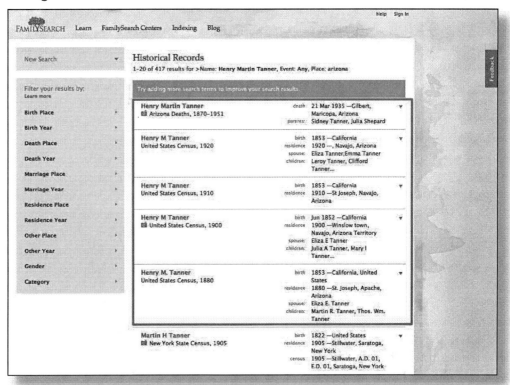

Of course your results may vary. I knew that my great-grandfather was in the database, but the point is that by working your way from general to specific in a search, you will ultimately have more accurate searches and more information. Along the left side you will see even more options in the form of a list of Filters:

- Birth Place
- Birth Year
- Death Place
- Death Year
- Marriage Place
- Marriage Year
- Residence Place
- Residence Year
- Other Place

- Other Year
- Gender
- Category

When selected, the Filters act to limit the number of results to the place, time or category selected.

In each case the choices are limited. For example, clicking on the Birth Place Filter shows the following options:

Figure 1.26.1

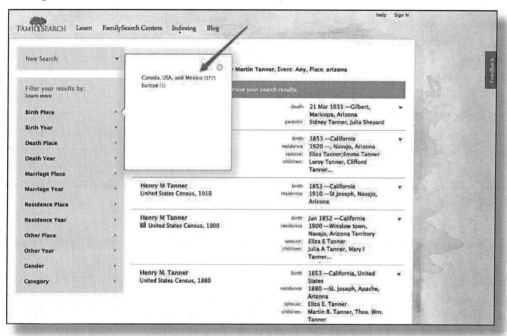

You will have to experiment with applying the Filters to see the results. In each case choosing a Filter will cut down on the number of results shown, however, you cannot use the Filters alone to find specific individuals. You need to have sufficient information in the Search Fields to find your family. The Filters primarily act as a way to get rid of irrelevant results.

There are more areas to cover in the Help Center, but those will be covered under #8 Feedback.

Now I will return to the items on the startup page.

#8 Sign In

You may ask why I left signing in to a position so far into the Guide. The main reason is that signing in is not needed to do searches and to otherwise use the FamilySearch.org website. As a contrast, the New.FamilySearch.org website is entirely limited to those who have registered and can sign in, but the FamilySearch. org website is open to everyone for free.

There are a few advantages to registering and signing into the site. Foremost, is the ability to contribute information to the Research Wiki. In addition there are some records that are only available if you sign in. When the records were originally microfilmed, the agreements with the various record repositories sometimes limited the use of the records. Some of those old agreements are still in place and effect and so a very few records require you to sign in before they are made available. It is also possible that you will never run into this issue. You do have to sign in to use the New. FamilySearch.org website.

LDS Account/FamilySearch Account

There are two different accounts. One is for members of The Church of Jesus Christ of Latter-day Saints and the other is for those who are not members. The main difference between the two accounts is access to the records of the Church concerning ordinances performed in the Temple. Since the early years of genealogy, there has been a concern about the sacred nature of the ordinance information. In the early days of genealogy, access to the Temple records was entirely limited to members who had a recommend to enter the Temple which was only available to members of the Church who qualified. As the records became more accessible, there were still restrictions on the access to some of the records. The old FamilySearch.org website also had a registration function and if you were not a member of the Church, you could not sign into the site and obtain access to Temple record information. That restriction persists today in the New.FamilySearch.org program. Until very recently only members of the Church were allowed access to the program. As those who are not members are allowed access, the Church ordinance information will not be viewable.

Hence, there are two separate accounts; the LDS Account for members and the FamilySearch Account for those who are not members. Except for access to the Church records, there is no difference between the two accounts. Everything on the FamilySearch.org website is available to both accounts as there are no Temple records on the website. At some point, the New.FamilySearch.org website will be integrated into the FamilySearch.org website and will cease to exist as a separate entity, however, the LDS Account/FamilySearch Account distinction will still apply.

The introduction of New FamilySearch program to members of the Church took more than two years, during which there were constant modifcations made to the program. The program, as it appears today, is quite different from the early versions and it is not unlikely that future changes will modify the program even further. The login procedures have now been implemented across the entire spectrum of FamilySearch online programs and are the same as those used in other Church websites not related directly to any of the FamilySearch sites. It is unlikely that future changes in the websites will include any basic changes to the method of applying for and maintaining an online account.

If you do not have either account, you will need to click on the Sign In link to go to the registration form. Here is a screen shot of the sign in/registration page:

Figure 1.27

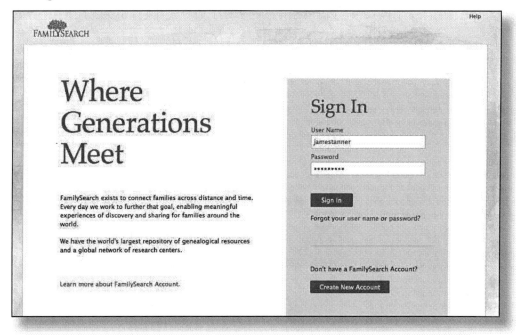

If you need to create a new account, you will get the following screen by clicking on the link:

Figure 1.28

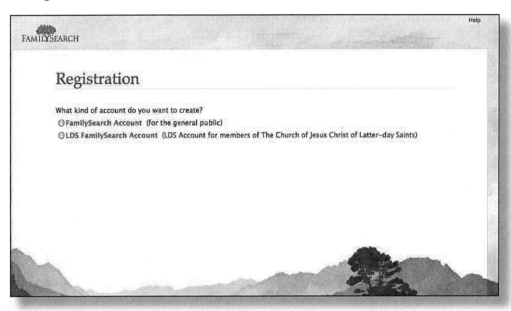

Here is a screen shot of the registration form. All that is needed is a name, a user name, a password and an email address for a FamilySearch Account:

Figure 1.29

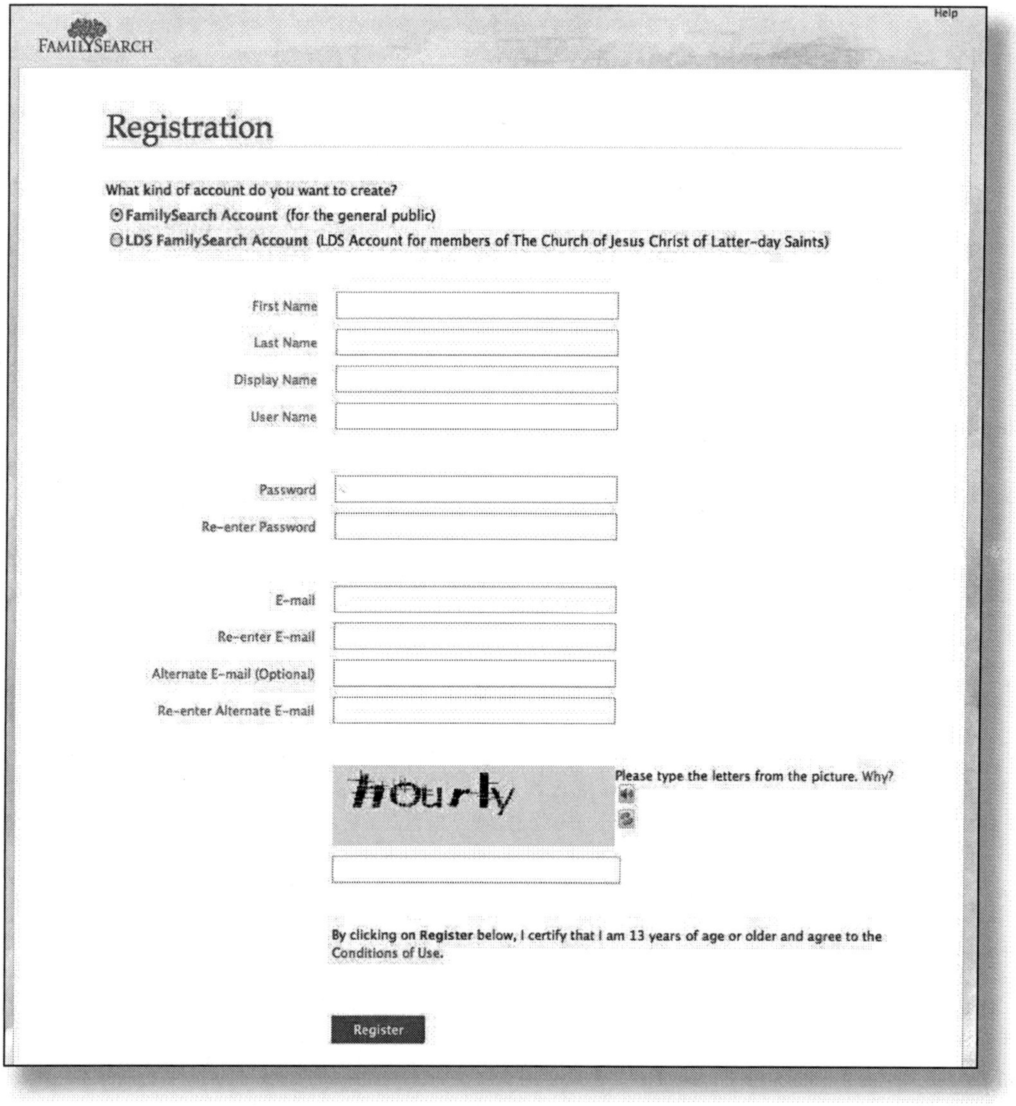

Registration is effective immediately. Your email account will be sent a message asking you to verify the registration, so that will have to be done before you can use the account. By registering you agree to abide by the Conditions of Use of the account. You can read the conditions of use by clicking on the link just above the Register button.

#9 Feedback and Assistance

Clicking on the Feedback link on the extreme right hand side of the startup page shows the following screen:

Figure 1.30

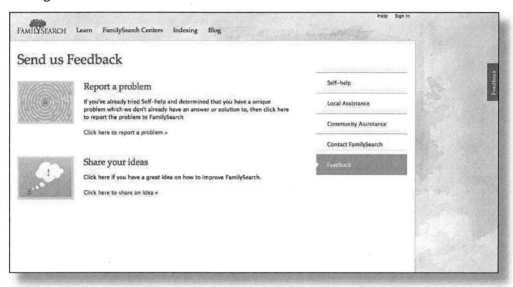

Feedback is part of the Help Center. On the right there are four links in addition to the Feedback link. The Local Assistance link, the Community Assistance link and the Contact FamilySearch link are also available by clicking on #6 Help. These links provide more places to get assistance from FamilySearch.org. The Self Help link takes you to the same page as the #6 the Help link.

Clicking on the Local Assistance Link show you the following screen:

Local Assistance

Figure 1.31

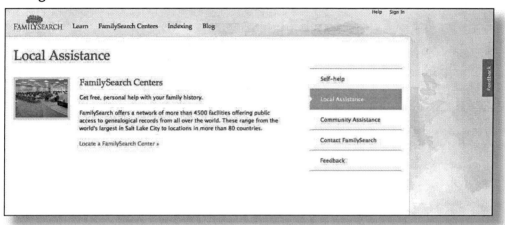

As you can guess, clicking on the Locate a Family History Center will take you to the same search screen available by clicking on #3 FamilySearch Centers. This link illustrates the web-like nature of the website. Many of the functions of the site are interrelated and so they are linked to more than one page.

Community Assistance

Figure 1.32

The Community Assistance link takes you to a page that refers you to the Forums.FamilySearch.org. Later in the Guide, I will cover in more detail the Forums, the Research Wiki and the Family History Library Catalog.

Contact FamilySearch

Figure 1.33

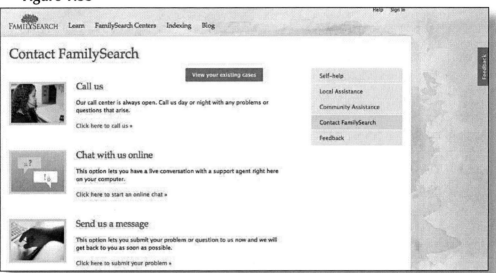

You can call for help from FamilySearch representatives 24 hours a day, 7 days a week. Clicking on the Call us link will give you a list of telephone numbers to call from any place in the world. Here is a screen shot of the call numbers:

Figure 1.34

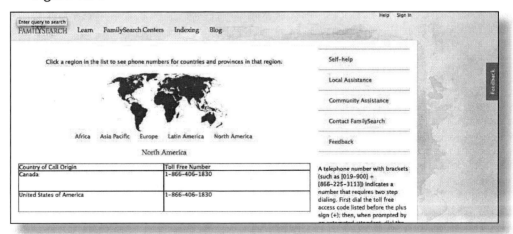

Please be aware that these numbers may change. You can find the rest of the numbers for other parts of the world by clicking on the links under the map.

You can also join an online chat with representatives of FamilySearch and others asking questions about the program. Even if you are not familiar with chatting online, you can click on the link and there will be instructions about how to proceed. Chatting in real time can require a faster Internet connection and a newer, faster computer.

One other way to contact FamilySearch is through email. Every time you contact FamilySearch you will be given a case number and you can view your existing cases and the status of the answers by clicking on the link on the Contact FamilySearch page. You must sign in to view the status of your existing cases.

What I have found is that nearly everything you can imagine is now in a Help Center document. By carefully searching for documents, you can avoid calling most of the time. However, there are problems, especially with New.FamilySearch.org, that are not readily answered and it is a comfort to know that you can talk to a real live person any time, day or night if you have an unanswered problem.

Note for members of the Church in North America only: The help number is 1-866-406-1830 or April 6, 1830.

• • • • • • • • • •

Another Note on Change and Feedback

If you are the type of person who is disturbed by changes or has difficulty adjusting, you will never be happy with a living, breathing website. One of the reasons for this is the issue of search engines. I have mentioned search engines in conjunction with doing searches on the FamilySearch.org website, but search engines are a much larger issue on the Internet. Essentially, a search engine is a program that searches documents or web pages for words and returns a list of the documents where the words can be found. When you type a search term into a blank search form, the program searches through the target documents and returns a list of places where your term may be found. The term "search engine" is used to describe a general class of programs. Not all search engines are the same. A website that employs some kind of search has to have its own search engine or searching program. It is possible for a website to use another search engine and you do see sites using Google's search engine or some other developers' search engines from time to time.

Often, the term "search engine" is applied to the huge programs like Google, Alta Vista and Excite, but these programs are different only in the scope of their search. Typically, these larger search engines employ another program called a "web spider" that systematically searches every web page on the Internet and feeds its information into another program called an indexer. The accuracy of the search engine and its ability to return relevant content is dependent on the ability of the programmers to write programs that will find what you want to find.

One reason websites have a feedback function, like that illustrated at #8 Feedback, above in the Guide, is to give the programmers information about what does and does not work. When you use the Feedback link to report problems with the program, you are helping to make the program work more efficiently.

● ● ● ● ● ● ● ● ●

Share Your Ideas

Clicking on the link #9 Feedback, takes you to the screen shown in figure 1.30. You will see a link to Share Your Ideas. Clicking on Share Your Ideas brings up some questions concerning whether or not your suggestions pertain to the Church's Temples or Temple work. If you answer no, your inquiry is re-directed to Get Satisfaction, a separate website. A Get Satisfaction account is automatically created for you and you are then directed to the website. You will get something similar to the following screen shot:

Figure 1.34.1

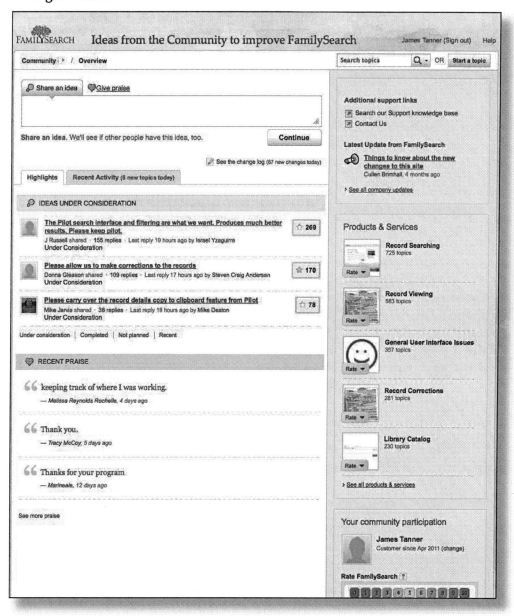

There are a number of items on this page including several links. This is essentially an online forum. It is different from the FamilySearch Forum discussed later in the Guide in conjunction with the FamilySearch Research Wiki. This Get Satisfaction Forum is designed to give specific suggestions directly to the Family-

Search developers and programmers. This page and all its associated pages will likely change frequently as new suggestions are made and as some issues are resolved. If you would like to see how FamilySearch organizes it programming and support activities, you can click on the right-hand side where it says "See all products and services." This is a screen shot showing Page One of Products and Services:

Figure 1.34.2

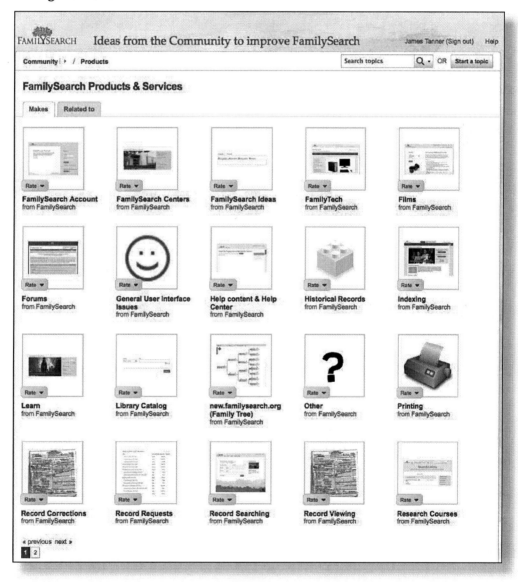

It should be noted that these so-called products and services are not always specific to a particular website or collection. If you look carefully, there is a drop-down menu on each of the icons allowing you to rate each one of the products and services on a scale from one to ten. The same rating system appears on the Ideas page for FamilySearch as a whole.

If you click on a product or service, the Topics list appears. Here is the list for the FamiySearch Forums;

Figure 1.34.3

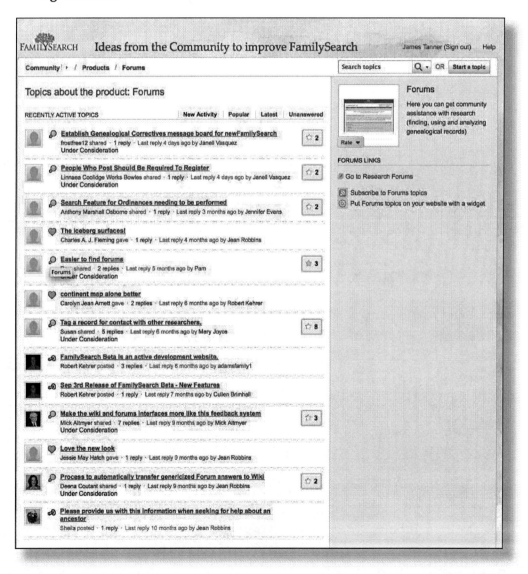

Even though this site looks a lot like a forum, it is not entirely a two-way conversation. It is a pretty fancy way of making suggestions. If you share an idea to change or improve any of the FamilySearch "products" then others have the opportunity to join your suggestion. The more people that join in, the more likely it is that FamilySearch will put the suggestion onto its list of things to change or do. The link shown on the Get Satisfaction startup page to "Search our Support knowledge base" takes you to the FamilySearch Help Center.

Now we are back to our review of the startup page. Just for reference, I am inserting another copy of Figure 1.3 with the numbered areas. Remember, #6 is missing until you sign in.

Figure 1.3 *(Repeated on purpose)*

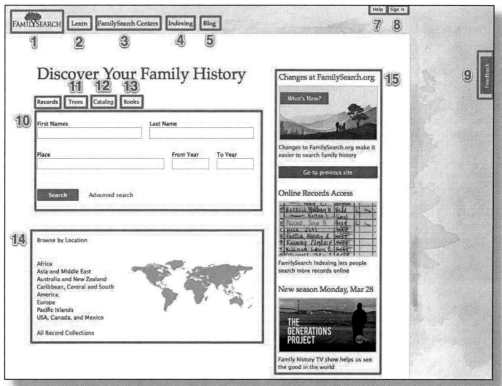

#10 Records (Historical Records and Search Historical Records)

Although the FamilySearch.org website has several search engines and their respective search fields, some of the searches they perform are overlapping and search some of the same records. This is not confusing in practice since you can use them all and may find additional information by simply searching with different terms or word order. However, since most of the searches on the website are for names, you should always remember to try variant spellings.

#9 Records is not a link; it is the reference to the records searched by the search fields in #12 Search Historical Records. The search fields recognize the basic fact of genealogical searches. To identify any individual, you need three things: a name, a date, and a place. Even if you have all three, that may not be enough. If you enter a name and a place with no date, you are likely to get many people with the same or similar name listed. The place can be as general as an entire state. Likewise the date can be approximate. The name is also important, but if you don't know a given name, entering a surname is sufficient to get you started.

If you enter a name and click the Search button, you will get a list of records possibly containing information about your person. As an example, I will use my great-grandfather again, Henry Martin Tanner. I also added a place, Arizona. Here is a screen shot of the blanks filled in with the name and place:

Figure 1.35

The next screen shot is the results. Notice the additional search terms available on the left side of the screen in addition to what was on the startup page. You can get a more expanded list by clicking the Advanced search link on the startup page. See the arrow in Figure 1.35 above. Here is the results page from a basic search:

Figure 1.36

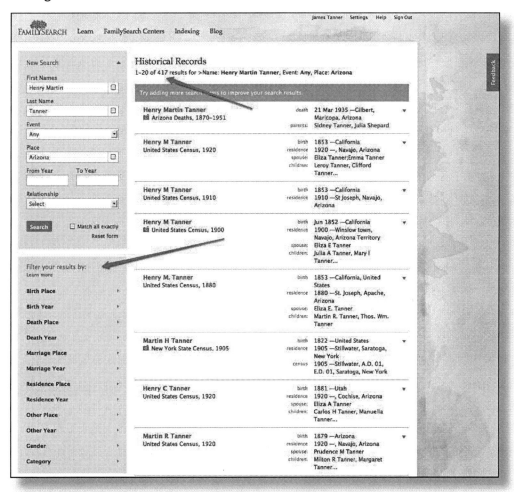

Notice two things about these results, first, as indicated by the top arrow, there are 417 records listed. If you look closely at the list, however, you will see that although the first few names are Henry Martin or Henry M Tanner, continuing down the list, the names change to Martin H and Martin R Tanner. These are not the same individual so it is unlikely that you will need to look at all the results.

If you look at the lower arrow, you will see a list of Filters. Clicking on the Filters gives you further selections for limiting the number of search results. I will have more to say about Filters later in the Guide. Here is an example of the choices offered by clicking on a Filter:

Figure 1.37

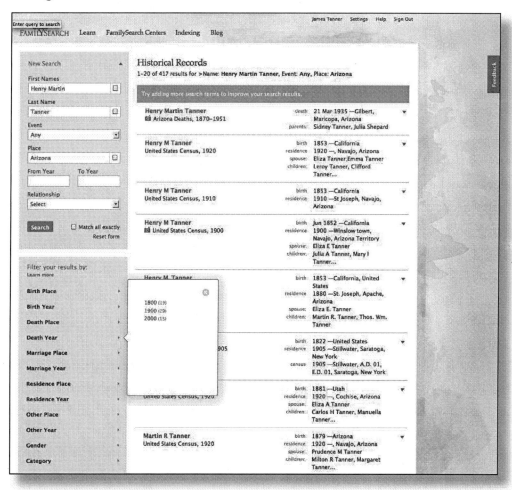

When you first see the results of your search, the list of fields in the upper left-hand corner are not selected. You have to click on the little triangle next to the "New Search" title to see the list. Here is screen shot before the triangle is clicked:

Figure 1.38

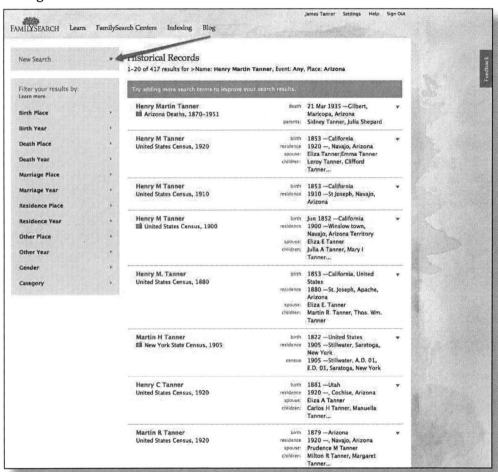

What do we learn from this? Filters are a valuable way to obtain more results from a search. You will also note that there is a bar across the search results that states, "The following results don't strongly match what you searched for, but may be of interest." As a matter of note, the suggested results do identify another Tanner relative, the wife of my cousin, Seth B. Tanner. In my opinion, as you gain experience using the search fields and analyzing the results, you will become much more proficient in finding relevant information in the databases.

• • • • • • • • • •

A Note on Wild Card Searches

Name searches allow you use a wild card character * in place of any unknown letters in the name fields. In order to use the wild card character, you must have the first three (3) letters of the name. For example, you could search for "Hen* Tan*"

• • • • • • • • • •

How do you find out about Henry M. Tanner in the 1880 U.S. Census? You do this by clicking on his name in the results list. Clicking on Henry M. Tanner gives the following information:

Figure 1.39

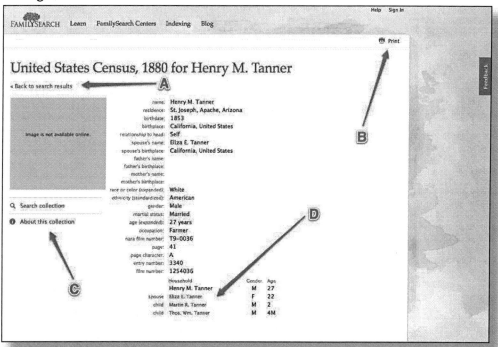

This is the search return for Henry M. Tanner in the 1880 U.S. Census. There are still more options. By clicking on the link "Back to the search results" as shown by arrow "A" you can return to previous screen. You can get a print out of what is on the screen by clicking on the link indicated by arrow "B." If you click on the "Search collection" link it will take you directly to the search page for the 1880 U.S. Census in the Historical Record Collections . You can also click on the "About this collection" link to go to a FamilySearch Wiki page explaining, in detail, the United States 1880 Census. In the case of the links marked by the arrow "D," you can also see the expanded search for each of the individuals listed.

Just as the title suggests, the Historical Records search searches the Historical Record Collections for instances of the search name, place and date, but a search with the default search fields on the startup page will also search the "Trees."

The following is a screen shot of the bottom of the screen of the search shown in Figure 1.37:

Figure 1.40

As can be seen from the following screen shot, clicking on one of the names shows that the information is coming from an Ancestral File Record. The Ancestral File Records come with a strong disclaimer: "Ancestral File is a collection of genealogical information taken from pedigree charts and family group records submitted to the Family History Department since 1978. The information has not been verified against any official records. Since the information in Ancestral File is contributed, it is the responsibility of those who use the file to verify its accuracy."

The following shows the Ancestral File Record with the arrows showing the disclaimer and the link to learn more.

Figure 1.41

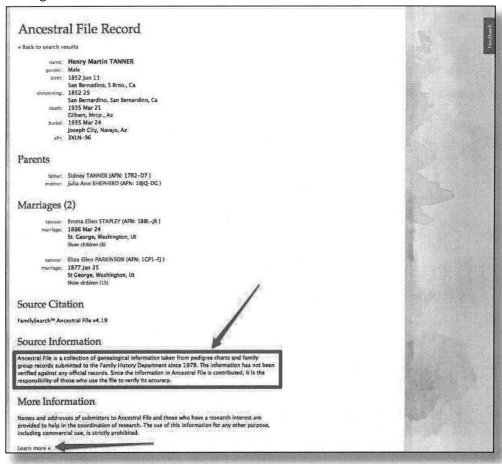

Clicking on the Learn More link takes you to a page in the FamilySearch Research Wiki explaining the Ancestral File. The following screen shot further illustrates the interrelated web-like nature of the FamilySearch.org website. We will come back to the Research Wiki later in the Guide.

Ancestral File page in the FamilySearch.org Research Wiki

Figure 1.42

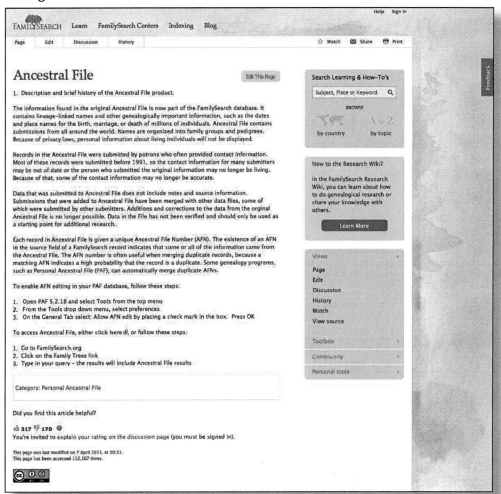

As you can see, clicking on further links will continue to take you to different parts of the website. Remember, if you get lost, click on the logo in the upper left hand corner of the screen and you will go back to the startup page. In writing this Guide, I had to make some arbitrary decisions as to where to stop following links in order to have some organization to the Guide. This is one of those cases when I decided that the explanation of the Wiki would take place later in the Guide.

#11 Trees

Figure 1.43

Interestingly, clicking on the Trees link brings up expanded search fields as seen in the following screen shot. I have already added in a potential search, again, for my great-grandfather to use as an example of the results.

Figure 1.44

At this point, you need to look carefully at all of the potential search fields and not forget what I said earlier about the search strategy of entering only one or two items at a time before each search to narrow down the search results. Clicking on the Search button returns the following search results:

Figure 1.45

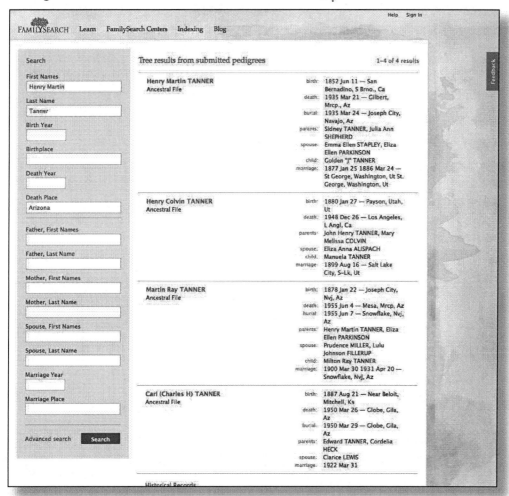

Listed at the bottom of the page, off of the screen shot, it shows 25,845 results. You may also note that the search put the Trees at the beginning of the search and the Historical Records at the bottom. This time putting in the name and one location produced thousands rather than hundreds of results. But it is noteworthy that the first entry in both the Trees and the Historical Records is in fact, my great-grandfather.

Clicking on the Advanced search link adds additional search fields. You might try adding a little more information at this point, to see what effect it has on the results. I added a birth year of 1852 and a birthplace of California and the number of results dropped precipitously to 7539. Adding a father's first name reduced the number of results to 7330. As I kept adding information the number of results kept dropping. But here is the real question, if you already know all this information about the person, why are you searching in the first place? An expanded search is mainly to allow you to put in other facts you might have available, such as a marriage place when you do not know the birthplace. Having all those fields in not really an invitation to add in everything you might know or can guess about the individual.

I still suggest the same strategy of starting out with only a minimum amount of information and then adding a little at a time.

Also, remember the statement quoted above about the reliability of the Ancestral File records. These are contributed records with no consistent citations to sources.

* * * * * * * * * *

A Note About Search Results

No matter where you are searching whether it be in FamilySearch, Google or wherever, you will often be confronted with numerous search results, sometimes many more than you will care to look at. Most of my Google searches return results in the millions. Yet, I almost always find my answer or person, if I find it at all, within the first page or so of results. A good example is the search above for Henry Martin Tanner. Although there were over 24,000 results for the first search, the results had my person in the first few results shown. What if this hadn't been the case? My first step would be to apply the filters (located on the left side of the screen below the search fields) depending on the type of record I was searching for. If that didn't work, I would be inclined to search individual collections rather make a general search of the entire database. In some instances, with a very common name, for example, a general search will be useless. You will have to focus on a particular type of record in a particular place and not hope that your person surfaces at the top of your search by shear luck. As we will see later in the Guide, each collection in the Historical Record Collections has its own search fields.

A Note on the Titles of the Links

At the time of the writing of this Guide, the New.FamilySearch.org website was not yet integrated into the FamilySearch.org website. The integration of the two sites has been discussed extensively by FamilySearch representatives and may occur by the time this Guide is available for sale. The program presently called New FamilySearch has also been referred to as FamilySearch Family Trees. The name of present link #10 Family Trees is somewhat ambiguous. It appears from the search results that it is intended to mainly search the old Ancestral File. It is possible that the names of these links will be changes as the program continues to develop.

●　●　●　●　●　●　●　●　●　●

More About #11 Trees

Figure 1.44 shows the screen for a basic search. Here is another screen shot with an arrow showing the link to an Advanced search. The main difference is the addition of search fields.

Figure 1.46

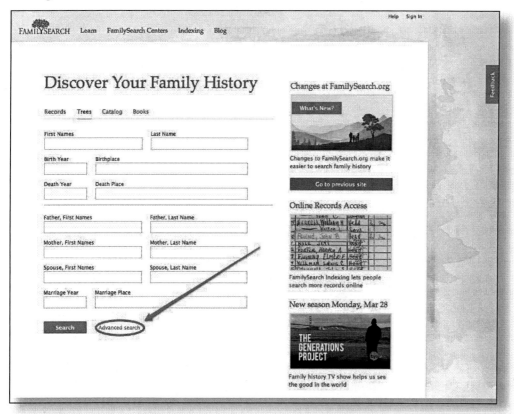

Clicking on the Advanced search link expands the search options as follows:

Figure 1.47

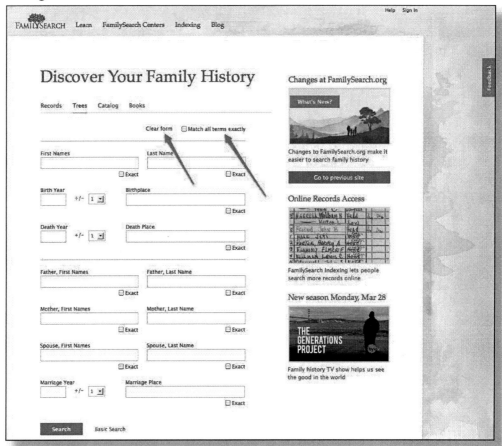

Remember, just because the search fields are showing and empty does not mean you have to try to fill them all. The expanded options are provided so that different combinations of information can be used for a search. For example, you may only know a name and a marriage date and none of the other information. The form allows you to enter as much as you know, but do not infer that the additional information is necessary for a valid search.

You can see two other buttons indicated by the arrows; one that will clear the form to start over and another limiting the search to the exact terms you enter. Limiting the search to exact terms should be used as an alternative, not as a routine selection. Historically, spelling changes indiscriminately and using the exact terms button may eliminate many valuable results.

#12 Catalog

With the increased complexity and size of the FamilySearch resources, the world famous Family History Library is transitioning to a new name, the Family-Search Library. Located in downtown Salt Lake City, Utah, the library has over 2.4 million rolls of microfilmed genealogical records; 727,000 microfiche; 356,000 books, serials, and other formats; over 4,500 periodicals; and 3,725 electronic resources. All of these resources are searchable through the Family History Library Catalog.

The Catalog's search function was entirely re-written for the present website and at the time of the writing of this Guide, was still under development. It is likely that the search function will be considerably expanded. It is also important to note that some of the search strategies available on the older website are no longer available on the updated site. The differences pertain primarily to the use of the wild card character * and the ability to do searches on partial names.

Presently the Catalog is accessed from a link on the startup page:

Figure 1.48

Clicking on the Library Catalog link brings up the present search screen:

Figure 1.49

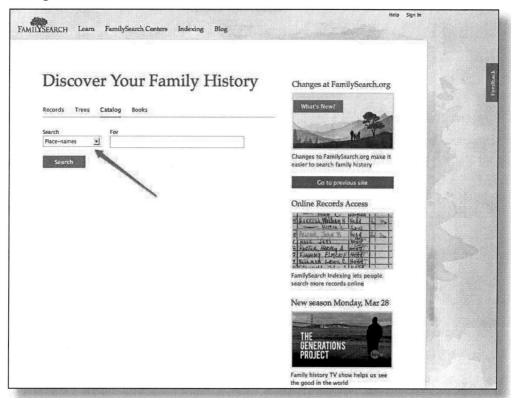

As shown in Figure 1.49 above, the search field opens to a default for Place-names. Click on the small downward triangle and the Place-name field becomes a pull-down menu with the following items:

- Place-names
- Last-names
- Titles
- Author information
- Subjects
- Call numbers
- Film numbers
- Keywords (Beta)

Place-names:

By entering a place, the search box will automatically bring up a list of associated or similar places to select from. You do not have to use any of the selections, clicking on the Search button or using the Enter/Return key on your keyboard will take you to a list of possible matched Catalog Entries.

You can also enter places in the following format, although it is not required:

[Country or State], [County or district], [City or town] such as: Arizona, Maricopa, Mesa

As you begin to type a name into the search field, you will automatically see a drop down list of suggested places. You can either keep typing or select one of the suggested options. The suggested entries are not a pull-down menu, they will change or disappear if you keep typing or if you click somewhere else on the page.

In the Family History Library Catalog the names of countries are in English. The names of states, provinces, regions, cities, and other jurisdictions are in the language of the country.[11] If you try to use a wild card character * , you will find that they do not work with place name searches. Do not use the words "country," "county," or "city" unless they are actually part of the name of the place. For example, "Salt Lake" will return a list of counties because Salt Lake is a county name as well as a city. Typing "Salt Lake City" will give you the city. But if you type "Provo City" you will get a message that says "No matching places." You do not have to type all of the words of the name of a place, typing any of the words will show you a list of options.

• • • • • • • • • •

A Short First Note about Beta Testing

You may note that the last entry on the pull-down search categories menu is marked as (Beta). A Beta test is a programmer's way of indicating that the program is still in the pre-release or testing stage. There will be another Note later on in the Guide with a more complete explanation of Beta testing.

• • • • • • • • • •

Here is an example of a Place-names search on the word "Arizona." The screenshot can only show a small portion of the categories returned by the search:

Figure 1.50

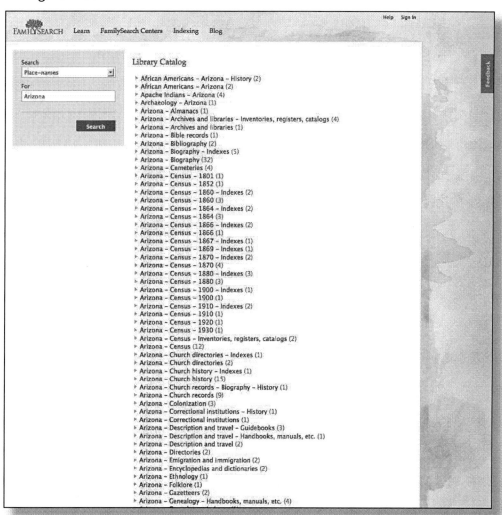

What is shown in the results are categories with the number of items in the catalog for each category shown in parenthesis after the entry. Clicking on a category expands the category to show all of the entries:

Figure 1.51

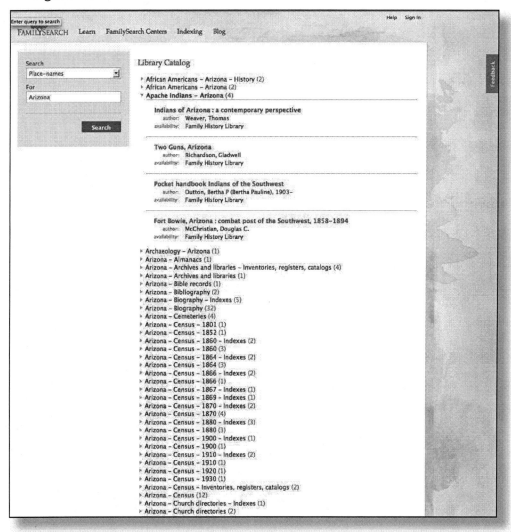

Further clicking on any entry will take you to an expanded listing for the Catalog item. The following screen shot shows part of the screen for *Indians of Arizona a contemporary perspective*:

Figure 1.52

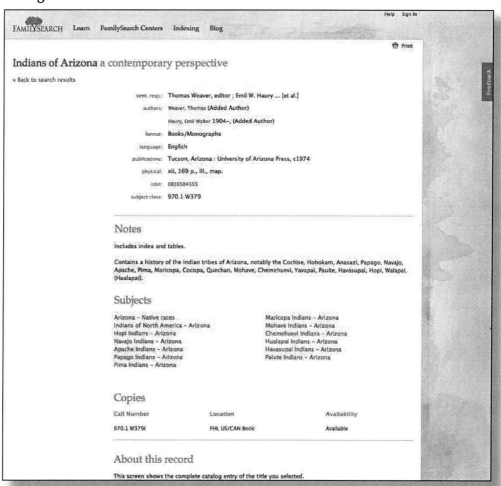

There are a large number of links to additional subject headings in the Catalog. For a list of Family History Library Catalog subject subdivisions see: https://wiki.familysearch.org/en/Locality_Subject_Subdivisions

.

Last-names:

This selection refers to surnames or family names. Entering a name in the search field when this choice is selected will return a list of any document in the Catalog containing information about that family or person. For common surnames the lists of results can be very long and you may have to click on the "Next" link to see all of the pages of catalog items. The search results will also include books and documents where the family surname may only appear someplace inside the book. Clicking on the title will show the entire catalog entry and list the subject, i.e. the additional surnames, contained in the work.

Remember that the catalog search is very literal. If you type in the word "Tann," the search results will only contain entries with those exact letters. But if you add the wild card character , like this, "Tann*", the results will include any entry with the first letters of "Tann." The following screen shot shows the results of a name search:

Figure 1.53

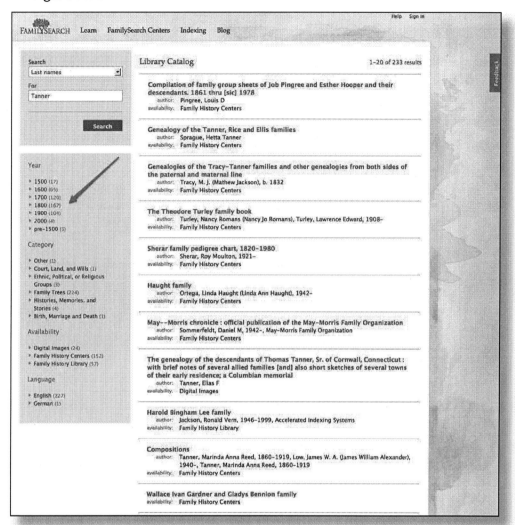

Notice the filters along the left side of the screen. Clicking on any one of the filters will reduce the number of results to the number contained in the parenthesis. Clicking on more than one filter will further decrease the total number of results.

Title:

This selection refers to searching for the title of a book or other document. You can enter a whole title or just one or more words from the title and the search will return all of the items in the Catalog containing the entries in the title of the book or document. The wild card character * also works with title searches. Even though a Last-name search results will include books and documents by title as well as surnames included in the books or documents, the title search will be limited to books and documents by titles only. If you are not sure of any of the words in a title, then you should use the keyword search. Following is a screen shot of the results from a Title search on the surname "Tanner."

Figure 1.54

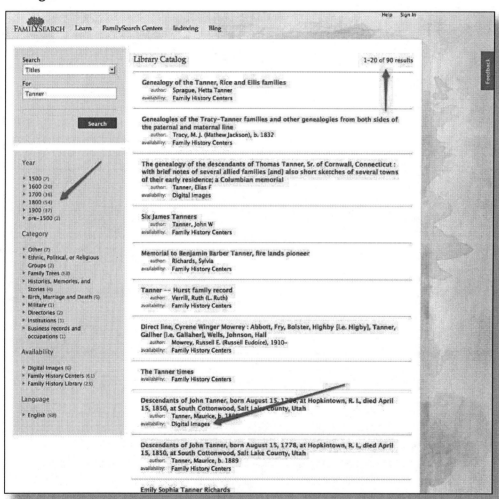

As with the Last Name search above, there are a number of filters along the left side of the screen. But there were far fewer results because the Title search only searches books or documents with the search term in the title. You can see from the arrow that there were only 90 results. Also note that fact that one of the entries is available as a digital image. This means the entire book is online and searchable and that every word in the book is indexed and you can search for any word, including names, in the book.

Author Information:

You can enter all or part of the name of an author and can search by first and last name or by corporate name. The reference to "corporate" name is not just limited to corporations but to any organized entity such as churches, historical societies, and other entities. Just as with the other searches, realize that there are a lot of entries in the catalog and part of a name may not find what you are looking for. If you only enter part of a word, it is likely that the search will not return any results unless you also use the wild card character * in your searches.

Once you do a search from the main page, you may have additional options, including Author and Subject numbers. Although, these search catagories exist, they do not seem to be numbers that are readily available unless you have done previous research at the Family History Library. If you do not happen to know the number, these extra search categories are not useful. Looking at a screen shot of an Author search, it turns out there are more books written by Tanners than those with "Tanner" in the title. Notice the list of filters along the left hand side of the screen.

* * * * * * * * * *

A Note on Digital Images

The revolution in genealogical research is the availability of online digital images of original source records. The images of older documents acquired on microfilm, are not much better than the original images. But as digital images which were acquired directly from original documents become available , the images will be as good as the originals or sometimes even better.

In the FamilySearch catalog, if a document is available online in a digital image format, the entry will state "Digital Images" on the Availability line. The Historical Record Collections mark the availability of digital images with an icon of a small camera to the side of each entry. As time passes, more and more documents will be available in digital image copies.

* * * * * * * * * *

Figure 1.55

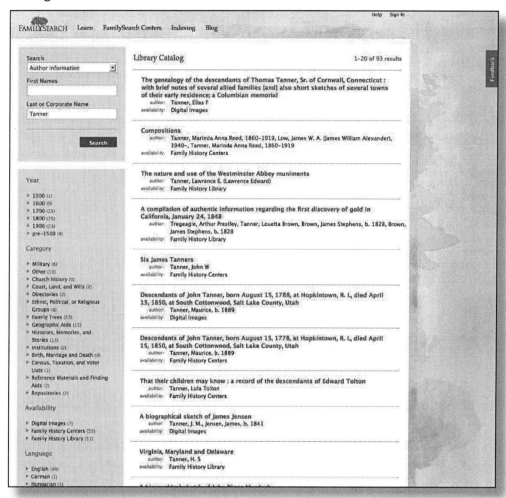

Subjects:

Since you do not know all the subjects listed in the Catalog, using the subject search field is hit-or-miss at best. It is somewhat difficult to distinguish between a subject and a keyword. In libraries, there are standard lists of categories used by the catalogers to catalog the books and other documents. When a book or document is cataloged, the cataloger assigns one or more categories or subjects. Unless the subject you use agrees with one of the categories or subjects used by the library, you will only get a very general return or none at all. In that case you should use the Keyword search category. Just as with the Author Information search, once you do a search from the main page, you may have additional options, including Author and Subject numbers. If you do not know the number these extra search categories are not useful.

In the following screen shot, notice the list of filters. In searching by subject a general search category such as "biographies" returned 20,986 results, so I added a modifier with the word "Arizona" and the number of results was reduced to 80, a far more manageable number of items to review.

Figure 1.56

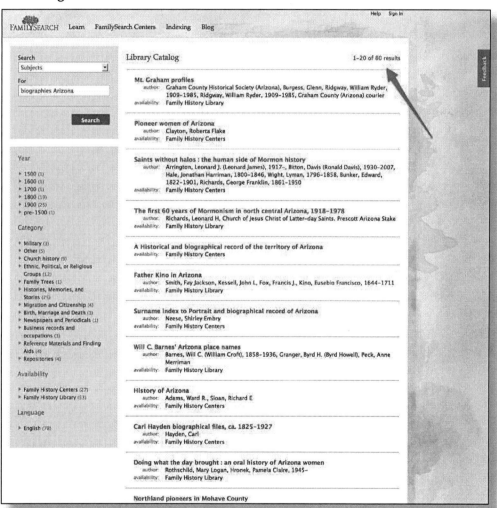

Call Numbers:

Books and other printed materials in the Family History Library are cataloged by the Library call number. The Library call numbers are based on the Dewey Decimal Classification and are used on books, maps, periodicals and other printed materials. They are different from the microfilm or microfiche numbers. Call numbers must be entered exactly and you cannot put in part of a number or use the wild card character *. Usually the Catalog is used to obtain a call number; if you already know the call number, you can use that number to physically find the book in the Library because the books in the Library are arranged by call number on the shelves.

Here is a screen shot using a call number search:

Figure 1.57

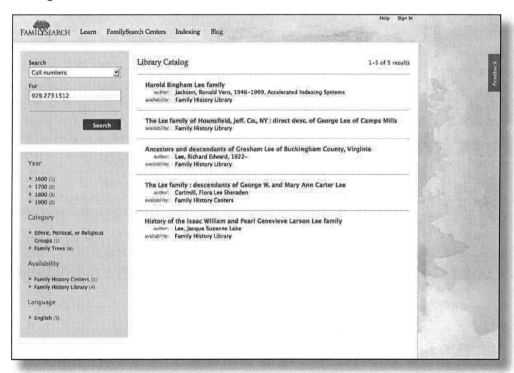

The subjects of the target book are listed as filters on the left side of the screen shot. Clicking on a title of a book expands the listing into the full catalog information that will not fit entirely into the screen shot.

Figure 1.58

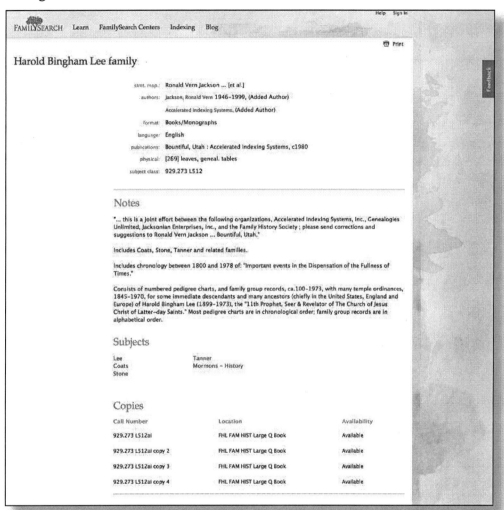

You can also see the subject headings, the number of copies of the book and further information including a brief description of the contents.

Film Numbers:

As with Call Numbers, microfilm and microfiche numbers are usually found through a Catalog search, not the other way around. If you happen to have a microfilm number and don't know what the number pertains to, you can use the Catalog search to find the item from the number. Microfilm and Microfiche numbers are assigned at the time of acquisition of the items and are arbitrary numbers. One good use for a Film Number search is to find related films. If you enter a number and the film is part of a series, the records page will list all of the related film numbers. The following screen shot shows a microfilm number search using a random microfilm number:

Figure 1.59

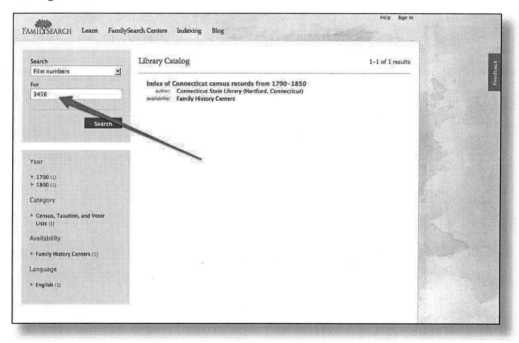

Clicking on the title of the microfilm will expand the entry to show all of the available microfilms.

Here is a screen shot of the same Index showing a partial list of the all of the related microfilms:

Figure 1.60

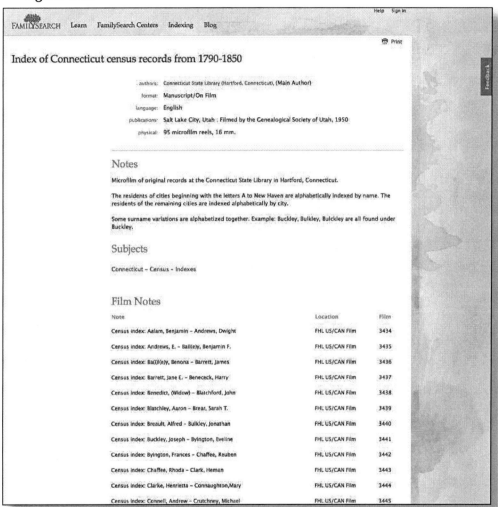

Keywords:

If none of the other searches find items you are searching for, you can always try putting in one or more keywords, even using the same words you used previously. On the other hand, if you are looking for a general category of materials, you might want to search first by keyword or words. You can vary the results of your search by adding or subtracting words. It is difficult to suggest any particular keywords since almost anything you are looking for might appear as a keyword. Here is an example of a search using a surname as a keyword:

Figure 1.61

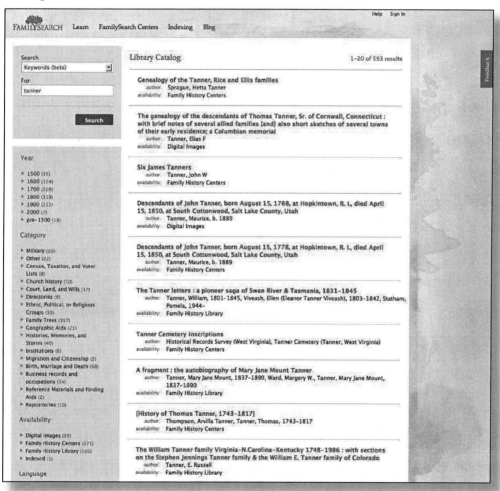

You can see that some of the entries have the availability as Digital Images, indicating that the entire book is scanned and online for searching. You will also see an extensive list of filters along the left-hand side of the screen. Even though there are a large number of results, you can further filter the list by clicking on the subjects listed in the filters to limit the list just to those entries that correspond to the filter. For example, if I click on the filter for a date of 2000, I will only have 7 items in my list. Here is a screen shot showing what happens:

Figure 1.62

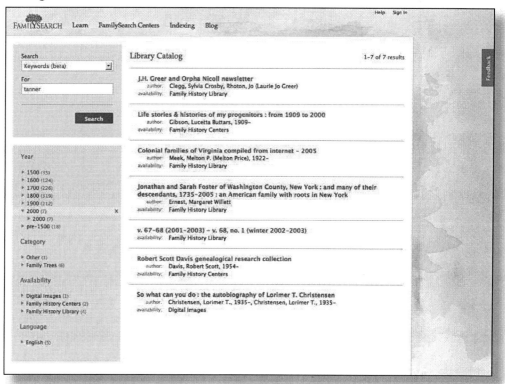

Even though the list does not seem to pertain to the keyword search, each of the entries shown must have a reference to "tanner" somewhere in the book or document. For example, clicking on the last entry for "*So what can you do: the autobiography of Lorimer T. Christensen*" you can see in the following screen shot the reference to the Tanner connection. Also note that the publication is available online.

Figure 1.63

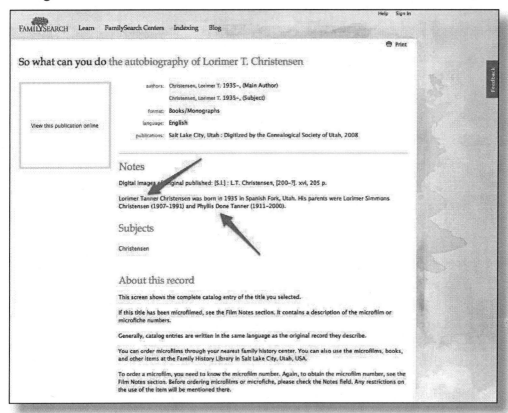

If you have a question about how to improve your search capabilities, may I remind you of the Help Center. Click on the Advanced Search and Filter by the Family History Library Catalog. You can then ask specific questions about how to do searches such as How to search for an item by number in the Family History Library Catalog.

#13 Books (The Family History Archive)

Link #13 is entitled Books and is a link to the Family History Archive, also known as the BYU Historical Books Collection. The Family History Archive is a website maintained by Brigham Young University. Here is a screen shot of the link on the startup page:

Figure 1.63.1

The startup and search page of the Archive is at: http://lib.byu.edu/fhc/index. php. Quoting from the website, "The Family History Archive is a collection of published genealogy and family history books. The archive includes histories of families, county and local histories, how-to books on genealogy, genealogy magazines and periodicals (including some international), medieval books (including histories and pedigrees), and gazetteers. It also includes some specialized collections such as the Filipino card collection and the "Liahona Elders Journal." The books come from the collections of the FamilySearch Family History Library, the Allen County Public Library, the Houston Public Library – Clayton Library Center for Genealogical Research, the Mid-Continent Public Library – Midwest Genealogy Center, the BYU Harold B. Lee Library, the BYU Hawaii Joseph F. Smith Library, and the Church of Jesus Christ of Latter-day Saints Church History Library."

The Family History Archive collections are integrated into the Family History Library Catalog. Each of the entries for the Family History Library Catalog shows the item's availability. This refers to the place where the original item is available and whether or not the item is on microfilm, a physical document or book, or digitized and available online. The digitized items include those books and documents that have been scanned by the Family History Archive project. If an item has been scanned and is available online the availability will be listed as "Digital Images." You can view the images by clicking on the title of the item, which will take you to the items catalog page and then by clicking on the link that says, "View this publication online."

The link to the Family History Archive goes outside the FamilySearch.org website to the Brigham Young University website where the Archives are located. The link is http://www.lib.byu.edu/fhc/index.php. Ultimately, the collection will include all of the books available at the listed libraries plus books held by the various Family History Centers scattered across the world. Estimates of the ultimate number of books to be added to the collection exceed 400,000 volumes.

Here is a screen shot of the Link to the Family History Archive startup

Figure 1.63.2

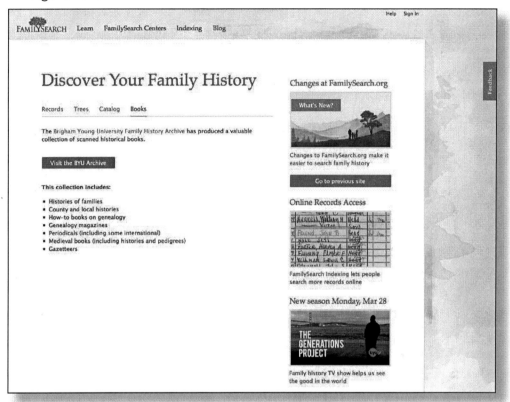

The link takes you to the Family History Archive site. Although there is nothing on the page identifying it as a website at Brigham Young University, the URL is http://www.lib.byu.edu/fhc/index.php.

Here is a screen shot of the search fields:

Figure 1.63.3

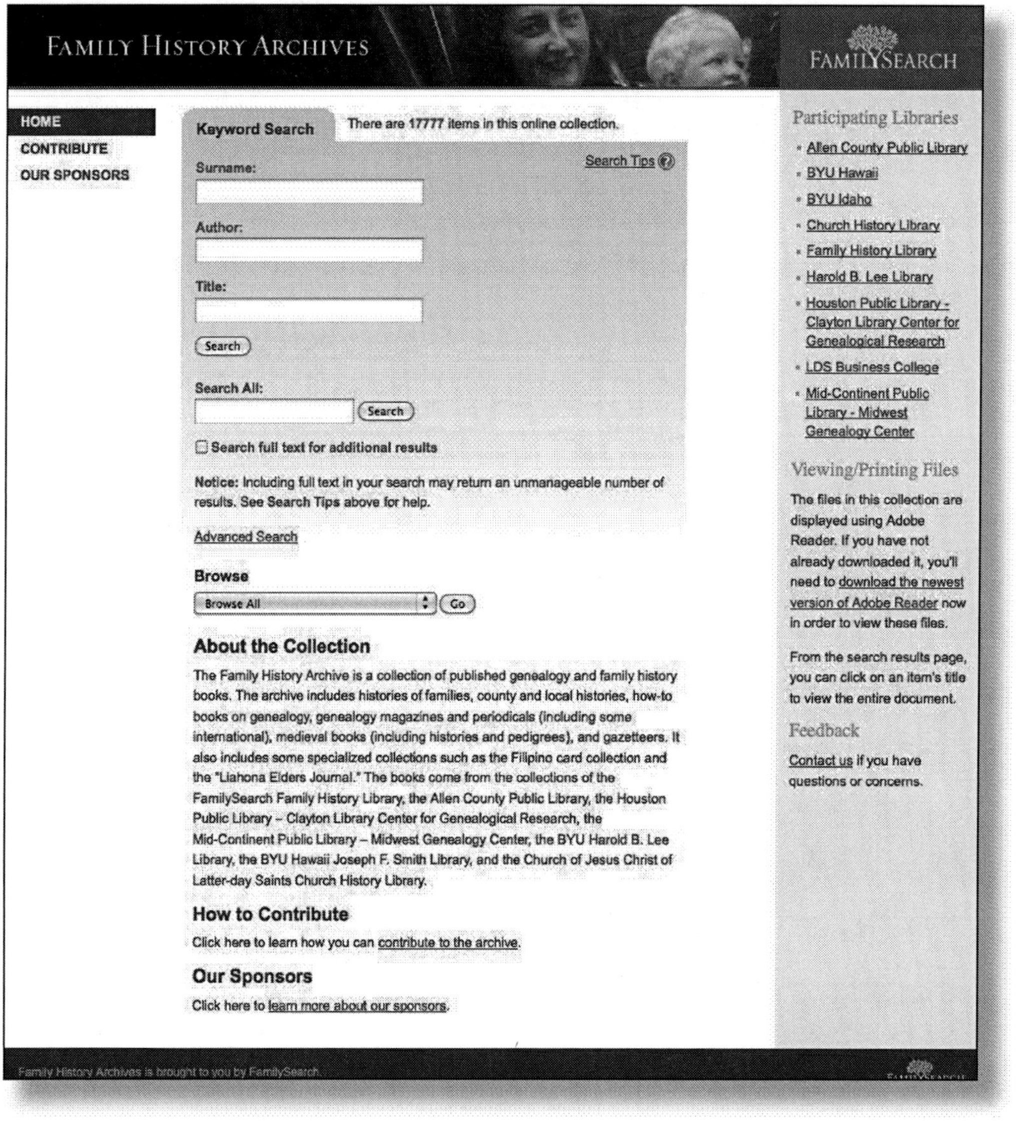

The digitized books and documents in the Family History Archive are fully searchable on any word. Books are also downloadable in PDF files. Clicking on the Advanced Search link brings up another search page that includes all of the Digital Collections in the BYU Library system. Following is a screen shot showing the Digital Collections search fields. As you can see, this link takes you outside of the normal FamilySearch websites and there is no way to return to FamilySearch.org without using your browser's back button or re-typing the URL.

Figure 1.63.4

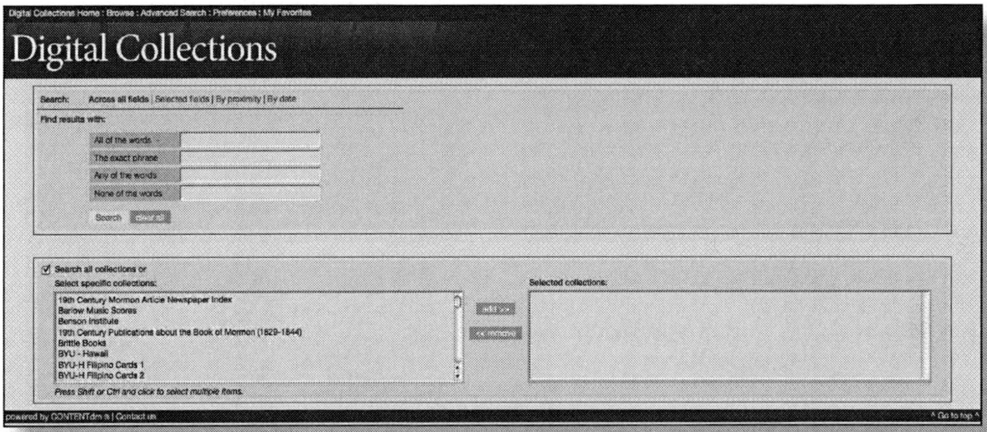

#14 Historical Record Collections

One of the most remarkable resources of the updated FamilySearch.org website is the ever growing Historical Record Collections. Many of these records are available online for the first time. Here is a screen shot of the FamilySearch.org website startup page showing the links to the Historical Record Collections"

Figure 1.64

You may remember earlier in this Guide when I talked about the Search form for Historical Records at #10. In addition to a general search, you can examine the Collections individually. To do so, you can either click on a specific geographical area or you can see the entire list of all of the Historical Record Collections. Each Collection may contain millions of records. New records are being added weekly to the Collections, so the lists will change as the records are added. Clicking on the link "All Record Collections" brings up a list like the following figure, however, the screen shot can only show a small portion of the list.

Figure 1.65

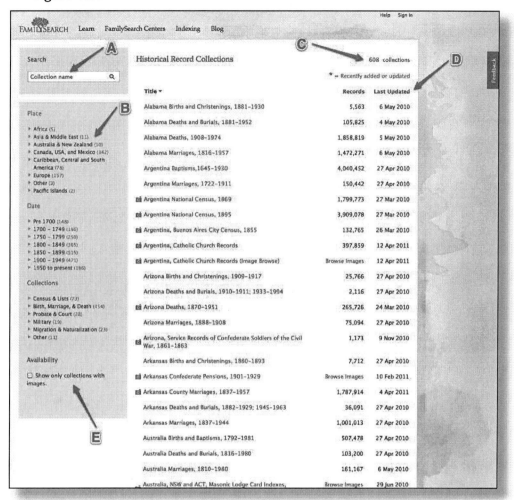

As you can see from the results, there were, at the time this screen shot was made, 608 collections. There will be many more by the time your read this. See the arrow marked "C." The search field at the arrow marked "A" allows you to make a search by collection name. For example, put in the name of a country and see only those Collections with that name in the title.

The list of items marked with the "B" arrow are filters. Selecting a filter will limit the list to the items selected. For example, the items marked Europe show 157 items. If you click on the Europe category you will get a further list of only those records from Europe, but you will also get a list of the European countries showing the number of Collections from each country. Further clicking will limit the list only to that particular country. Here is a screen shot showing what happens when you click on "Europe."

Figure 1.66

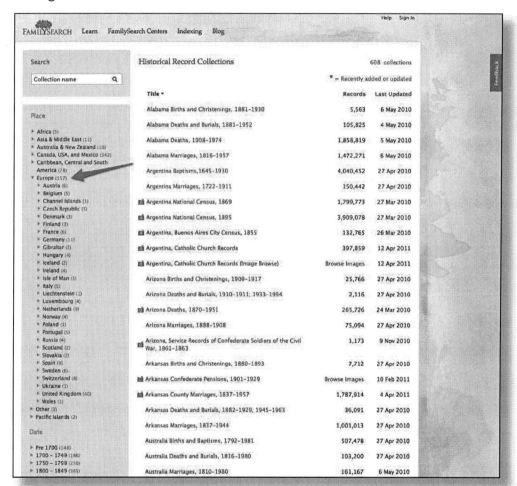

The list of countries shown by the arrow are listed in alphabetical order and the number in parenthesis is the number of Collections available for that country.

Going back to Figure 1.54, the arrow marked with "D" indicates the date of the last update for each of the Collections. Clicking on the column head, "Last Updated" will sort the column by date with the most recent collections on top.

The final arrow is marked "E" and it is a button to limit the list only to those items with scanned digitized images.

About the Historical Record Collections

As I have mentioned before, the Historical Record Collections is growing extremely rapidly. New Collections are being added almost daily. The Records are presented in three different formats depending on record availability. Here is a screen shot showing the three different formats:

Figure 1.67

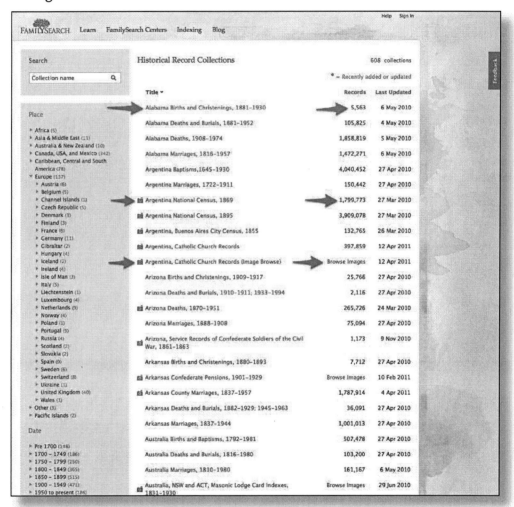

The first kinds of records are those that are represented by the first arrow. These are records that are available only as an index. The second arrow points to a Collection with images of the original records as evidenced by the camera icon, as well as an index as shown by the number of records. The third arrow points to a

Collection with images but no index. The Records column has a notation to Browse Images indicating that the Collection only has images. Here are some examples of screen shots illustrating the three different kinds of Collections. I will give an example of what happens when you click on the links. I have chosen to give only one example of a Collection, because all other choices will be very similar in all of the other Collections. The first screen shot is the results of clicking on the Argentina National Census, 1869 link.

Figure 1.68

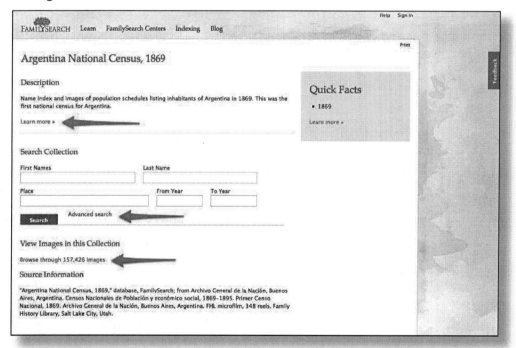

There are three things to specifically note. Since this Collection had both a camera icon and a number of records, this indicated that the Collection had both an index and images of the records. The arrow at the bottom of the screen shot points to a link showing the number of images. Clicking on this link to browse through the images, takes you to the images through a series of filters, as can be seen from the following screen shot:

Figure 1.69

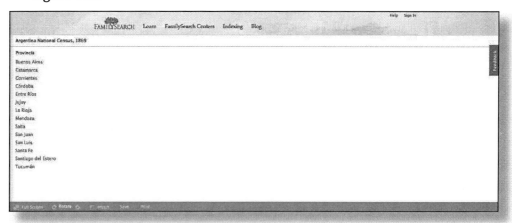

The list gives you the choice of selecting a particular Argentine Province for records. Clicking on a Province, such as Santa Fe, brings up the next screen:

Figure 1.70

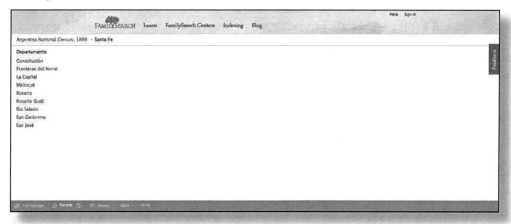

As you can see, now you have a list of the Departments in the Santa Fe Province.

Further clicking, in this case on Rosario, brings up the next smaller political or religious subdivision, depending on the subject of the records. The next screen is a list of the sections and districts in the Rosario Department:

Figure 1.71

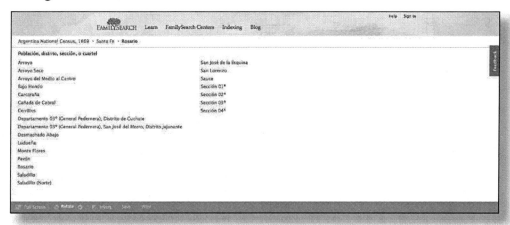

This further selection illustrates an important feature of the Historical Book Collections, even in the Collections that are not indexed: the organization of the individual files gives you a structure to narrow down your search to a small, manageable geographic area.

Clicking again on Rosario, brings up the beginning of the actual records:

Figure 1.72

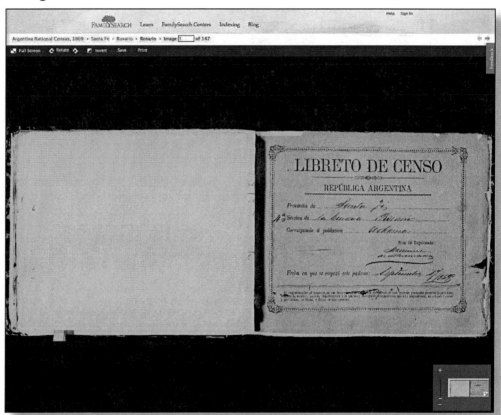

If you look at the top of the screen, above the image of the record, you will see the history of the search; Argentina National Census, 1869 > Santa Fe > Rosario > Rosario > Image 1 of 147. Also note in the lower right-hand corner of the image screen, there is a thumbnail image with a slider bar from minus to positive. Moving that slider bar zooms in on the image as shown in the next screen shot:

Figure 1.73

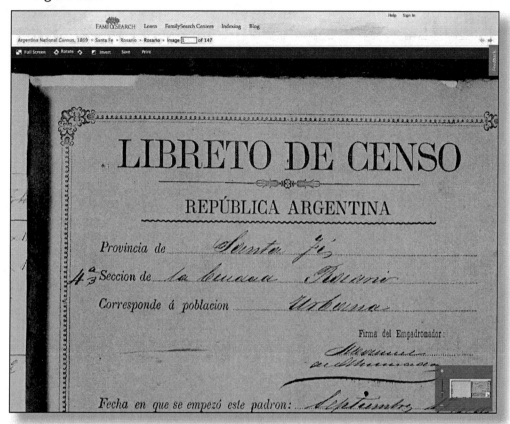

The thumbnail view in the lower right, shows the location of the zoomed area. The scanned images are extremely good quality and preserve almost all of the information in the original microfilm, but the scanned images have the advantage of allowing you to zoom in on details which is not easily done with microfilm readers. There is also an advantage to having the image generally available for free on the Internet as opposed to paying to rent the film, waiting while it is delivered, and then spending time at a microfilm reader. As you can see from the menu bar, you can save the image to your disk. These saved images can also be attached as media items to entries in most of the popular genealogy database programs.

You can also invert the image. Sometimes inverting the image makes the text or handwriting more legible. Here is what happens when you invert the text:

Figure 1.73.1

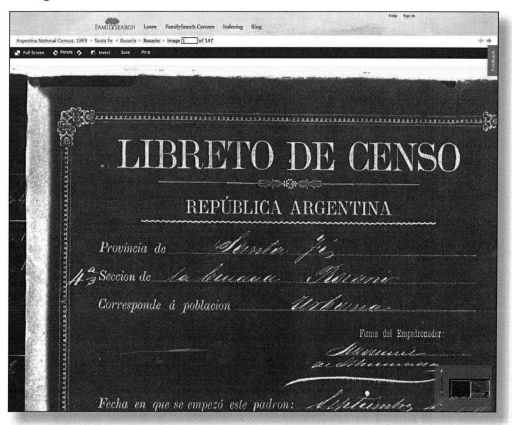

Going back to Figure 1.68, there are two other links of importance on this record that also appear on all of the other individual Collections in the Historical Record Collections: the link to "Learn more" and the "Advanced Search."

Clicking on the Advanced Search link adds additional search fields as shown in this screen shot of the Argentina National Census, 1869:

Figure 1.74

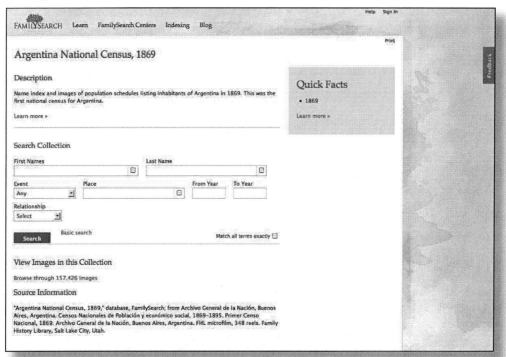

As with any of the other search functions of the FamilySearch.org website, there is a basic search strategy. The rule that I suggest is always start with entering information into one or two fields then narrowing the search by continuing to add information if necessary. Also, I suggest not clicking on the exact search box unless you have exhausted all other options. There is no guarantee that the compilers of the records spelled your ancestor's name the way you think it was spelled. Be sure and try different optional spellings of all names.

The next link on the Collections window invites you to "Learn more" about the Collection. Clicking on this link takes you to a page in the FamilySearch Research Wiki that describes the details about the Collection. There is a Wiki page for each Collection in the Historical Record Collections.

Here is a screen shot of the Argentina 1869 Census page from the Wiki that appears when you click the "Learn more" link: (not all of the page will show in the screen shot)

Figure 1.75

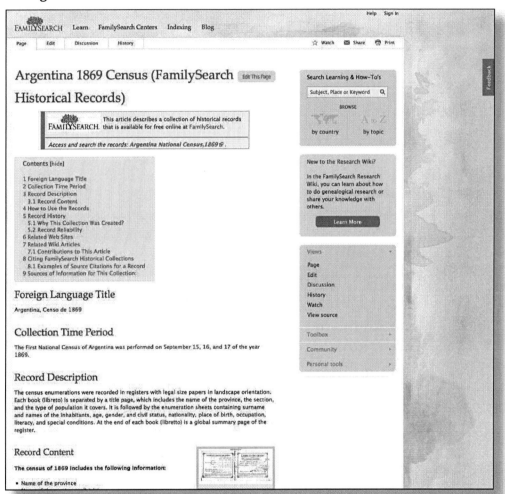

Most of the pages relating to Historical Record Collections contain similar information, including the Collection time period, the record content, how to use the records, the record history, why the collection was created?, the record reliability and related websites and links. I will get into the Wiki in more detail later on in the Guide, but the links from the Historical Record Collections to the Wiki work both ways. In a real sense, the Wiki becomes the master index of all of the Collections.

Going back to the FamilySearch.org startup page, here is the reference screen shot:

Figure 1.3 *(Repeated yet again)*

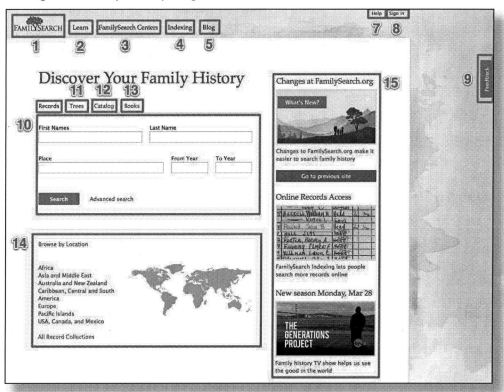

#15 Links to featured content

In the short time the updated FamilySearch.org website has been online, these large display links have been used for a variety of purposes and have changed. As you look at the screen shots in this Guide, you might notice changes in the details of the pages in different shots. During the time this Guide was being written the picture/link on the top of #15 brought up a blog page from December 2010 when the site was first introduced. Since that time the What's New Blog has been updated from time to time. During May of 2011, there was a link to the U.S. Civil War Project. Here is a screen shot showing that link:

Figure 1.75.1

Clicking on the U.S. Civil War Project link brought up the following page:

Figure 1.75.2

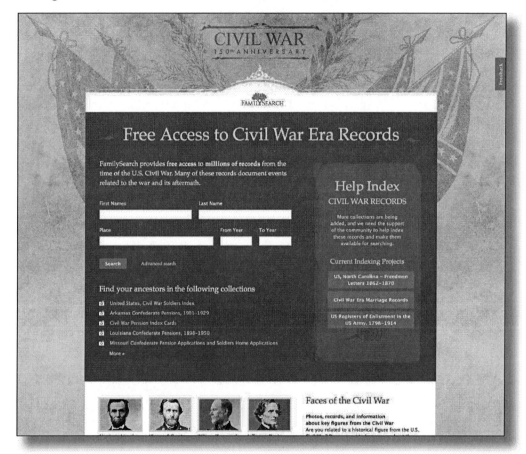

Even though this link may disappear at some time, the record collections cited will be still available on the site under the Historical Record Collections link.

#15 Link to Previous Version of FamilySearch.org

The link to the previous version will likely become less obvious and less visible as the site develops. Here is a screen shot showing the links to the old website as indicated by the arrows:

Figure 1.76 - 1.77

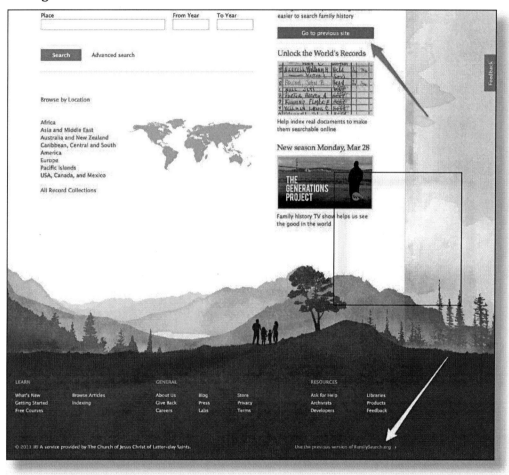

Items at the Bottom of the Startup Page

The screen shot 1.76 - 1.77 also shows the links at the bottom of the startup page. At the time this Guide was written there were twenty-two different links, more than the total of all the links on the rest of the page. Also included is the link to the previous version of FamilySearch.org, and other useful and informative resources accessed through the remaining links.

Starting on the left-hand side of the screen there are five links grouped under the "Learn" heading. Following is a list of those links with an explanation and screen shot if necessary.

Learn Links at the Bottom of the Startup Page

What's New:

Presently the link goes to a summary page with three additional links to some of the pages we have already covered. Interestingly, this link to "What's New" is different than the What's New display link in Item #15. Here is a screen shot of the results page from the What's New link at the bottom of the page:

Figure 1.78

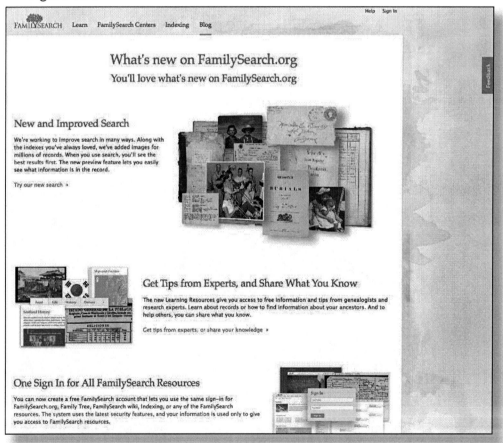

The first link option takes you to the main startup page for a search. The second option goes to the Learn page with the links to the Wiki. The third option goes to the information page for an LDS or FamilySearch Account. Here is a screen shot of the informational page:

Figure 1.79

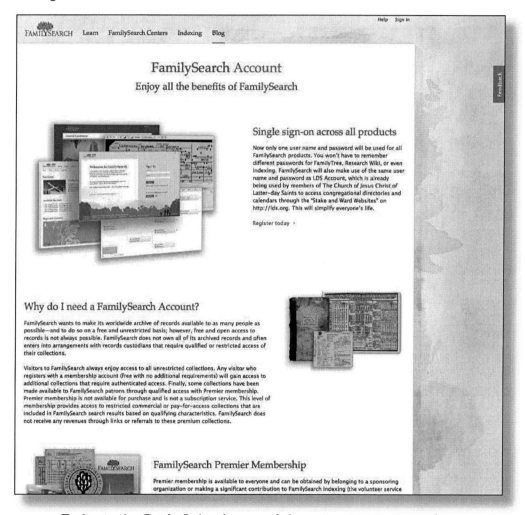

Earlier in the Guide, I already covered the registration process and pages above with reference to #8 Sign in. The bottom of the screen shot above, mentions the FamilySearch Premier Membership.

Record collections in the Historical Record Collections are available for viewing in the following categories:

1. Unrestricted collections; images available and viewable by everyone.
2. Collections with images available only to registered FamilySearch users.
3. Collections with images available only to registered FamilySearch users with premier membership.
4. Third-party collections with varying restrictions to images, some of which require a fee.[12]

Premium or Premier Membership is available to those who index records through FamilySearch Indexing and earn 900 points or more during a calendar quarter. By visiting the FamilySearch Indexing website and signing into the site, you can view your sign-in status and whether or not you qualify for Premium or Premier Membership. Points are earned for each record that you index. The points for any given project are determined by the number of records you index, based on a scale of points for each record. As of the date of the writing of this Guide, I have yet to find any records that require a premium membership.

Getting Started:

This link takes you to a page introducing you to the process of starting your family history. This is the same page that you can access by clicking on the Get Started link shown in Figure 1.6. The Getting started with family history page is as follows:

Figure 1.80

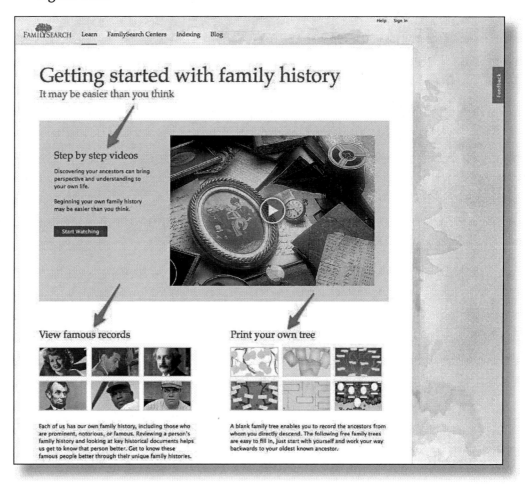

There are three helpful sections; Step-by-Step videos, Links to view records of famous people and an option to print out a blank sample family tree form. Clicking on the Videos link brings you to a list of introductory videos:

Figure 1.81

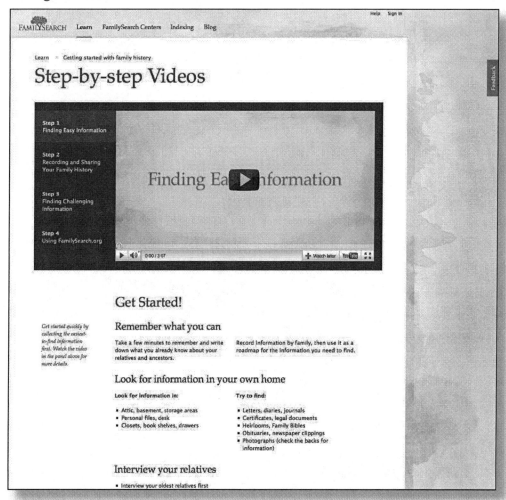

You can choose to watch the videos or simply following the instructions. There are two forms which can be downloaded from links at the bottom of the page (not showing): one is a guide in how to collect your information at home and from other people, the other is a guide for conducting a family history interview.

• • • • • • • • • •

A Repeat of the Note on the Changing Face of FamilySearch.org

All active websites change over time. As I pointed out earlier in this Guide, FamilySearch.org is under active development. Pages and links may change at any time. Then why is this Guide useful if the website is going to change? All websites have a basic structure. While the information and links may change as information is added or updated, the basic structure of the website will not change unless there is a major overhaul. FamilySearch.org underwent such an overhaul in December of 2010 when the updated site was activated and dropped its Beta status. It is unlikely that there will be such a major overhaul of the entire website in the near future. There may be additional pages and additions such as the TechTips.FamilySearch.org website, but these additions will not change the overall look and feel of the site.

From time to time, FamilySearch does add new features to the websites, often without any public announcement or fanfare. If you discover a new feature, consider it a bonus. One new feature added without any particular notice to the public was the Chat function added to the Help Center. I was attending one of the online Webinars for the Research Wiki when I learned about that addition.

• • • • • • • • • •

Free Courses:

Just for reference, here is another screen shot of the startup page showing the list of links I am discussing indicated by the box:

Figure 1.82

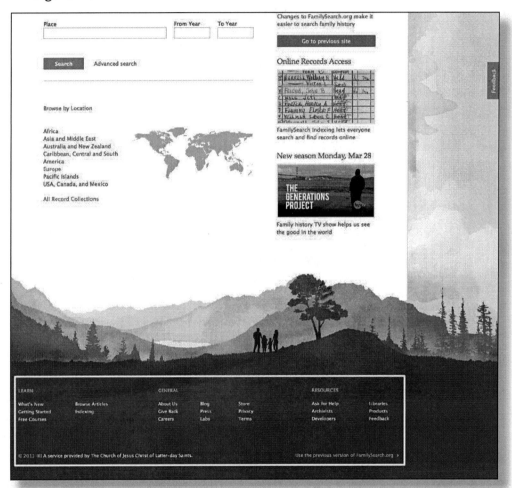

As I mentioned above, there are presently twenty-two links to additional information from FamilySearch. This is one reason why I stated back in the beginning of this Guide that the FamilySearch.org website looked deceptively simple. In fact, there are links to huge and complex databases as well as other resources.

The Free Courses link takes you directly to the list of Research Courses shown in Figure 1.11 above.

Browse Articles:

This link takes you directly to the Browse by Country page of the Family-Search Research Wiki. Here is a screen shot of a portion of the page, but I will be discussing the Research Wiki later on in the Guide.

Figure 1.83

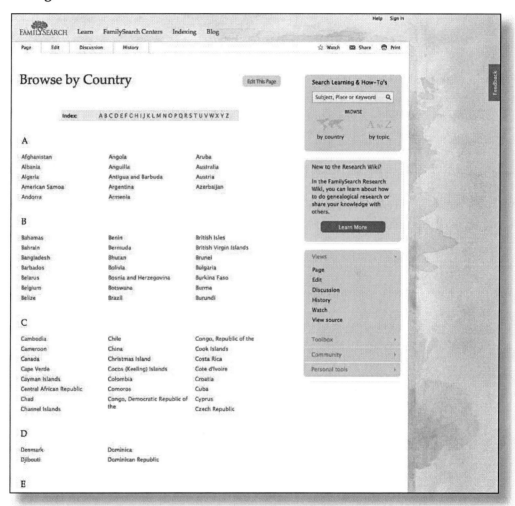

When I discuss the Research Wiki below, I will explain all of the links along the right side of the page.

Indexing:

This bottom of the startup page link takes you directly to the Worldwide Indexing page shown in Figure 1.84 below. I will be discussing the Research Wiki later in this section and the Indexing program in the next sections of this Guide.

General Links at the Bottom of the Startup Page

About Us:

Nearly all websites have a link identifying the sponsoring organization and FamilySearch.org is no exception. Although the name of The Church of Jesus Christ of Latter-day Saints is not prominently featured on the website, there is no particular effort to conceal the fact that FamilySearch is a Church sponsored and owned corporation. With the exception of some areas pertaining to the Church's Temple ordinances, all of the information from and access to the website are free and are offered without any obligation on the part of the users. There are several links to the Church's website, LDS.org, scattered throughout the FamilySearch.org website.

There are two links on following page to the Privacy Policy and Terms of Use, shown with arrows, but there are also links to these same pages on the startup page:

Figure 1.84

Give Back

This is another link to the page shown in Figure 1.15 Giving Back. The page has links to FamilySearch Indexing, Research Articles which is the FamilySearch Wiki and FamilySearch Evaluation.

The FamilySearch Evaluation page is a link to the survey. Here is a screen shot of the Evaluation page:

Figure 1.84.1

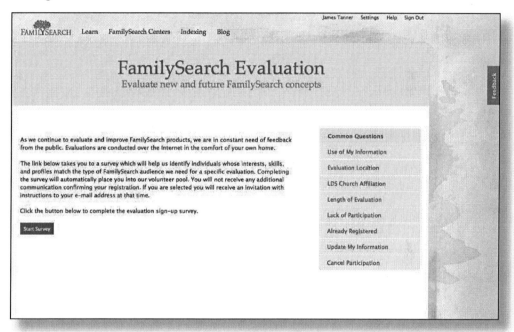

The information requested is fairly detailed. Along the right side of the page are answers to some "Common Questions" about the use of the information and other pertinent information in a series of pop-up windows. The information indicates that not everyone who signs up to Evaluate FamilySearch will be selected to do so.

Careers

The Careers link goes to a page listing the job openings within the Family History Department of The Church of Jesus Christ of Latter-day Saints. The jobs listed are primarily in the engineering/programming area of expertise.

Blog:

The link to the Blog postings is redundant of the link on the top of the page I have marked as #5 Blog. The postings change almost daily and here is another screen shot, note the links on the right-hand side to Subscribe to the Blog and to Follow the Blog on Twitter and Facebook.

Figure 1.85

• • • • • • • • • •

A Note on Subscribing and Following

Subscribing to a website is a way to keep up-to-date with any changes or additions. Before you subscribe you need to have a Reader program running in your browser. One of these programs is Google Reader, a free program from Google. You can obtain a copy of Google Reader free by signing up for a Google Account. Go to the Google startup page and search for Google Reader or go to the pull down menu under "More" on the Google startup page. Follow the instructions and install the Reader, then when you subscribe to the website or Blog post, you will receive automatic notice of new items. This is especially helpful if you have friends or family members who Blog. Remembering to look at their Blog posts can be difficult. You can go overboard with adding post subscriptions to your Reader and end up with hundreds of notices a day. Caution is advised.

Following is similar to subscribing but uses two different programs on the Internet, Twitter and Facebook. Both of these programs can become a full-time job if you following too many feeds. To follow in either program you have to have an account.

• • • • • • • • • •

Press:

Another link at the bottom of the startup page takes you to a webpage with the official news and press releases regarding FamilySearch.org. Here is a screen shot of the top of the page. You can probably guess that this page will change frequently.

Figure 1.86

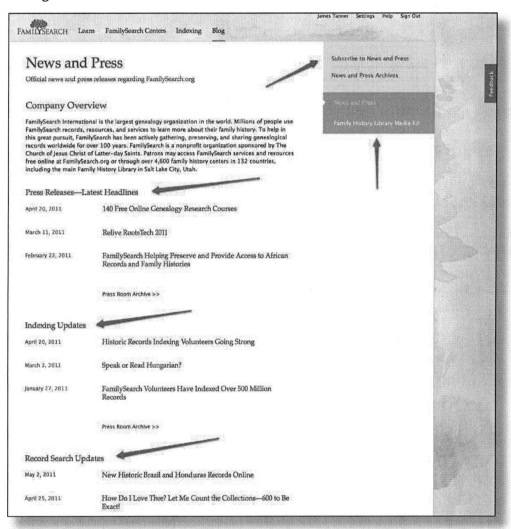

There are several things to note about this page. The press releases are separated into general categories. The reference to "Record Search Updates" is to the

Historical Record Collections, using the older designation before the FamilySearch.org site was updated. It will take some time for these smaller details to be worked out and maybe by the time you read this Guide, the terminology will have changed and the format may have changed also.

As with the Blog posts, you can subscribe to the News and Press posts as shown by the arrow in the upper right-hand corner of the screen. The information also indicates that FamilySearch.org also has a Media Kit for the Family History Library. Here is a screen shot of the Family History Library Media Kit page:

Figure 1.87

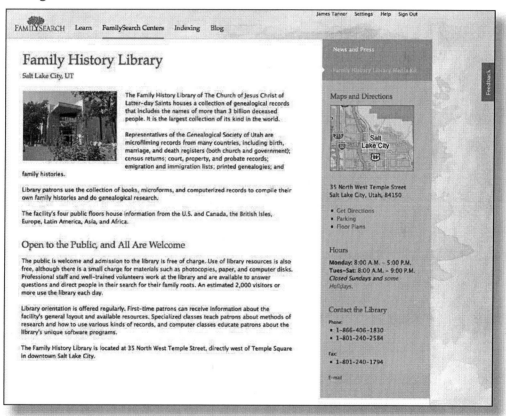

This is a different page than the pages accessible by clicking on the link to #3 FamilySearch Centers on the startup page.

Labs:

FamilySearch Labs is a separate website used by FamilySearch to feature online products that are under development. I will be discussing the Labs website in the following sections dealing with the separate websites.

Store:

Clicking on the Store link opens the FamilySearch Store, a separate website. At the time this Guide was written, clicking on the Logo from the Store did not take you back to the main website. In addition, there were only two items in the store for sale. I would assume that the entire layout and content of this page would change. Here is a screen shot of the current page:

Figure 1.88

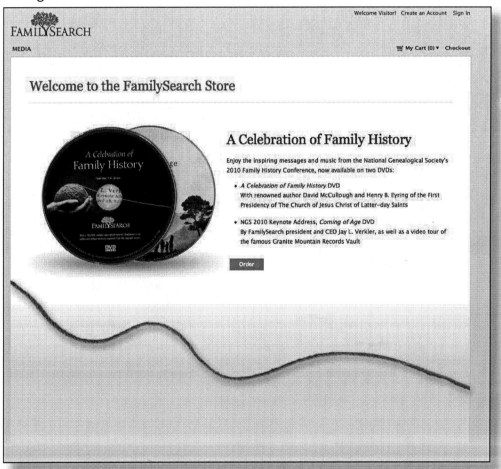

You can see that there is a link to create an account. This is not the same account as your FamilySearch or LDS Account you previously created, so you will have to create a new account. Also note that there is a link to Shipping and Returns information at the bottom of the page. When you sign in to create an account you will be asked for your name, your email and a password. Here is a screen shot of the Sign-in screen:

Figure 1.89

If you are creating a new account, you click on the Register button and get the following screen:

Figure 1.90

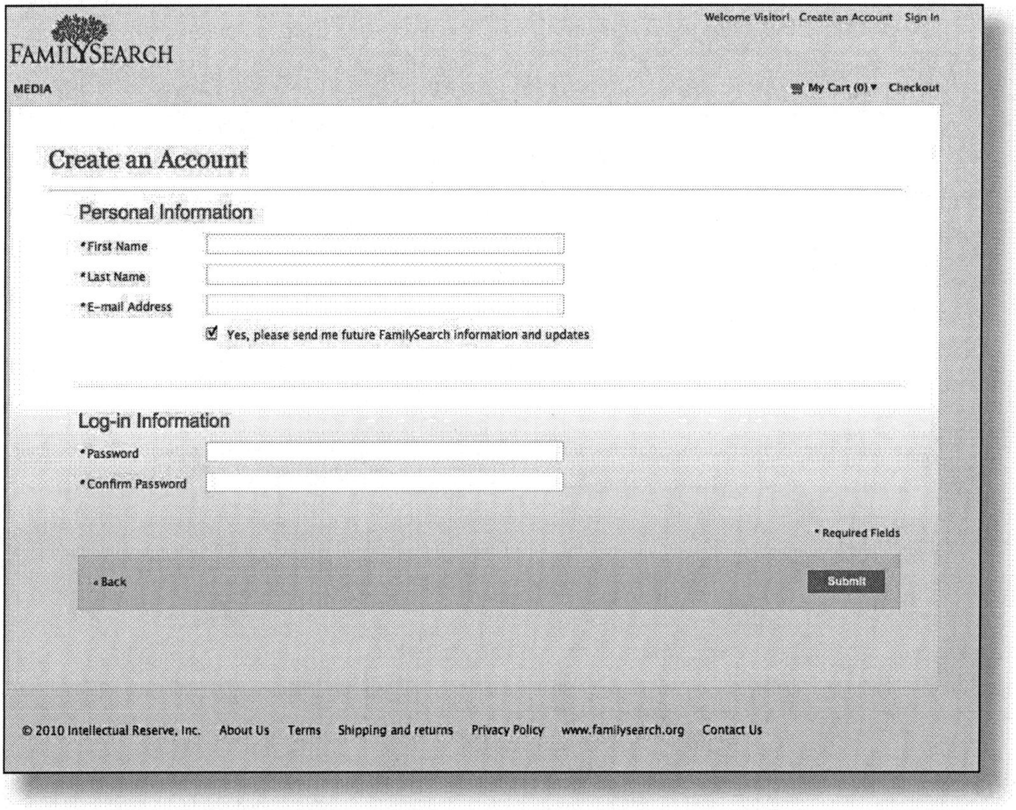

After filling in the information, you will get a screen with fields to add your billing and shipping addresses and other information. These fields will contain your private billing and shipping information as well as a record of your orders.

Privacy:

The Privacy page is long legal explanation of important issues dealing with the use of the website. Here is a screen shot of the top of the page which goes on for quite a while:

Figure 1.91

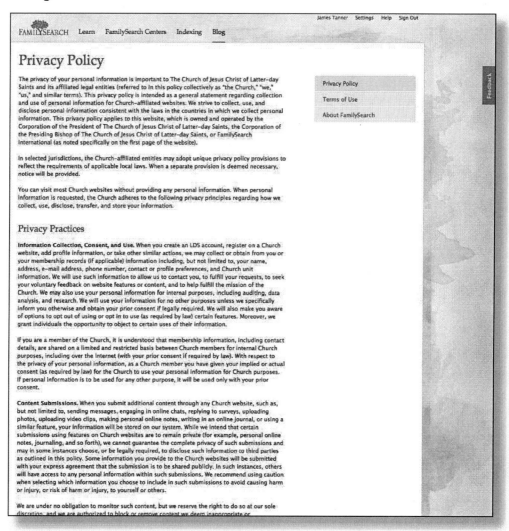

There are links on the right top of the screen to Terms of Use and About FamilySearch. The Terms of Use link goes to the same place as the Terms link on the startup page, as does the About FamilySearch link that I already discussed above. If you have any questions about the legal implications of any of the Privacy Policies, I suggest you discuss the issues with competent legal counsel. It is not at all unusual for websites, especially those as heavily used and complicated as FamilySearch.org to have this type of disclaimer. I did not include all of the terms contained on the page in my screen shot. You must refer to the page to read all of the Privacy Policies.

Terms:

This Terms of Use page is another long page of important legal issues. If you have any legal issues, once again, I suggest you discuss them with competent legal counsel. Just as with the Privacy Policy, I did not include all of the Terms contained on this page. You must refer to the page to read all of the Terms of Use. Here is a screen shot of the top part of the page:

Figure 1.92

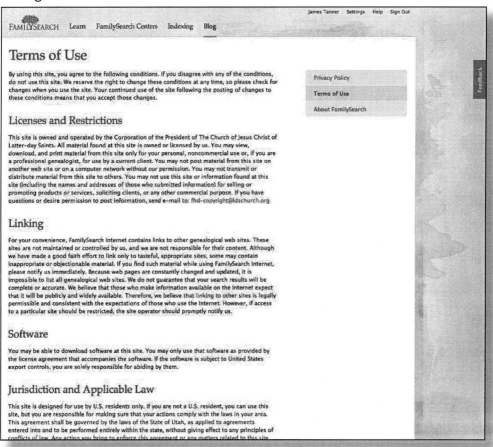

Resources Links at the Bottom of the Startup Page

Ask for Help:

This is the same link as #7 Help discussed above. See Figure 1.19 above.

Archivists:

This link shows the history of FamilySearch.org with a link to the Home screen of The Genealogical Society of Utah. As the site says, "For over 100 years, we have served record custodians around the world. We pioneered industry standards for gathering, imaging, indexing, and preserving records. Advances in technology and the emergence of our digital world now provide an opportunity for us to combine the resources of GSU and FamilySearch.org under a single name: FamilySearch."[13] Here is a screen shot of the page showing most of the information.

Home:

Figure 1.93

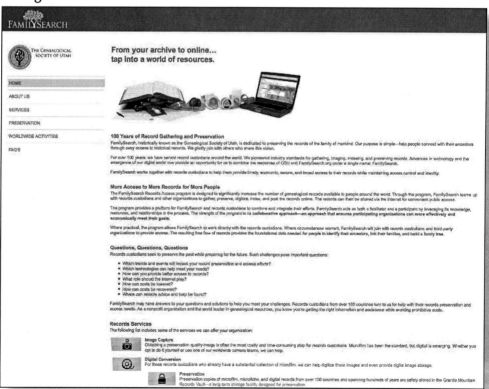

About Us:

Figure 1.94

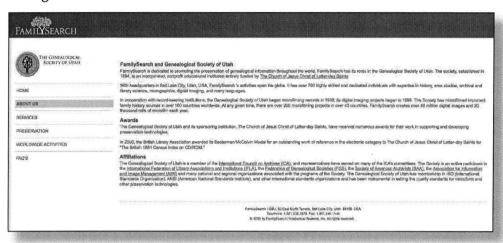

Please note the copyright data at the bottom of the page which includes a reference to Intellectual Reserve, Inc. Like FamilySearch, Intellectual Reserve Inc. (IRI) is a non-profit corporation wholly owned by The Church of Jesus Christ of Latter-day Saints. IRI is the holding company for the Church's intellectual property including copyrights and trademarks. According to the website Tradmarkia, IRI owns over 60 trademarks associated with the church.[14]

Services:

Figure 1.95

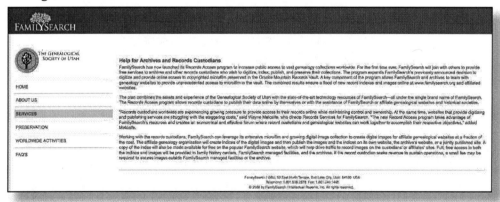

This website is aimed at archivists and record custodians. It is an explanation of the benefits of FamilySearch's ability to provide digitization services.

Preservation:

Figure 1.96

A common concern of all records custodians is the preservation of their books and documents. As this page states, "FamilySearch's microfilming and digital imaging technology programs have preserved millions of volumes of manuscript materials. In conjunction with cooperating institutions, FamilySearch uses the preservation technology and equipment that best meets the needs of both FamilySearch and its affiliates."

Worldwide Activities:

Figure 1.97

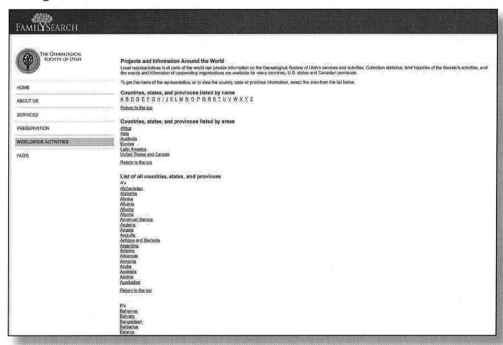

This extensive list of countries illustrates the international influence of FamilySearch. Each of the place names in the list is a link to a FamilySearch representative who has the responsibility for that particular geographic area. This page is probably the most graphic example of the extent of FamilySearch's activities.

FAQs:

Figure 1.98

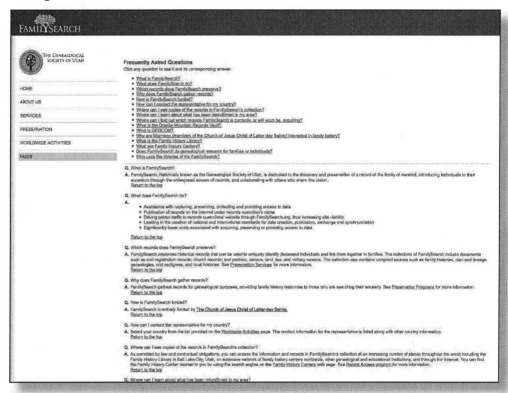

The page shown in this screen shot contains an interesting summary of the work of FamilySearch and answers some basic questions about the record acquisition program. At the time of the writing of this Guide, this site was not yet completely integrated into the main FamilySearch.org website. Some of the links went to the older website.

Developers:

The Developers link at the bottom of the startup page goes to the separate website known as the Developer Network for Software Programmers. Devnet.FamilySearch.org. This is another site that will be discussed in a later section of this Guide.

Libraries:

Clicking on the Libraries link takes you directly to the "Find a FamilySearch Center" page. See Figure 1.9 above.

Products

If you were wondering what ever happened to Personal Ancestral File, it is still available on the Family History Products page. Since there are a large number of third-party products listed, I have omitted a screen shot. But there is a list of products for the Web, Windows, Mac and Mobile devices. This is another page that will have frequent changes.

Feedback:

Clicking here takes you to the same page as #9 Feedback on the right-hand side of many of the pages. See Figure 1.30 above.

This concludes the links on the startup page of FamilySearch.org. The following subsections will talk about each of the separate but integrated websites I skipped in the previous discussion.

FamilySearch Indexing

FamilySearch Indexing was previously an independent website, but with the introduction of the updated FamilySearch.org website in December, 2010, the Indexing site was partially integrated into the newer website. I say partially, because the site is still mostly independent. You can still go directly to the Indexing site by typing in the URL, *Indexing.FamilySearch.org* (the capital letters are ignored). Interestingly, the startup page from the link on FamilySearch.org goes to a different page than the direct URL. Here is the linked page from FamilySearch.org:

Figure 1.99

If you type in the URL directly rather than clicking on the links, you get a different page that does not have the same look and feel as that of the updated website. The Indexing program will be covered in greater depth in Section Two of this Guide.

Figure 1.100

There are over 100,000 volunteers throughout the world participating in the FamilySearch Indexing program. All of the indexed information is available for free in the Historical Record Collections on FamilySearch.org unless the documents are restricted in some way. FamilySearch Indexing requires that you register with an LDS Account or a FamilySearch Account. After registering you must also install the Indexing software on your computer. Once installed, the program runs from the icon of the installed program.

The process of Indexing serves a valuable purpose, that of indexing the scanned images of the microfilm scanned in the Historical Record Collections. To start Indexing, double click on the program icon installed on your computer. You will then download a batch, that is, a set of related records, and can then review the images and instructions. You then begin typing in the requested information in the fields provided on the Indexing forms. After entering the data from a record, you run the quality checker and submit the batch to the Indexing project.

Each batch of records is entered by two separate indexers. The resulting files are then reviewed for consistency by an arbitrator. Indexing is done by projects, that is large groups of related records such as Census records for a particular state. The projects are broken down into batches. Each batch is a group of records that can usually be completely indexed in less than an hour. Indexing applies a rating of beginner, intermediate or expert depending on the degree of difficulty. Your first batch is pre-selected. At each stage of the process there are detailed instructions for every entry you are asked to make. If you have questions, you can click on the link to each field's help. After each series of entries in a batch, there is a quality check before you submit the batch. While you are working, the work you do is automatically saved. You can always get telephone support from the support operators. More specific instructions are available in the Users Guide and in the instructional materials.

Here is a screen shot of the instructions to double-click the program icon to begin the program:

Figure 1.101

At the time this Guide was written, FamilySearch Indexing had 73 international indexing projects underway in 12 different languages, the most recently added program being Hungarian. The projects are originated by a project manager who makes the decision based on the type of contract with the record custodian and the overall goals and plans for the Indexing project as a whole.

The program keeps the work moving along. As an Indexer, you have seven days to complete your batch. You will be warned when the batch is about to expire. If you do not complete the batch, the program will automatically retrieve the batch and make it available for another indexer.

An extensive number of resources are available to help with indexing such as Indexing Tutorials, a Resource Guide linked to instructions, handwriting helps, and language helps.

There is a more extensive discussion of the Indexing program in Section Two.

The FamilySearch Research Wiki

The following information about the FamilySearch Research Wiki will only make complete sense if you follow along with your computer open to the pages indicated. Some of the links are redundant with multiple links to the same information. Other links may be interesting, but not something you will be interested in looking at regularly. If all you want to do is search for information, you can ignore most of the links entirely. However, once you begin to see how the Research Wiki works, I believe you will find the links to be very useful.

•   •   •   •   •   •   •   •   •   •

A Note on Program Redundancy

In order to be more "User Friendly," most computer program are written with some degree of redundancy, that is, duplicate links and functions. The FamilySearch.org website has a fair degree of redundancy built into its screens and links. As you will see below, the startup page for the #2 Learn link has four different links to the Research Wiki, three of which are identical. Rather than being a mistake by the programmers, this redundancy is intentional. So don't be surprised if clicking on various different links takes you to the same page in the website.

•   •   •   •   •   •   •   •   •

The FamilySearch Research Wiki is the heart of the FamilySearch.org website. It is accessed from the startup page by clicking on the "Learn" link, which is located at the top of the FamilySearch.org startup page. See #2 Learn above in this Guide. There are four separate links to the Research Wiki on the Learning Resources page as shown in this screen shot:

Figure 1.102

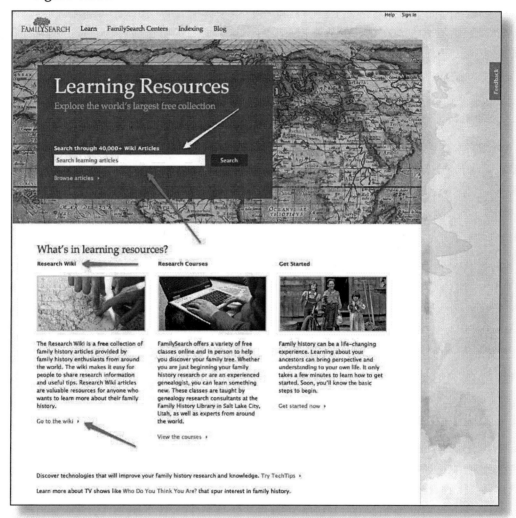

The first arrow shows the search field. Entering a search term into this field will take you to a list of similar terms found in the Research Wiki. The other three arrows go directly to the startup page for the Research Wiki as shown in the next screen shot:

Figure 1.103

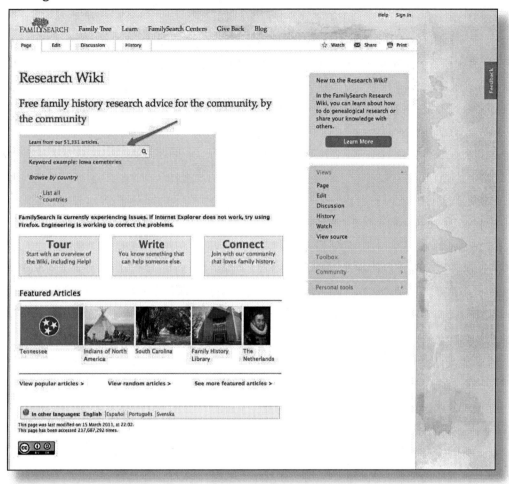

The arrow in Figure 1.103 shows the search field. This is essentially the same as the search field on the Learning Resources page shown in Figure 1.102.

· · · · · · · · · ·

A Note about Wikis in General

A "wiki" is a particular kind of program that runs on the Internet as opposed to running on your individual computer. The term "wiki" is a Hawaiian word for "quick," and was named after the wiki-wiki Shuttle at the Honolulu International Airport by the developer of the first wiki, Ward Cunningham.[15] A wiki is a collaborative website that allows the creation and editing of any number of interrelated and linked web pages by using a browser. In editing a wiki, you use a simplified mark-up language called wikitext. The wiki program also recognizes some of the standard HTML (Hyper-Text Markup Language) used throughout the World Wide Web. The first wiki developed by Ward Cunningham was called the WikiWikiWeb and is still active online.

Wikis became a driving force on the Web with the introduction of Wikipedia.org run by the Wikimedia Foundation.[16] Wikipedia is a compilation of user submitted articles or pages and, as of the date of writing this Guide, had over 18 million articles. Wikipedia is ranked in the top ten websites by the amount of traffic.[17]

Studies have shown that a highly cooperative Wiki-model can provide information of the highest quality. In an article entitled "Assessing the Value of Cooperation in Wikipedia," authors Dennis M. Wilkinson and Bernardo A. Hubeman of the Information Dynamics Laboratory of the Hewlett-Packard Development Company, L.P. found the following:

"Since its inception six years ago, the online encyclopedia Wikipedia has accumulated 6.40 million articles and 250 million edits contributed in a predominantly undirected and haphazard fashion by 5.77 million unvetted contributors. Since it is not obvious that this kind of large-scale, voluntary effort can produce good results, we measured the correlation between the 50 million edits in the English-language Wikipedia and the quality of its 1.5 million articles. We found that article quality is indeed correlated with both number of edits and number of distinct editors. An analysis of editing patterns shows a heavy-tailed distribution of articles, in which relatively few articles having disproportionally high numbers of edits and editors end up at the forefront in terms of quality and visibility."[18]

* * * * * * * * *

The Research Wiki articles contain almost unlimited information about where to find or research records, localities, subjects and research methods. The Research Wiki does not contain pedigree charts or family group records. Individual pages in the Research are referred to both as "articles" and as pages. By design, the articles on the Research Wiki are largely confined to historically and genealogically related subjects. It is organized in two ways; by geographic location or by subject matter. This distinction will become more clear as I show how the Research Wiki operates. I will start with a discussion each of the elements and links on the startup page with arrows or markers to indicate where the links occur.

Elements on the Research Wiki Startup page

Figure 1.103 shows a screen shot of the Research Wiki startup page before you sign in. To sign in you use your LDS Account or FamilySearch Account. See #8 Sign In, previously discussed. You do not have to sign in to use the Research Wiki. You can search and use many of the features without being registered at all. In order to edit any of the articles or contribute information you will need to be registered and sign in. When you do sign in, if you look at the right hand side of the page, you will see an expanded Personal Tools section. Everyone who signs into the Wiki automatically has a User page. Part of the Personal Tools is a "My preferences" link. This page includes a link called "Skin" that gives you two options for viewing the Wiki: the view in FamilySearch or a different view entitled "FamilySearch Wiki". The main difference between the two options is that the FamilySearch view includes all of the FamilySearch.org website links while the FamilySearch Wiki view does not. Since you can make this choice in your preferences, how you view the pages is a matter of personal preference.

To change the view, you will have to sign in. Once you sign in, click on the Personal Tools link to show the list of Personal tools which includes the following options:

- Your Userpage title with your user name from your FamilySearch or LDS Accout
- My talk
- My Presferences
- My watchlist
- My contributions
- Sign Out

I will go into more detail about the Userpages and the other links later in the Guide. Right now the only thing you need to know is that you can chose the view you get of the pages in the Research Wiki by clicking on the "My preferences" link and choosing the "Skin" tab or link at the top of the page.

Because it is the default view, I will discuss the elements of the FamilySearch view as opposed to the FamilySearch Wiki view of the startup page. Note that on both views there are a large number of options and links. If you change your preferences to the FamilySearchWiki view, some of the menu items will change but the basic functionality of the website will not change. To avoid navigational issues, I suggest leaving the default FamilySearch view of the site.

Here is another screen shot of the FamilySearch view with the first set of arrows and markers:

Figure 1.104

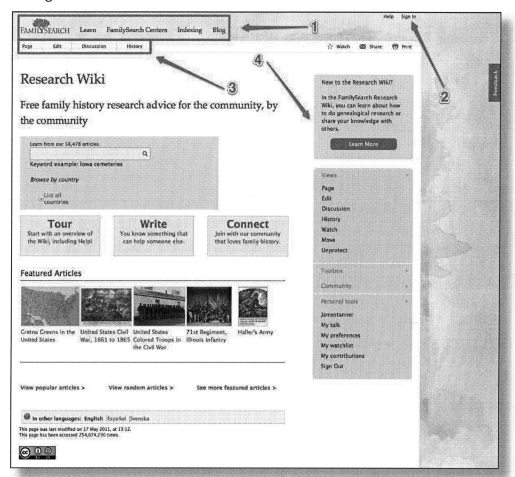

Here we go with the links on FamilySearch view startup page. The links marked #1, as indicated by the box and arrow, are the same as those on the Family-Search.org startup page. Clicking on any one of these links will take you to exactly the same set of pages as any of the other pages with similar links in the website. If you continue to click on links you may be asked to sign in. Here is an example of the sign-in link:

Figure 1.105

If you do not wish to sign in, you can get back to the Research Wiki by clicking the back arrow on your browser. Clicking the other links takes you directly to the FamilySearch.org website pages for those links. Although, as I said earlier, you can use the Research Wiki to search for information without signing in, there are various functions of the FamilySearch.org website as whole, including the Research Wiki, that require you to sign in. Since registering requires only a minimal amount of information, I suggest signing in so that this is no longer an issue.

* * * * * * * * * *

A Note on Referring to the Research Wiki

For simplicity, I will refer to the Research Wiki, from here on, as the Wiki. In order to avoid confusion between references to the specific Wiki here and the generic term, I will capitalize the word whenever I am talking specifically about the Research Wiki as opposed to wikis in general.

* * * * * * * * * *

In Figure 1.104 the arrow marked #2 is where you click to sign in. Once you have signed in, you automatically return to the FamilySearch Wiki startup page.

The arrow marked #3 points to tabs for functions of the Wiki. These functions are not particular to the Research Wiki but are basic functions of the wiki program itself. Those functions are:

- Page
- Edit
- Discussion
- History

There are three more functions that are also on the same level but not indicated by arrows: Watch, Share and Print.

You can see duplicate links to these functions by clicking on the Views drop-down menu as shown in the following screen shot:

Figure 1.106

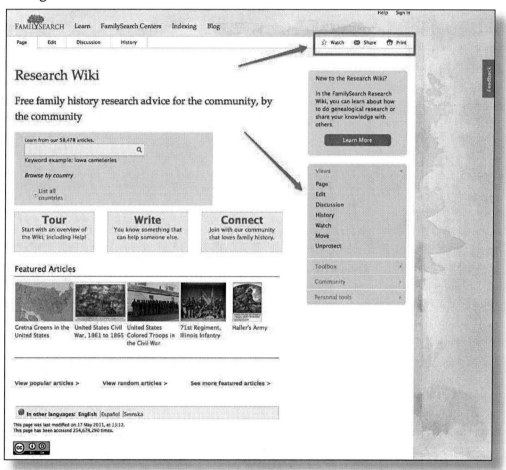

The arrows point to the functions for Watch, Share and Print, as well as the expanded list of items under the Views drop-down menu. By comparing the links to those in the right-hand column, you can see that the functions are duplicates of most of those already listed.

The Page link, both in the tab and in the drop-down menu, takes you to the page view of the Wiki. A wiki page is made up of several layers of information. The main page (also called article) is the normal or default view. Each article or page also has an Edit view that allows a registered user who is signed in to edit any of the content of the page. I am going to use the page from the Research Wiki for Mesa, Arizona as an example:

Figure 1.107

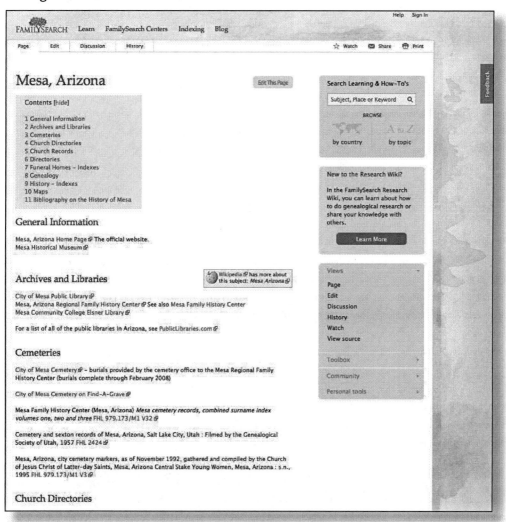

You can see from Figure 1.107 that each page of the Research Wiki has most of the same elements. The menu bars, the list of links on the right-hand side of the page and other page elements, like the Contents, are all generated by the program and appear on every page. The information added by the users is in the center part of the page and, in this case, consists of information about Mesa, Arizona.

If all this, so far, seems confusing, it is because it is confusing. There are so many choices with different links, that only by working with the program for a while will you begin to understand how it operates and how everything fits into the structure.

Searching in the Wiki

Searching is available to anyone. Registration is only necessary to edit or contribute to the Wiki. Although the search field seems simple, only a blank space for an entry, you can use a lot of different strategies for finding information. First and foremost, you can search by keyword, such as a place, a subject, a record type, or the name of an article, the same way you would do a basic Wikipedia search. Remember that the Wiki primarily has information about genealogy. It does not have information about individuals. Do not use sentences or phrases. You can use phrases or sentences in Google and other search engines, but the Wiki does not return good results when searched in this manner. Also, the Wiki is not a place to ask questions about your family. You may wish to try using the FamilySearch Forums for questions and support. I will explore the Forums website later on in the Guide.

To begin a search, type the term or terms you are searching for in the blank search field and click the search button or hit enter on your keyboard. Here is the first part of the results for a search on the word "Mesa."

Figure 1.107.1

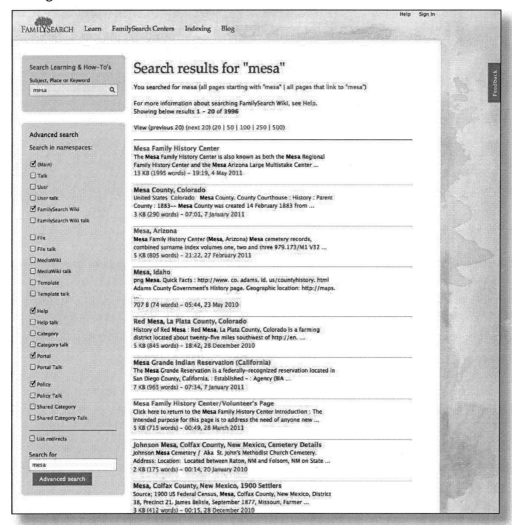

To go to any one of the entries click on the name of the article or page. Once you click on one of the results, the program changes the color of the entry so you can tell which entries you have already clicked. At the top of the page you can see that there are 3996 returns for the word "Mesa." If you don't find what you are looking for in the first list, then you need to narrow the search by adding one or more terms. I suggest using the general search strategy, entering the fewest possible terms at first and then slowly adding terms as you need to narrow the results. You can look at the next group of search results by clicking on the View (previous 20) (next 20) (20 | 50 | 100 | 250 | 500).

Along the left-hand side of the results page, there is a long list of options with checkboxes titled "Advanced Search." This is a list of the namespaces in the Wiki. (See Note below). When you did your initial search, the Wiki program searched only those pages or articles in the namespaces with the check marks. If you want to expand your search to include more pages or articles in the Wiki, you need to check additional boxes. You can also set the number of boxes checked as a Preference on your User page. See below.

*   *   *   *   *   *   *   *   *

A Note about Wiki Namespaces

In computer programming, a namespace, sometimes called a name scope, is a term used to refer to an abstract container or environment created to hold a logical grouping of unique identifiers or symbols. In the wiki world, the term is used to refer to a collection of pages, which have content with a similar purpose or where the intended use is the same. Namespaces are essentially partitions of different types of information within the same wiki. All of the wiki pages exist within a namespace and this can be distinguished by using the namespace prefix of a page that forms part of the title of a page, separated with a colon.[19] For example: Figure 1.109 below in the Guide, "Talk:Mesa, Arizona." There are a number of different namespaces including the "Talk" pages. A Talk page is a separate page associated with a main page that is provided to make a place where a discussion or talk can occur about the content of the main page. Here is a list of some of the namespaces in the Wiki:

Main	File Talk
Talk	Template
User	Template Talk
User Talk	Help
Project	Help Talk
Project Talk	Category
File	Category Talk

Learning the functions of each of the namespaces is part of the challenge of learning about a Wiki. You do not need to know any of this to use the Wiki to look up information, but if you start contributing to the Wiki, you will need to understand these pages. More information can be found in the Help:Namespaces page in the Wiki.

*   *   *   *   *   *   *   *   *

Before we go on, I need to show the alternate skin for the startup page chosen in the User Preferences. Here is the Research Wiki startup page after I have signed in and after I have chosen the skin for the FamilySearch Wiki:

Figure 1.108

Because I have selected the FamilySearch Wiki view in my preferences, after I sign in, the pages change by reducing the number of elements. The menu bar is much reduced, but most of the same functions and links are still listed on the right side of the page. At the bottom of the list you can see the Personal tools which I will discuss shortly. After signing in with the FamilySearch Wiki skin, here is the Mesa, Arizona article:

Figure 1.109

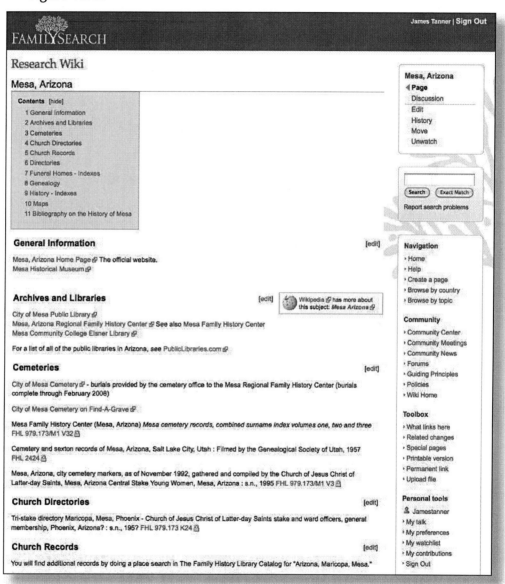

As you can see, the FamilySearch items at the top of the page have disappeared and the options on the right side of the page have expanded. Although the information about the City of Mesa entered on the page can be changed by the user, the basic elements, such as the links on the right side of the page, do not change.

The first heading in the list on the right-hand side shows the list of page optionsalready noted. Each of these options is associated with the subject page, here Mesa, Arizona.

The following paragraphs contain a discussion of the underlying pages to the Mesa, Arizona article as listed in the Menu box in the upper right corner of the screen:

Discussion Link

The Discussion or Talk page is where the Wiki users can discuss issues regarding the content of the article or page. Every page in the Wiki has a Discussion link. If there is no content in the Discussion or Talk page then the link will appear red in color rather than blue. I entered a comment to show content in the Discussion or Talk page:

Figure 1.110

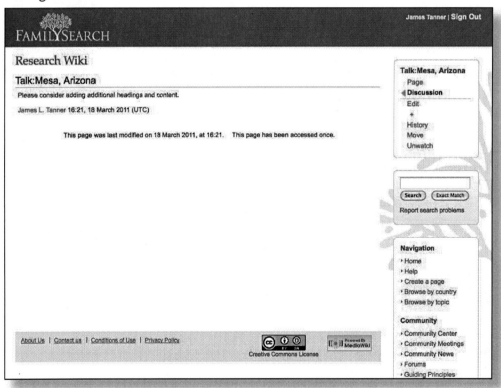

In most cases, it is probably not necessary to have a discussion about a particular page. However, if there is any controversy over the contents or if the information is in any way unacceptable in the Wiki community, then the place to express those opinions is on the Discussion or Talk page. If you try to click on the Discussion link, you cannot edit the Discussion or Talk page without signing on to the Wiki.

Edit Link

Next is an example of the Edit page for Mesa, Arizona:

Figure 1.111

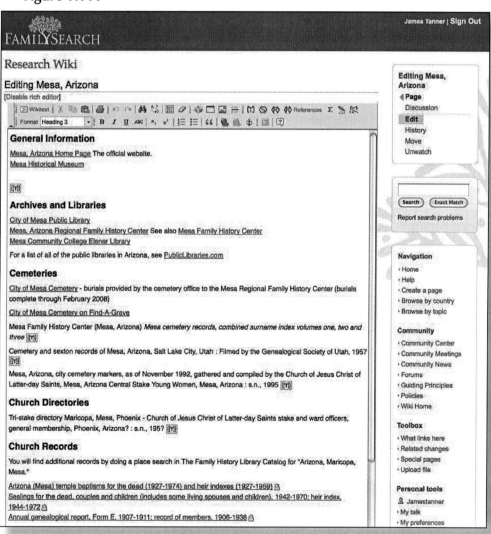

History Link

The History page shows all of the edits, additions or changes made the article or page listed in chronological order. You can compare revisions by clicking in the buttons and then clicking on the "Compare selected revisions" button. Each edit entry identifies the person who made the edit or changes the size of the edit and then includes an undo link. Clicking on the undo link reverts the changes to the previous version. Here is a screen shot of the Mesa, Arizona article's History page:

Figure 1.112

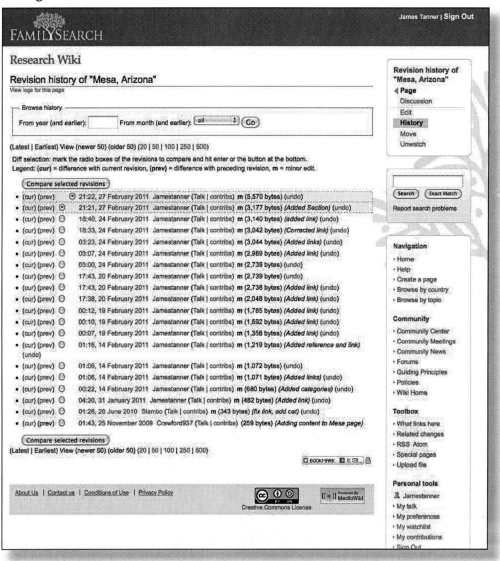

• • • • • • • • • •

A Note about Why Wikis aren't a Mess

One of the most common concerns expressed about a wiki by first-time users is why the whole thing doesn't just turn into a complete mess or junk pile. The answer is relatively complex. Part of the answer lies in the structure of the wiki. Even though the information is collaborative, the structure is relatively static and predictable. The real key however, lies in the way the wiki is organized. One key to how the program works lies in the Edit pages' undo link. Every change made to the wiki is recorded on an Edit page. Anyone who disagrees with a change or edit, can almost instantly revert the page or article to its pre-change condition simply by clicking on the undo button. So any vandalism or inappropriate material can be quickly and easily eliminated.

The rest of the story lies with the wiki community. The wiki is a totally voluntary organization. But there are always those who have some special interest in the content, goals, policies and procedures of the wiki. In the FamilySearch Research Wiki, this support is provided in part by Family-Search staff members, but there are also many volunteers who contribute time and effort to maintain the integrity of the Wiki. Most of the pages in the Wiki have a moderator, which is a person responsible for the pages or articles. The moderator watches all of the wiki pages in his or her area and is notified by email of any changes. If there is a issue with an entry, the moderator can correct the entry or raise the issue with the administrators on up the line. Issues concerning the overall appropriateness of the content or article can be discussed on the Discussion or Talk page. If there is a problem, the issue can also be discussed in the FamilySearch Forum.

All of these options will be discussed more fully in the context of the Guide.

• • • • • • • • • •

Move Link

As you can see in Figure 1.112, each addition, edit or change to the article or page is documented and reversible. You can also see a new item in the page functions, Move. This is a drastic measure and should be used only rarely. Here is a screen shot of the Move page with its explanation:

Figure 1.113

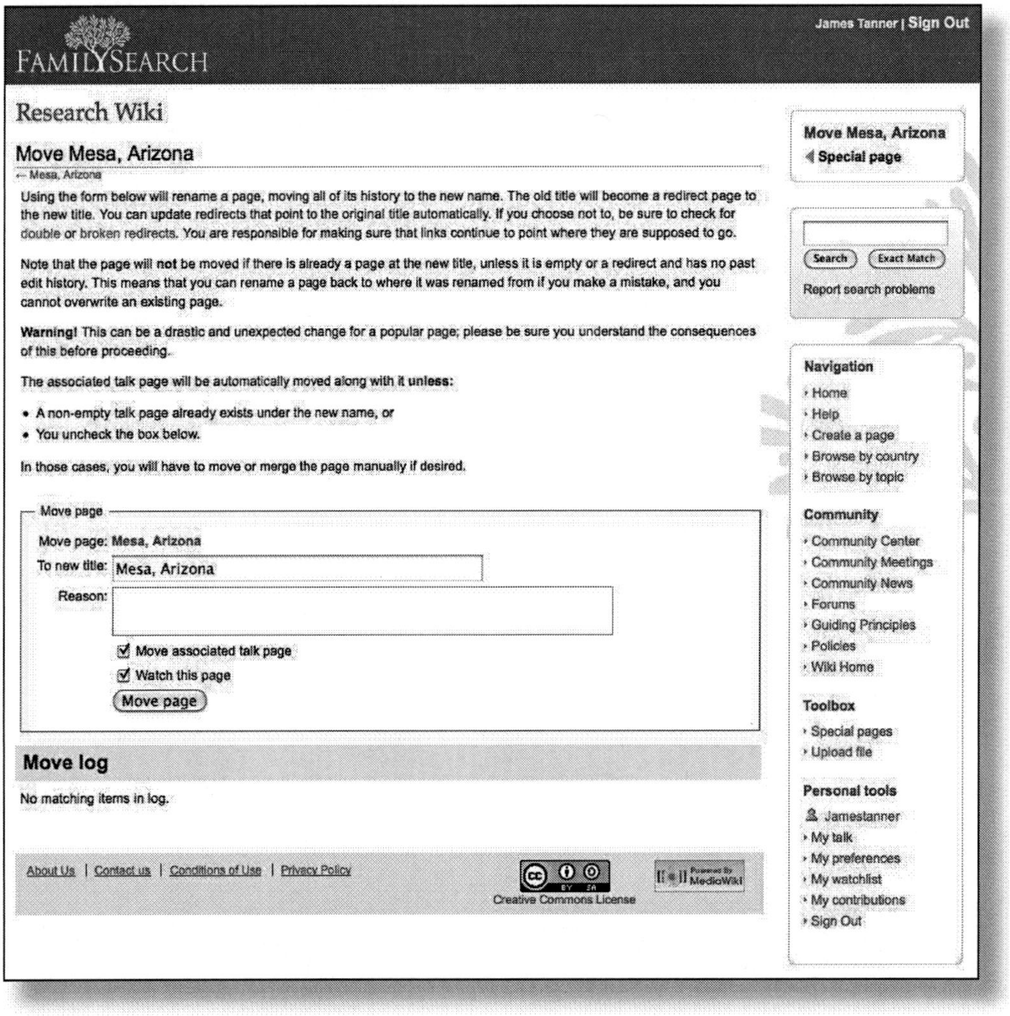

Watch/Unwatch Link

The last item in the list is the Watch link. Once you have made a change or edit to an article or page, the Watch automatically changes to Unwatch. What this means is that you are now automatically watching the page to which you made the changes. Watching means that any time there is a change to the page, the program will send you an email notice of the change with a link to the newly changed page. This is one good reason why the Wiki does not disintegrate into a junk pile. Everyone has the opportunity to watch any pages they have an interest in maintaining.

Back to the Wiki FamilySearch Skin

Now, back to elements on the startup page. Please don't get helplessly confused, but I am switching back to the FamilySearch skin. It is sufficient to understand that there are two ways to view the Wiki, that is, two different "skins" or designs. If I sign out, the page design immediately reverts to the FamilySearch skin. To avoid further confusion, I will stick with the FamilySearch skin as much as possible.

Here is another shot of the startup page for the Wiki for reference:

Figure 1.114

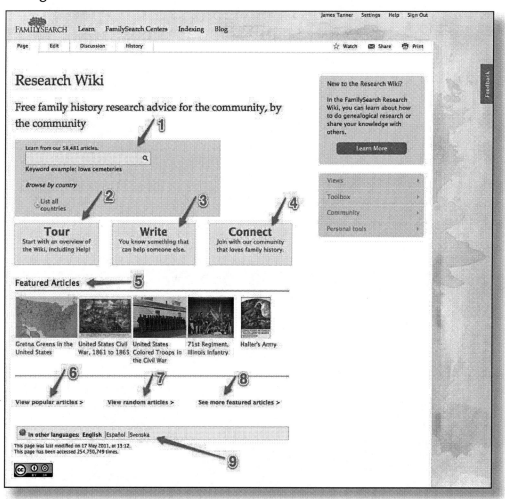

Nine of the elements on the page are indicated by arrows and numbers.

#1 is the search field. This is where you can search for almost any term dealing with genealogy. The search looks for any article or page containing the term. Searching on the Research Wiki is straightforward and quite simple. All you do is type in a search term into the search box; you can type a subject, a place or keywords. For example, you can search for records in Arizona, by typing the word "Arizona" into the search box. You will get better results if you list the words you are interested in finding rather than using phrases such as, "Where can I find records about Arizona?" If you are looking for a specific type of record, probate records, for example, try typing in just the word. If you are looking for a certain kind of record in a particular location, type in the word followed by the location, for example, "Probate Arizona," Do not use complete sentences or punctuation.

#2 is a link to a tour of the Wiki. There is really no way to adequately represent the dynamic functions of a complex website in written text. Clicking on the link will take you to the Help:Tour page containing dozens of subsequent links to information in the Wiki about how the program works.

#3 is a link to the page "Help:Edit and Contribute" an extensive guide to getting started as a new contributor. Each of these pages has numerous additional links to more specific information.

#4 is a link to the Wiki community including the Wiki Forums that will be discussed later on in the Guide.

#5 indicates a number of links to featured articles. These change frequently. They are featured because they are a good example of what the Wiki is trying to accomplish.

Numbers 6, 7 and 8 are also examples of different articles in the Wiki for illustration purposes. If you have any curiosity about what kind of information you might find in the Wiki, clicking on some or all of these selections will give you a good idea of the nature of the Wiki and its scope. I find it interesting that some of the pages in the Wiki with the highest number of visits have the least information.

#9, the last arrow on Figure 1.114, points to the three other languages that are supported by the Wiki. You will have to sign in separately for each of the languages.

* * * * * * * * *

A Note about Neutral Point of View

One of the guiding principles of the Wiki is a neutral point of view. See the page called FamilySearch Wiki:Guiding Principles. All articles in the Research Wiki must fairly represent, and as far as possible without bias, all of the significant views of family history related topics that have been published by reliable sources. A neutral point of view also implies that all of the information in the Wiki will be based on and cited from sources that are authoritative and verifiable. The Wiki is not a soapbox for personal views or opinions. It is also not appropriate to include personal experiences, testimonials, and stories of research successes or to advertise goods or services. All of the submissions to articles on the Wiki should avoid dogmatism and any overly religious, political, ethnic, cultural, and nationalistic discussions. As the FamilySearch Wiki:Guiding Principles page states, "The best way to avoid being personal or dogmatic is to write with a neutral point of view and cite authoritative sources for the ideas you express. Strive to fairly explain any competing points of view that differ from your own. Even though this site is sponsored by a religious entity, it is neither reviewed nor correlated for doctrinal correctness, and therefore, should not become a forum for doctrinal discussions or discourses—even ones that are purely informational in nature."[20]

* * * * * * * * *

This is a very busy page with lots of links.

At the very bottom of the page there are additional links which may vary from time to time. Here is a screen shot with an arrow pointing to an additional link, the Creative Commons License.

Figure 1.115

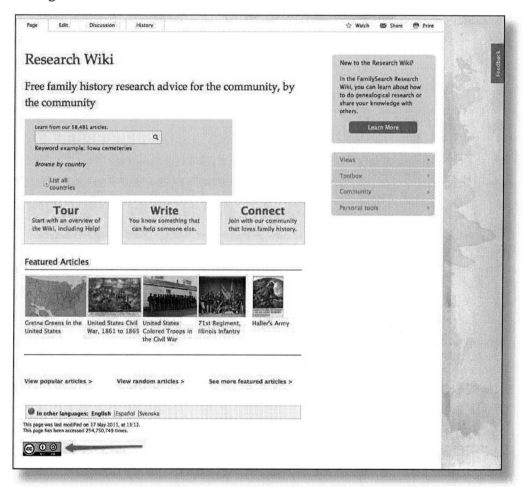

Creative Commons License Link

On the Creative Commons License there are three small icons, the first that looks like a CC is the Creative Commons, a non-profit organization that has developed a set of free public licenses to enable authors to share their work with others. The Creative Commons License gives the consumer (user) more freedom than

Federal Copyright Law.[21] The two smaller icons indicate first, that you are free to copy, distribute and transmit the work but you must attribute the work in the manner specified by the author or licensor (but not in any way that suggests that they endorse you or your use of the work).[22] In addition the second little icon indicates that if you alter, transform, or build upon this work, you may distribute the resulting work only under the same or similar license to this one. The license also requires that the user must make clear to others the license terms of the work for any reuse or distribution. The best way to do this is with a link to the Creative Commons web page just as the Wiki has done.[23]

• • • • • • • • • •

A Note about Wikitext

Wikitext is a markup language. A markup language is a system of annotating text in a way that it can be syntactically distinguished from that text. One simple example is the revision instructions to authors by editors, traditionally written in blue pencil on an author's manuscript. More modern examples included HTML or HyperText Markup Language commonly used to format web pages on the World Wide Web.[24] Wikitext is known as a lightweight markup language because it has a simple syntax in order to be easy for a person to enter with a text editor. Wikitext is also considered to be a presentation oriented markup language that is uses code embedded in the document to produce a "what you see is what you get" (WYSIWYG) effect.[25] The Wiki uses both Wikitext and HTML to create the format seen on the website. The page view showing all the embedded codes is accessed through the "Edit" link on the page functions.

Wikitext is used in the Edit mode to format pages or articles, create links, build tables and other design functions. There are two modes of editing, one using a Rich Editor where most of the functions are automated, and another in native mode that reveals all of the Wikitext and HTML commands. There will be more about this subject later in the Guide.

• • • • • • • • • •

Links on Right-hand Side of the Pages

The links along the right-hand side of the page are extremely useful but may be confusing. The first issue is that the links change depending on your personal preferences and depending on the page you are viewing. Since there are two very different ways to view the Wiki, the FamilySearch View and the FamilySearch Wiki view, I will cover both of these views and the differences and similarities. Like everything about a dynamic website, the selections and menu items may change at any time. If you have any doubt about a link, simply click to see where it goes. If you get lost, either click on the logo or type the address in your browser.

First I will discuss the older FamilySearch Wiki view of the links with comments and comparisons to the FamilySearch view, then I will go through the links again, using the FamilySearch View. Once again, these views may change at any time, but the general categories of links and the links themselves will still be in the Wiki.

The categories of links in the two different lists are as follows:

FamilySearch Wiki View Links

- Navigation
- Community
- Toolbox
- Personal Tools

FamilySearch View Links

- Views
- Toolbox
- Community
- Personal Tools

As you can see, the lists are similar but have some differences. One is not better than the other but it is just a matter of preference. If you want to find out more, jump ahead to the Personal Tools section and read about the "My preferences" link.

Links in the FamilySearch Wiki view of the website:

Navigation Links

Starting at the top of the column the links are as follows:

- Home
- Help
- Create a page
- Browse by country
- Browse by topic

For the most part, these links are self-explanatory, but I will give a short explanation of each .

Home Link

This link does exactly what it says; takes you directly back to the Wiki home or startup page. This can be confusing because even though the Wiki is integrated into the FamilySearch.org website, Home does not mean back to the startup page for the whole website. Normally, you would click on the FamilySearch Logo and it would take you back to the whole website startup page, for example, when you are in the Wiki, clicking on the Logo takes you back to the FamilySearch.org startup page. But, as you will see shortly, there is yet another link on every page to the Home page.

Help Link

The Help link is another redundant link. Redundancy is not bad, it is really very good thing, but until you get some experience in using the Wiki, you may not realize the extent to which links are duplicated. This link does not go to the main FamilySearch.org help page; it goes to a separate Wiki article with links to resources. The links on the Help Link page go to additional pages in the Wiki. You can always return to the Help Link page by clicking on the Navigation: Help Link.

Here is a screen shot of part of the Help Link page:

Figure 1.116

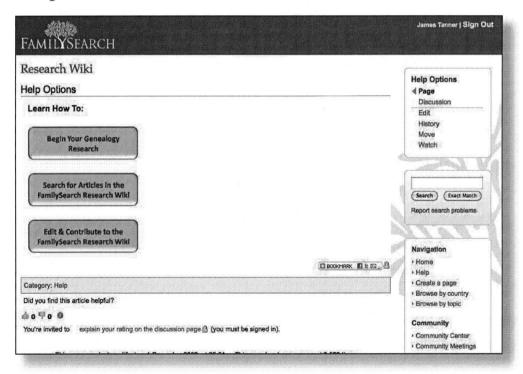

Create a page

This link takes you to a very simple way to create a new page in the Wiki, however, you should review all of the linked instructions before creating a page. If you create a page using this utility, you should realize that the page will not be linked to any other existing page in the Wiki. In essence, the page will be an orphan. It is much better to create pages using links from existing pages. You should always consider editing or adding to an existing page or article rather than creating a new page. You can also create a new page by adding a link to the title you want to give to the new page. Once the link is saved, you can click on the name of the new page and a new page will be added with that name. Using this method you can automatically link the information from the new page to existing pages Remember that the Wiki uses the terms "pages" and "articles" interchangeably.

Browse by country Link

The Wiki startup or home page has a link to "Browse by country" but the same link is also on every page. The link connects to a list of most of the countries in the world. Each of the countries is further linked to its individual country page. The amount of information available about some of the countries may surprise you. There are still countries where there is very little information. Here is a screen shot of the top part of the Browse by country page"

Figure 1.117

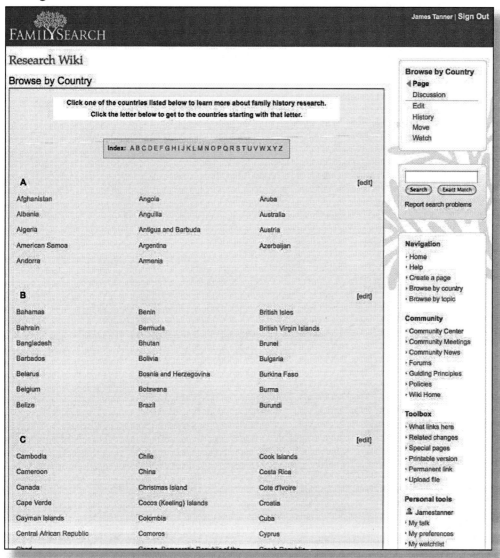

Browse by topic Link

Clicking on this link takes you to the list of the Wiki Subcategories and illustrates a little more of the structure of the Wiki. The title of the page is descriptive, Category:Contents and points out the need to understand the organization of the Wiki before naming new pages. Most of these Category links have subsequent Subcategory links. The first screen shot shows the Category:Contents page:

Figure 1.118

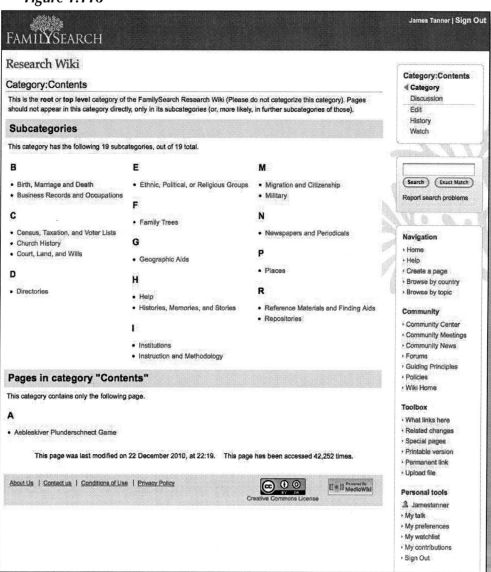

Here is the Subcategory page from the Birth, Marriage and Death Link:

Figure 1.119

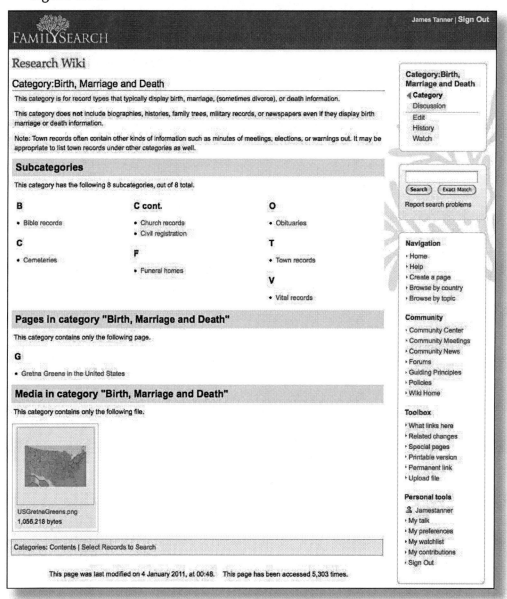

• • • • • • • • • •

A Note about Privacy and the Wiki

When you sign in and start participating in the Wiki and in the Forums, you may become concerned about your privacy. The guideline is simple, don't put anything on the Wiki or write anything in comments that you do not want the whole world to know about. Always remember in any interaction on the Web that includes FamilySearch.org, the Wiki, Forums and other sites, that you are in a sense performing before the world. Don't put things online that you might later prefer had remained unsaid or unexpressed.

• • • • • • • • • •

Community

Moving on to the next category of links along the right-hand side of the Wiki page, we get the following list:

- Community Center
- Community Meetings
- Community News
- Forums
- Guiding Principles
- Policies
- Wiki Home

Please note that this list is different than the one you will see with the Family- Search View selected in your preferences. Keep reading below for an explanation of that view.

The overall theme of these links is to emphasize the community nature of the Wiki. Although you can use the Wiki without ever participating in the community, once you begin to contribute information, you will find that there are a lot of topics that need discussion. This can be accomplished, in part, through the Discussion link on every page, but matters that concern large blocks of pages or policy issues that may affect the entire Wiki, need to be decided by consensus. The Forums are provided to have a place to interact in a more direct and specific way about matters concerning the entire Wiki. Neither the Wiki nor the Forums constitute a social networking site and messages should be confined to the matters at hand.

If you have signed into the Wiki and changed your "My Preferences" options, you will see a slightly different list. The Research Forums, Wiki Forums and Contributor Help links are replaced by one link to the Forums startup page. I will discuss this issue as we go along with this set of links.

Community Center Link

This designation is a convenient way to introduce the Wiki community related links. From the screen shot of the current Community Center page, you can see that this is a collection of links. Here is the screen shot:

Figure 1.120

The pictures do not particularly relate to the links or to the Wiki. They appear to be a way to add some variety to a Wiki page. The links are generally useful and are available either from a search or though other links. If you look carefully, you will see that some of the links have little arrow icons next to them. These small icons indicate that those particular links go to sites outside of the Wiki. To avoid confusion, you may wish to set your browser preferences to open a new window or tab when you click on an external link. How you handle opening external links is a personal preference issue.

If you are new to the Wiki, it is a good idea to take the time to look at most of these links. Even if you have some experience, many of them will be helpful.

• • • • • • • • • •

A Note about the Nature of Wiki Articles

The Wiki is not a pre-determined or pre-planned project. No one has an outline of what the Wiki should contain or how the information will be organized. To effect any major reorganization, it takes a consensus of the Wiki users. Pages or articles in the Wiki will reflect the abilities, opinions and knowledge of the contributors. If you find something in the Wiki that you do not think works as it should, then you have just as much right as anyone else to make the changes. If you think that more or different links are needed, then you can register, sign in and make any additions or changes you think are appropriate. If you aren't sure if you should make any kind of change, then put your thoughts into the page's Discussion or Talk page. If no one responds to your discussion in a reasonable period of time, you might go ahead and make the change and then see if someone comments. You do not have to be timid about making changes or additions but you do need to be considerate and polite.

• • • • • • • • • •

Community Meetings Link

Community meetings are held over the Internet by Webinars. A Webinar is a combined word for web based seminar, presentation, lecture or workshop that the transmitted over the Web. Special Web software allows you to not only watch and listen to the proceedings, but, by using a microphone attached to your computer, you can participate and ask questions.[26] If your computer does not support a microphone connection, you can also participate by telephone. FamilySearch offers weekly

Webinars to support the Wiki program. Here is a screen shot of the page giving the information about the weekly meetings:

Figure 1.121

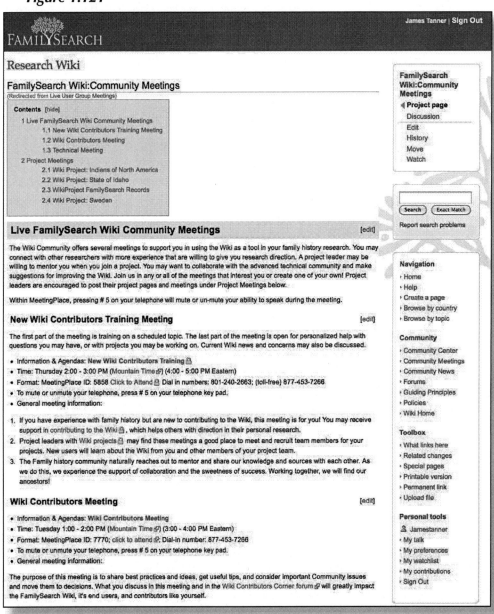

Please note that the dates, times and other information about the Webinars will likely change from time to time, but if you have questions or want to participate, this is a good way to get an introduction to the Wiki community.

* * * * * * * * * *

A Note on the Ongoing Wiki Dialogue

The nature of the Wiki allows the contributors, administrators and anyone else who is interested to participate in an ongoing discussion of topics concerning the Wiki as part of the community. The Community links open the door to this participation. However, participation is in no way required to use the Wiki's resources. Whether or not you become involved is a personal decision based on your interests and abilities. There is no fixed time commitment, but active participation does require you to spend some time, not only editing and adding to the Wiki, but discussing the issues involved. The Wiki itself is the medium for communicating these issues to the general public. In addition to the links shown under the Community, you can also do a Wiki search for additional community pages. Search for "Community."

* * * * * * * * * *

Community News Link

This link is exactly what it says; it is a page of news about anything noteworthy to the Wiki community. As is the case with all things about the Wiki, the content of the page is by consensus. Here is an example of the page; of course the content will have changed considerably by the time you read this Guide:

Figure 1.122

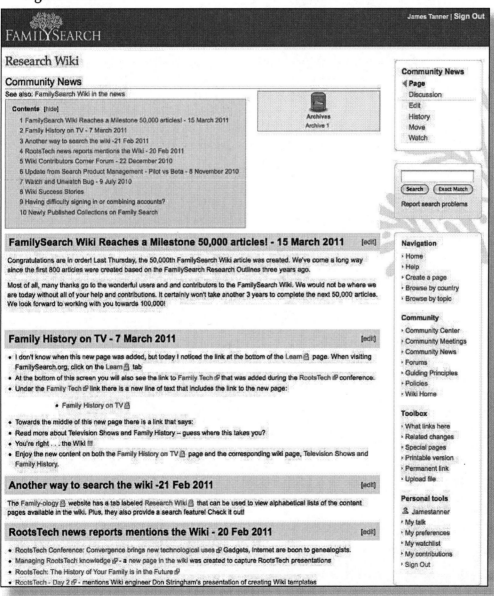

If you want to get an idea of who is contributing to the Wiki, look at the History page for any given entry. You will soon be able to recognize some of the more prominent contributors by their User Name. If the contributor has a User Page, you can always click on the name and see some additional information about that particular contributor.

Forums Links

Depending on the preference for "Skin" that you choose on your preferences page, this choice will be called either simply Forums or split into two links; Wiki Forums and Research Forums. All of these links go to the FamilySearch Forums pages but the "Forums" link goes to the general startup page for the Forums, while the Wiki Forums and Research Forums links go to the specific forums dealing with the Wiki or with Research. Although it might seem confusing to have three different formats for accessing the Wiki, there are not many differences and the differences are not significant. I will show the FamilySearch View a little later with these selections.

Here is a partial screen shot of the startup page for the Research Forums, as it appears when you have the FamilySearch preferences selected:

Figure 1.123

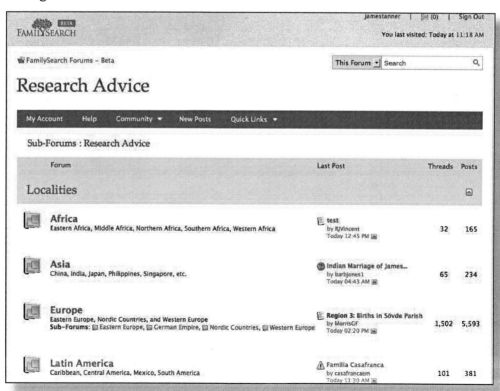

In the upper left-hand corner of the screen, there is a set of nested links showing the FamilySearch Forums – Beta with a further link to the Research Advice page. As you will see in the next subsection of the Guide, this is a way to keep track of where you are in the Forums website.

The next screen shot shows the screen when you click on the Wiki Forums link:

Figure 1.124

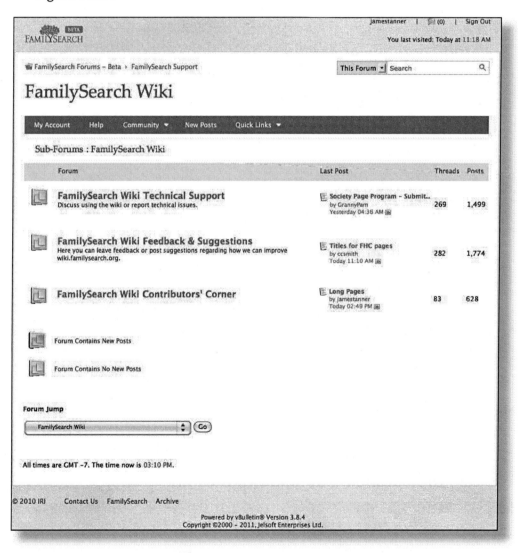

Once again, looking at the upper left-hand corner, you can see the nested links indicating where you are located in the Forums. These selections deal specifically with the Wiki. Note that there is a way to tell if new posts have been added; the icons change to show new content. This is helpful if you are monitoring or participating in a discussion.

If you are signed in and if you have selected the FamilySearch Wiki preferences your screen selections are slightly different as outlined above. Clicking on the "Forums" link takes you to the Forums startup page. This is not as confusing as it sounds since they are all essentially the same Forums website. Here is a screen shot of the upper part of the general Forums startup page:

Figure 1.125

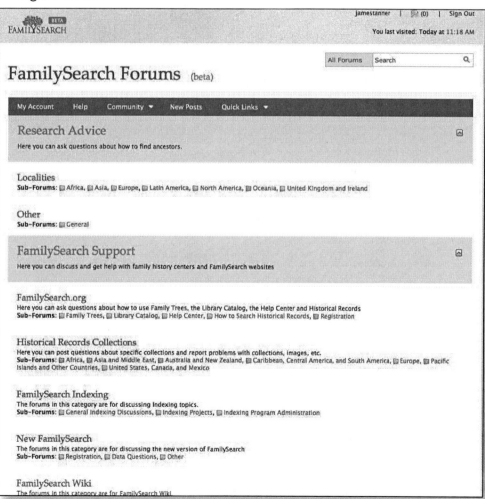

Note that the links in the upper left-hand corner are collapsed into the FamilySearch Forums –Beta. However, if you look down the list of Forums, you will see both the Research Advice set of the Forums and the FamilySearch Wiki set. Clicking on these links will take you to the two screens shown above. I will be discussing the Forums in more detail in the next subsection, but if you want to jump ahead, you certainly may.

*   *   *   *   *   *   *   *   *   *

A Note on Navigating the FamilySearch Websites

It helps to realize that each of the FamilySearch.org websites was developed separately and only fairly recently combined under the Family-Search.org umbrella. By the time you read this Guide, some of the issues with links and naming conventions may have been resolved, but there are very few areas where the slight differences in screens or links makes any difference in finding the information in the site. For example, presently, there is no back-link from the Forums website to FamilySearch.org or to the Wiki. Clicking on the logo in Forums doesn't do anything because it is not a link. So you must either use the back arrow on your browser, a bookmark from your browser or type in the address again to return to either the Wiki or FamilySearch.org

*   *   *   *   *   *   *   *   *   *

Guiding Principles Link

This link takes you to the FamilySearch Wiki:Guiding Principles page the top portion of which is shown below:

Figure 1.126

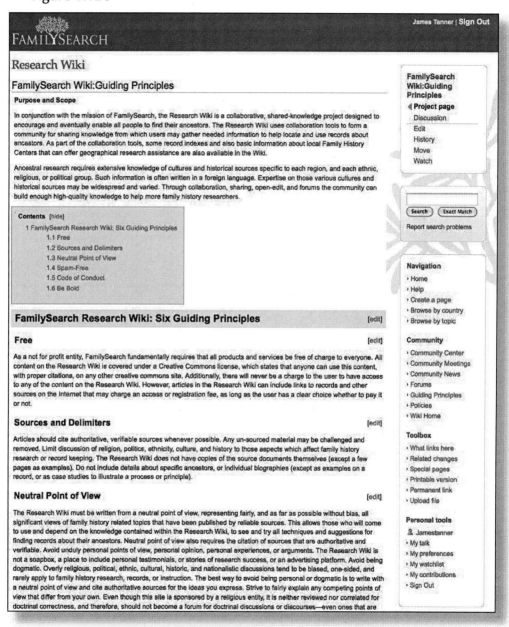

This is a very important page because it sets forth the basis of how the Wiki actually works. All contributors to the Wiki should be familiar with these Guiding

Principles and the Policies in the following screen shot, to avoid potential problems with the data entered.

Policies Link

This link goes to the FamilySearch Wiki: Policies page shown in this screen shot:

Figure 1.127

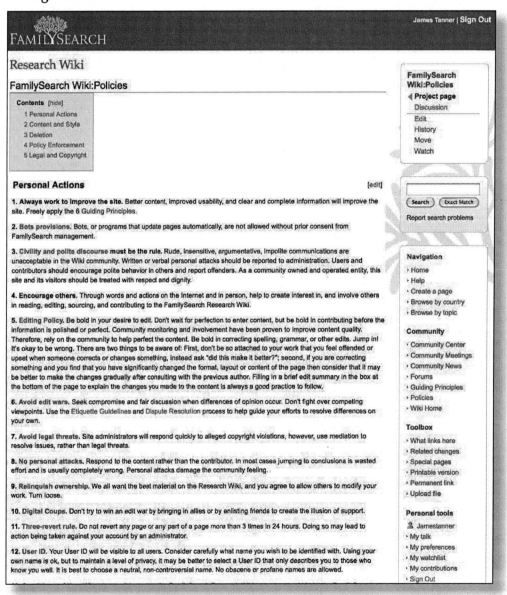

This is another very important Wiki page. The Guiding Principles and Policies are, in part, what make the Wiki a valuable genealogical resource. It is beyond the scope of this Guide to discuss either the Guiding Principles or the Policies in detail, so we will move on to the last link in this category.

Wiki Home

This link is like a few others, it does exactly what it says, takes you to the startup page for the Wiki. There are several screen shots of the startup page above in this Guide, so I did not include another one, but remember that the look of the pages will change depending on your choice of User preferences.

Toolbox Links

From the FamilySearch Wiki view in the "My preferences" choice of Skins (explained further on in the Guide), you get the following list of links:

- What links here
- Related changes
- Special pages
- Printable version
- Permanent link
- Upload file

These links relate more to the function of the Wiki than the content. I am using the Mesa, Arizona page as an example in the following screen shots.

Figure 1.128

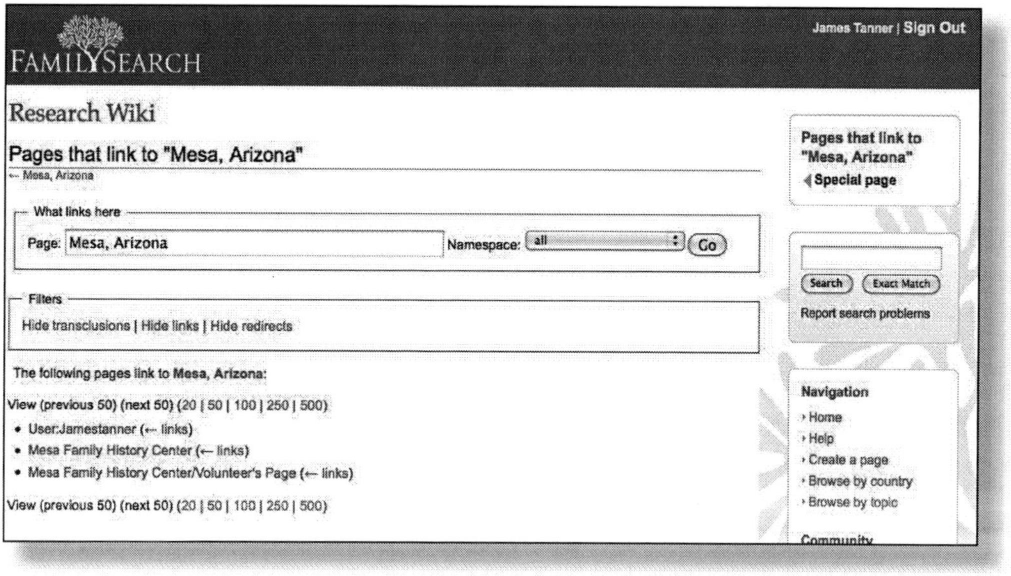

The list of pages might be short, as with this Mesa, Arizona page, or have hundreds of links. The value of this list lies in the ability to see where else in the Wiki you might search for information. The list also demonstrates the relative importance of the page in the Wiki. Pages with few links might have just the information you are looking for, but still not be very much in demand in the overall scheme of the Wiki. If you are contributing to the Wiki, this list gives you an instant reference of what additional links might be needed to make the page more valuable.

You will note that the list of options on the right-hand side of the screen continues to change as you navigate through the Wiki. In this case the list has condensed to only two choices: Special pages and Upload file. which will be discussed shortly.

What Links Here Link

Clicking on this link takes you to a page listing all of the pages or articles within the Wiki that are linked to that particular page. As you change pages within the Wiki, obviously, the list will change. I would suggest that you might get a long list of pages that have little of nothing to do with the topic of the main page, since depending on your Preferences, you may see a long selection of pages dealing with the structure and maintenance of the Wiki.

Related changes Link

Clicking on the History link gives you a list of all of the changes to the specific page but clicking on the Related changes link gives you a list of the changes to the pages that are related to the page under consideration. For example, clicking on the Related changes link from the Mesa, Arizona page gives the changes made to the Mesa Family History Center page as shown by the following screen shot:

Figure 1.129

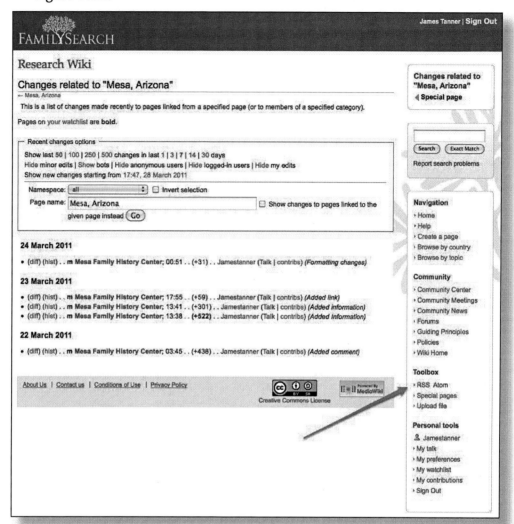

The arrow in Figure 1.129 points to a new link, RSS Atom, which was not previously available. This link lets you subscribe to any changes in this page through the RSS Atom feed. RSS is usually expanded to Really Simple Syndication, a method of providing computer users who have a "Reader" or "Aggregator" program to be notified of any changes to the page. The most used Reader program is Google Reader. If you click on this link, you will be taken to the sign-up page for the Reader or Aggregator you are using. If you do not have a Reader or do not even know what I am talking about, you can ignore this link entirely. But if you ever get to the point of having a Reader, you might remember that there is a way to subscribe to any changes in this page.

Special pages Link

This is a general maintenance link to a variety of pages categorized as "Special." Here is a screen shot of the upper portion of the page:

Figure 1.130

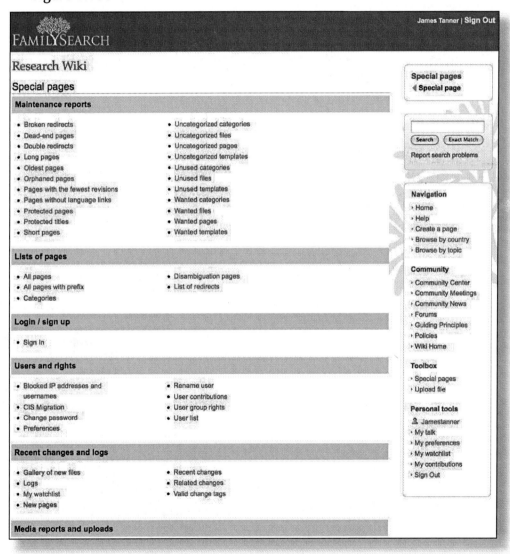

Although you may find some of these links interesting, a discussion of nearly all of them is beyond the scope of this Guide as they are mainly administrative or contributor links. Some of the links show lists of one or a very few pages, others list hundreds or thousands of pages in the Wiki.

Printable version Link

This is another link that does just what it says, that is, it formats the current page so that the page can be printed. When you click on this link with the Mesa, Arizona page showing, the following screen shot shows you what happens:

Figure 1.131

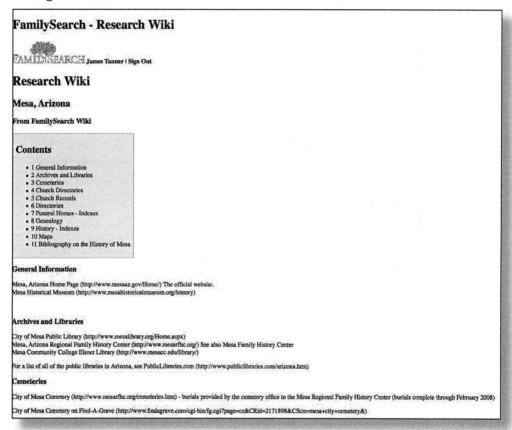

You can see from the screen shot that all of the HTML (webpage) formatting has been removed, leaving only the textual content of the page.

Permanent link Link

This link may take a bit of explanation. A permanent link is a unique address on the Internet that will not change if the page is moved or updated. In this case, clicking on the link generates a permanent link to the page at the time. The purpose is to provide a link to a specific revision of the page and also to maintain that link as long as the web page still appears on the Internet. Although this a way to prevent broken links in citing pages, it has a downside also. Not all pages will remain on the Internet, so a "Permanent link" is not always so permanent. As revisions are made to any page, the older versions pass into the archives and show up on the History page. If there is some specific information you wish to preserve, found on a particular page, you may wish to record the permanent link. The actual permanent link is shown in your Browser's address field. There is nothing to show in a screen shot, as the page does not change except for a notation as to the date of the revision as of the date the link was made permanent.

Upload file Link

This is yet another link that describes exactly where it goes and what it does. All images submitted to the Wiki must be approved before you can add them to a page or article. This is the one area of the Wiki where you cannot add information directly. Any graphics files must be approved before they are loaded into their corresponding pages. The approval process is not complicated nor does it take a long time. Here is a screen shot of the form you can use to upload an image for approval:

Figure 1.132

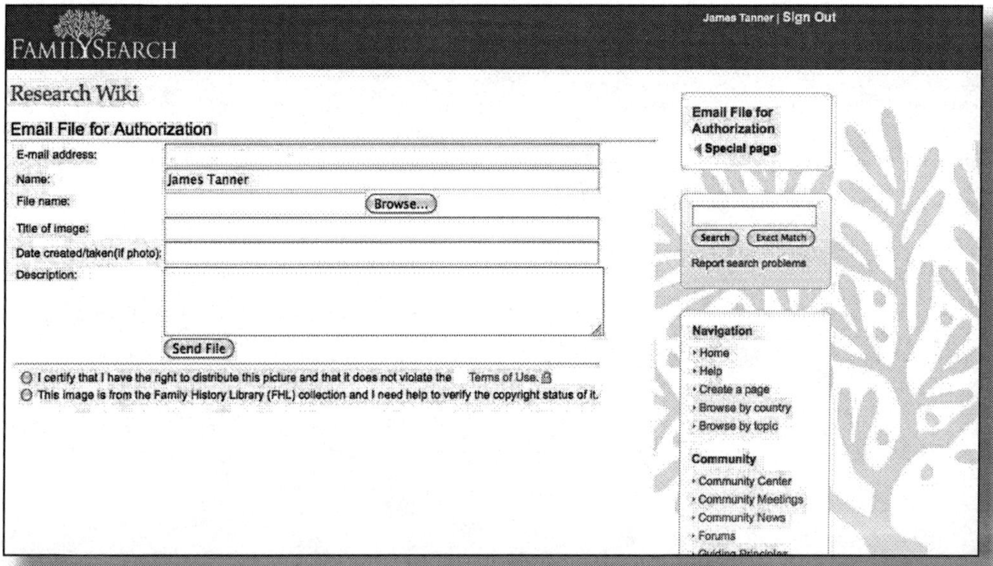

In approving graphics or photos, this is the only place where FamilySearch becomes apparently involved the process and administration of the Wiki.

Personal tools

The Personal tools menu when visible from the FamilySearch Wiki view, includes the following items:

> Username
>
> My talk
>
> My preferences
>
> My watchlist
>
> My contributions
>
> Sign Out

All of these items are useful but add functionality and not content. Everyone who signs into the Wiki should create a user page. You don't need any particular format, but you might look at some of the other User pages to get some ideas. You need to remember that the Wiki is a public place. Anything you put online goes to the entire world. If you don't want it known, don't put it on a public site.

As I wrote this Guide, I debated whether to include screen shots of my own User page and the other associated pages on the list and I ultimately decided it would not be a good idea from the standpoint of being only one example. I did not want to give you, the reader, the impression that this was an example of how it should or should not be done. So at this point, you will have to be content with word descriptions of most of the pages, but you can always view my User page online.

Username

This is the name you use when you sign up for an LDS Account or a Family-Search Account. The Wiki Policies say the following about the User ID or Username, "Your User ID will be visible to all users. Consider carefully what name you wish to be identified with. Using your own name is ok, but to maintain a level of privacy, it may be better to select a User ID that only describes you to those who know you well. It is best to choose a neutral, non-controversial name. No obscene or profane names are allowed."[27] Clicking on the Username link will either take you to a blank User page or to your User page if you have added any information.

To add information, just as with any other page in the Wiki, you click on the Edit link and start typing. Be sure to save your work. As soon as you save your additions, they will be published and available on the Internet.

My talk

This is the Talk or Discussion page associated with your User page. If someone wants to leave you a message, they can add a Discussion to your Talk page. This is not a social networking site, it is a way to communicate with Contributors to the Wiki. To add information to this page, you click on the Edit link and type whatever you wish to say.

My preferences

I have mentioned this section before several times. There is a pretty extensive list of options for you to choose from. The basic list is as follows:

User profile: This page contains your contact information and a link to your FamilySearch or LDS Account. You can, if you wish to do so, edit or change your login and password to the Wiki, by clicking on the link to your LDS or FamilySearch Account and making the changes there. You should note for future reference, that changing your login and password in the FamilySearch Forums would change your status in the Forum because participation is based, in part, on the number of your posts. I will go over this issue again in conjunction with the FamilySearch Forums.

Skin: In computer jargon, skin refers to the color and look of the program. Here is a screen shot of the Preferences Skin page with arrows showing the two choices:

Figure 1.133

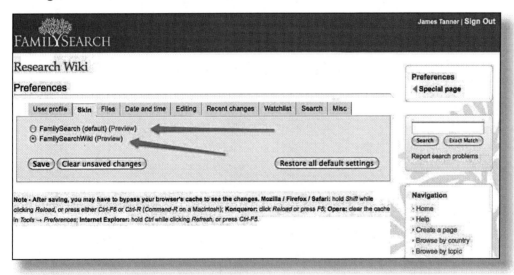

This may not be a choice in the future if FamilySearch decides to have only one interface.

Files: This is normally default information limiting the image size, but the size of the images can be changed.

Date and time: You can choose the format for the way the program displays date and time. You can also fill in your time zone. When you are on the Internet you may be dealing with people from all over the world so it is convenient to let the program know your local time.

Editing: There are a number of different editing options some of which should be left at the default settings. Here is a screen shot of the present options:

Figure 1.134

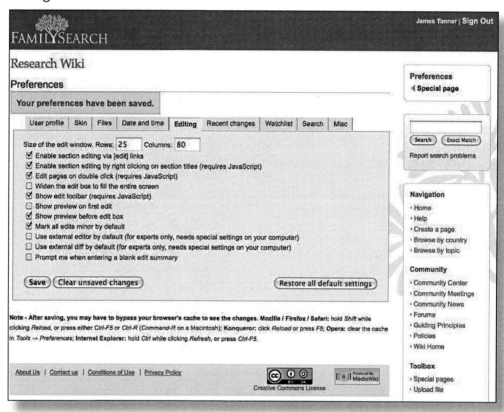

I suggest that you leave these selections in their default setting unless you understand what you are changing. Fortunately, there is a button to click to restore all default settings if you get something unexpected; the check box items are mostly self-explanatory.

Recent Changes: This is another set of options where you do not need to make any changes unless you know what you are changing. Here is a screen shot of the options:

Figure 1.135

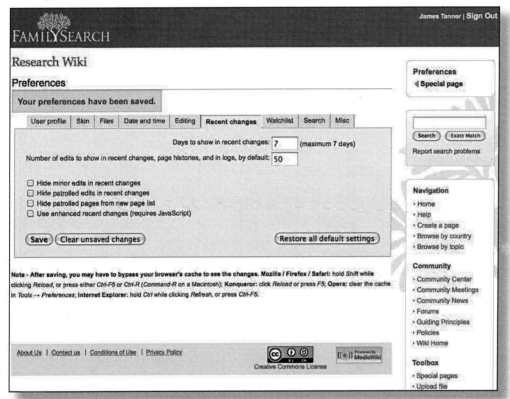

Watchlist: By watching a page in the Wiki, you will receive notifications of any changes made to the watched page or pages. If you don't like getting email, don't watch any pages, however, these settings will govern the time the changes are shown. The changes you make will affect the list shown under "My watchlist" discussed in the following subsection.

Search: This link lets you select the standard options you want to show on the Advanced Search menu. You may also wish to stay with the default settings until you get more experience with the Wiki and can make some choices. You can always restore the default settings by clicking the button at the bottom of the selection box. Here is a screen shot of the selections:

Figure 1.136

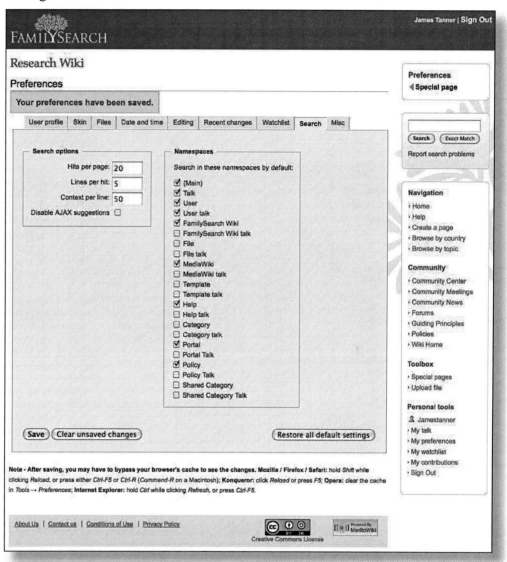

For an explanation of the terms used in the list of options, refer back to the Note on Namespaces. You will note that this view has a list of the various namespaces in the Wiki. Essentially, what you need to know at this point is that the choices add categories of pages to any search. The additional pages searched are mostly administrative or talk (discussion) pages and may be less likely to have valuable research information. If you find that you need to expand your search, you can always add additional check boxes when you do a search. Checking the boxes here will keep the boxes checked every time you open the program unless you change your preferences.

Misc: Here is a screen shot of the miscellaneous preferences:

Figure 1.137

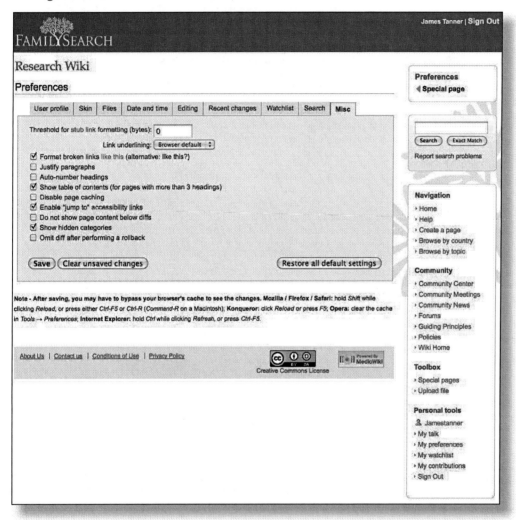

There are several choices here that are not obvious. The defaults checked should be left unless you are aware of what choices you are making. Essentially, there is nothing in these selections that will prevent the Wiki from functioning normally but if the views start to change in ways you did not expect, you might wish to go back to the default selections. As you look at the choices, the reference to "diffs" is to comparison pages that show the difference between two versions of the same page with the differences highlighted. Here is a screen shot of a History page for Mesa, Arizona with arrows showing the buttons for choosing versions of the changes to compare:

Figure 1.138

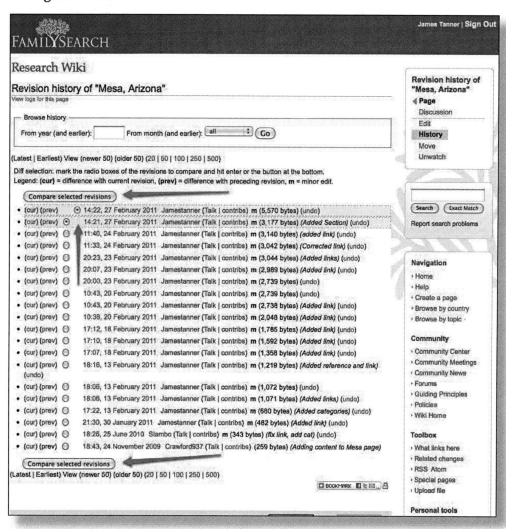

You can choose which versions of the page you want to compare by clicking in the selection buttons and then clicking the "Compare selected revisions" button. Here is the result from the first selection shown in the screen shot:

Figure 1.139

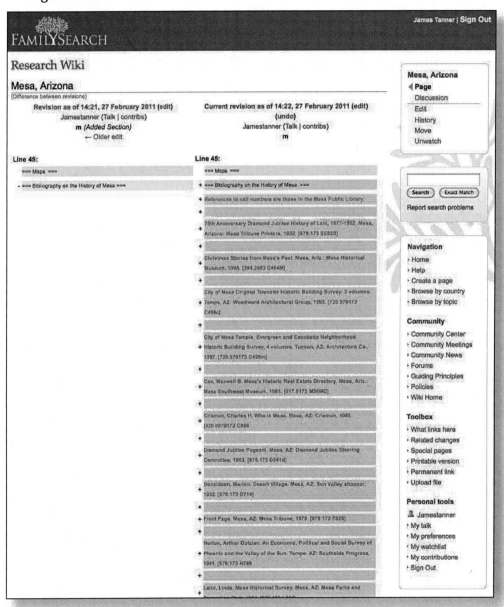

This screen shot shows the two versions of the page. The one on the left (the very short one) is what was there previously and on the right the list of changes. By this method you can very quickly determine what changes have been made to a page and whether on not you need to change something back. This page and those similar to it, are called the "diffs" pages.

Now back to the rest of the Personal Tools list of links:

My watchlist

When you click on a Watch link for any page, that page is added to your Watch list. The program automatically sends you an email notification of any changes to your watched pages. You can always take a page off of your watch list by clicking on the Unwatch link.

My contributions

This link goes to a page listing every change, addition or correction you make as a contributor to the Wiki. The length of the list obviously depends on the number of your personal contributions. The list is sorted in chronological order. The Wiki keeps track of every change you make to the Wiki and your involvement with the Wiki depends to some extent on the number of edits or changes you make.

Sign Out

Another self-explanatory link. Click on this link and you will be signed off the Wiki.

FamilySearch View of the Wiki

As I have already discussed above, you can choose your view or "Skin" of the Wiki as part of your "My preferences" page. See Figure 1.133 above. There are mainly changes to the menus and selections. The FamilySearch view, as differentiated from the FamilySearch Wiki view, incorporates more of the elements from the Family-Search.org webpage and is the default view unless changed. Here is a screen shot of the upper part of the page with arrows showing the links in the right-hand column that differ from what I have already shown above. Neither of the two views loses functionality and which one you choose to use is a matter of preference.

Figure 1.140

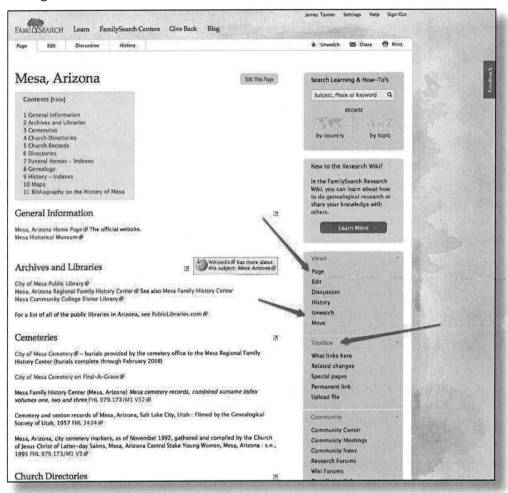

The differences are not significant. The Views portion of the links, has the items in a different order, Edit comes before Discussion, Move and Watch/Unwatch are switched.

In the Toolbox portion of the links, the FamilySearch version is missing the "Printable version" link.

The top portions of the page show the links from the FamilySearch.org website, but none of these links is unique and all of the functions of the page are available in both views, either directly or indirectly.

Here is the bottom half of the page:

Figure 1.141

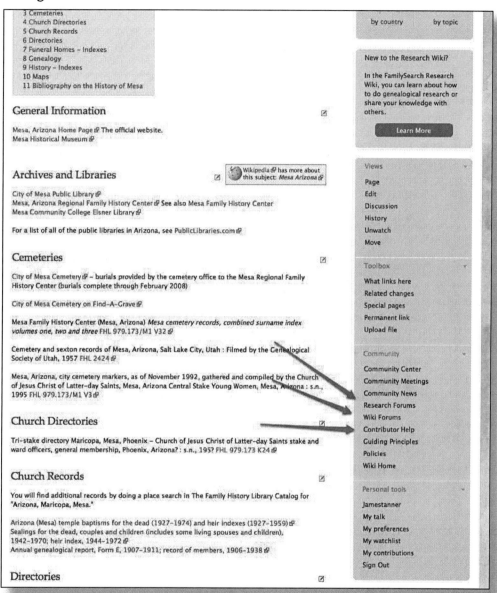

The rest of the list has similar differences. In the Community link list, the FamilySearch version has two more links going directly to the Research Forums and the Wiki Forums. There is also an extra link to Contributor Help. Clicking on

Contributor help, currently takes you to the Help:Edit and Contribute page, the top portion of which is shown in this screen shot:

Figure 1.142

As I have said periodically throughout this Guide, the screens may vary over time from the screen shots in the Guide, but the functions will likely remain the same.

●   ●   ●   ●   ●   ●   ●   ●   ●   ●

A Note on Editing the Wiki

I have already made a number of references to editing the Wiki. Detailed information about editing wikis and particularly the Research Wiki are beyond the scope of this Guide. If you want to know more, the process is summarized on the Help:Basic Editing page of the Wiki and its connected pages. Editing is not difficult but does involve some simple programming using HTML and Wikitext. There is no obligation for any user of the Wiki to do any editing, but you are missing a good opportunity if you don't take time to contribute. When you share what you know personally, your contributions will benefit the entire community of genealogists, not just those who are currently using the Wiki. The resources on the Wiki are more than adequate to answer nearly every question you could have about editing. But it is also important to realize that the FamilySearch Research Wiki uses the same wiki program as Wikipedia and the WikiMedia Foundation. See http://wikimediafoundation.org/wiki/Home. Nearly all of the reference materials available from the WikiMedia foundation also apply to the Research Wiki.

●   ●   ●   ●   ●   ●   ●   ●   ●

FamilySearch Forums

Bulletin boards or forums are some of the oldest programs to run on the Internet. Even before the development of the World Wide Web, the Internet was being used by groups of people interested in a certain subject to discuss and meet online. Forums are also referred to as newsgroups and sometimes as conferences.[28] The essence of a forum is that the users can post and receive messages from all those participating in the forum. The FamilySearch Forums, http://forums.familySearch. org, have been integrated into the Research Wiki under the Community links on the right-hand side of each page. Here is a screen shot of the startup page for the Wiki showing the link to the FamilySearch Forums:

Figure 1.143

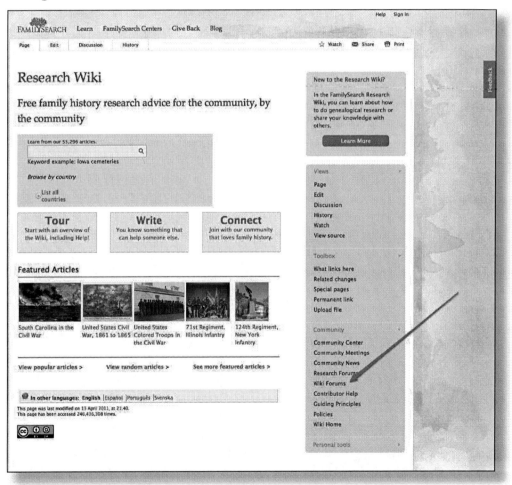

The arrow indicates the link. You can also access the Forums by entering the address in your browser: Forums.FamilySearch.org. In a forum you can ask specific and general questions about the subject of the forum or participate in a discussion. Obviously, the FamilySearch Forums are limited to mainly questions about genealogy and the FamilySearch programs. The FamilySearch Forums are not an open social networking site like Facebook but they are similar in that social groups can be formed around a specific topic. The topics are moderated and the moderators can limit or terminate inappropriate discussions. When you click on the link to the Forums, you get the main Forums menu. The following screen shot shows the top part of the startup page:

Figure 1.144

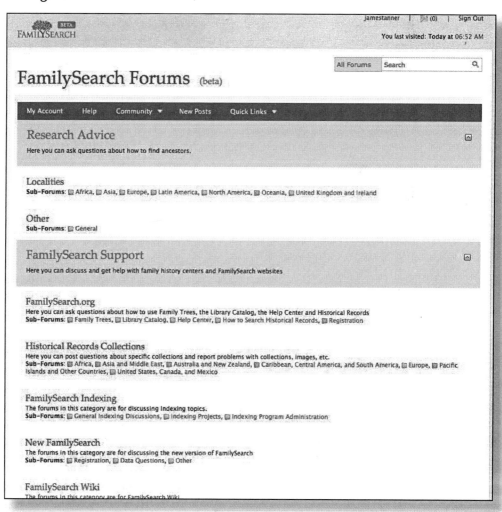

As you can see from Figure 1.144, there are a number of sub-forums listed in the different categories. It is helpful if questions are directed towards the applicable sub-forum. Inquiries or suggestions should be posted in the area relating to a particular on-going discussion, or community members can start a new discussion related to their query. It is important to find out the rules and understand them before participating as a forums member although you may also need to read some of the posts in a forum to determine which one would be most appropriate. For example, it is not proper to advertise products in a forum post or spam forum members. Such conduct may result in getting blocked from the Forum. As will be shown below, those who answer your posts can be professional genealogists or enthusiasts who have a good working knowledge of the topic.

It is also helpful before getting into the different sub-forums to understand some of the terminology. First is the term "thread." A thread is a series of "posts" or questions or comments revolving around a single topic. Starting one of these discussions is called starting or initiating the thread. You can read what is posted in the FamilySearch Forums without being registered, but if you want to participate or ask or answer a question, you will have to register and sign in. You can use your LDS Account or FamilySearch Account if you already have one. If you do not have an account, you will have to register before participating.

Merely clicking on the name of the sub-forum expands the category either to show additional levels of sub-forums or lists of active threads. Here is an example of the view if you click on the FamilySearch Wiki sub-category:

Figure 1.145

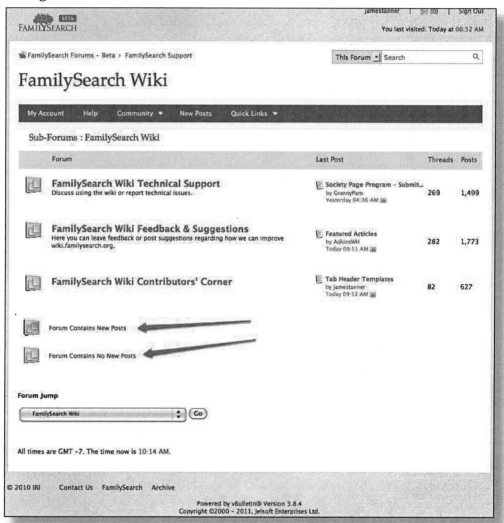

What you see, is a further list of three sub-forums. The page also shows the number of total threads (discussions) in each sub-forum and the number of total posts. There is a link to search the Forum on the right side of the screen, and just above that link another link to search the entire Forum site. The two arrows indicate the way the Forum marks the entries to show recent or unread contributions. The Forum page is loaded with links and can take some time to explore. But before looking at all the links, you should begin by clicking on each of the Sub-Forums. The Sub-Forums are split into two major categories: Research Advice and FamilySearch Support. The Research Advice Forums are further divided into Localities and Other. You can navigate through the Forums site by watching the upper left-hand corner of the screen where the path to the current window is shown. Clicking on any of the levels shown in the list will take you directly to that level. For example, in Figure 1.145, clicking on the FamilySearch Forums – Beta link, will take you back to the beginning level of the Forums website.

The Beta designation indicates that the website is still under development. This puts everyone on notice that the operation or layout of the site could change at any time. The screen shots I have in this Guide might appear to be outdated by the time you read this, but the general functionality of the site will remain the same.

In the upper right-hand corner of the screen, you find the login fields. As with all of the FamilySearch websites that are open to the public, you can log in with either your LDS Account or FamilySearch Account.

• • • • • • • • • •

A Note About Beta Software

When software developers have reached the point of testing their new programs, they often issue limited versions of the program to a select number of people to "test" the program's operation and features.

The initial phases of such a test are commonly referred to as an Alpha test. By analogy, the versions of the program that are in the basic developmental stages are called Alpha versions. By convention, all of the versions of the program are numbered and since the final first release version of a program is usually Version 1.0, earlier versions are numbered below 1.0 such as .60 or whatever. There is no standard method of numbering programs and the numbers assigned are nearly always arbitrary. When development of a program has progressed to the stage where it can be released to the public on a limited basis, it is termed a "Beta" version. The Beta designation lets the public know that the program is still under development and my not function entirely correctly. Family-Search has used both the Alpha and Beta designations extensively for its websites. Although the websites are not traditional computer programs, the websites function like programs and are going through the program development stages. You will note that the Forums website still has a Beta designation if you look carefully at the FamilySearch icon in the upper left-hand corner of the screens. At the time of the writing of this Guide, the TechTips website is still designated as Alpha and the New FamilySearch program was still in Beta testing. When a program reaches its release stage (Version 1.0), the Beta designations are dropped.

• • • • • • • • • •

Please note that the Forum information changes constantly. At any given time there may be hundreds of people online posting questions and responding to posts. If you post a question, be sure and check back regularly to see if an answer or comment has been posted. As I explain below, you can also subscribe to a Sub-forum and receive email notifications of any new posts. You can set your user preferences in the Forums so that the program will send you an email every time there is a change to a particular Sub-forum. In an active Forum you may get a lot of email messages if you chose this option. If you look at Figure 1.145 you will see that at the right-hand side of the screen there is a list of number of active threads and the number of posts. The number of posts can easily be in the thousands. Here is a screen shot of the top part of the Research Advice Sub-Forum expanded to show the Localities:

Figure 1.146

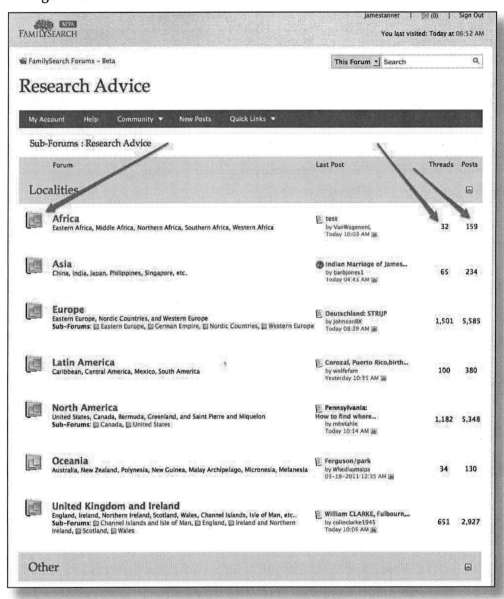

There are three arrows, the one on the left points to the markers indicating whether or not there are current unread messages or threads. Remember, that the term "threads" refers to a linked set of messages or posts. The other two arrows point to the number of open threads and the total number of posts on that particular subject.

* * * * * * * * *

A Note on Logins and Passwords

A login is an arbitrary designation used by a computer user to sign into a website or database. It is part of the security system of online databases that allows only registered users to utilize the services of the database. Most systems allow the user to choose both their login and their password. There are two opposite poles with regard to logins, those who choose logins that identify to some extent the name of the user and those who choose arbitrary and unidentifiable names or phrases. In some cases, the database will let the user choose a separate Username, different from the login. In other programs, the login becomes the Username automatically. Almost all programs, whether online or otherwise, provide a way to change both your Username or login and your password. In the case of both the FamilySearch Research Wiki and the FamilySearch Forums, changing your Username will have the effect of resetting your counters showing your involvement or activity in the Wiki or Forum.

Usernames and logins can be entirely personal and arbitrary. There is no reason to choose any particular form of login or Username other than your own ability to remember what you have used for any particular website. In the case of the FamilySearch websites, you choose both your Username and password from your LDS Account or FamilySearch Account. However, in the case of the Forum, there are some specific rules, quoting from the Forum Help on Forum Rules:

"User Names and Signatures:

Do not use Deity in your user names, signatures or avatars.

Do not select user names of famous or infamous individuals.

Do not use humor in signatures at the expense of others.

Do not select user names that indicate political preferences.

Do not select user names that refer to or promote a Web site or business.

Do not use links in your signature to promote Web sites or businesses."

System administrators may modify your user name, profile, avatar, or signature in order to bring it into compliance with these policies and the Terms of Use.

Passwords are a different matter. Most websites and some programs require a certain form of password to protect unauthorized entry. Passwords should be long enough and vary between the characters used that they will be difficult to guess or replicate. But that same difficulty of replication makes long or involved passwords difficult to remember. You should also take into account that you will likely be typing the password many, many times and you might want to take that time or effort involved into account when choosing one.

• • • • • • • • • •

Clicking on any one of the Sub-Forums will bring up a list of open threads. Below is an example of clicking on the Europe Sub-Forum. Bear in mind that the contents of the Forums change minute by minute, so you will hardly ever see the same list twice unless you click every few minutes. Also, the pages might be very long to contain all of the topics or posts, so my screen shots will not show the entire list of topics or posts.

Figure 1.147

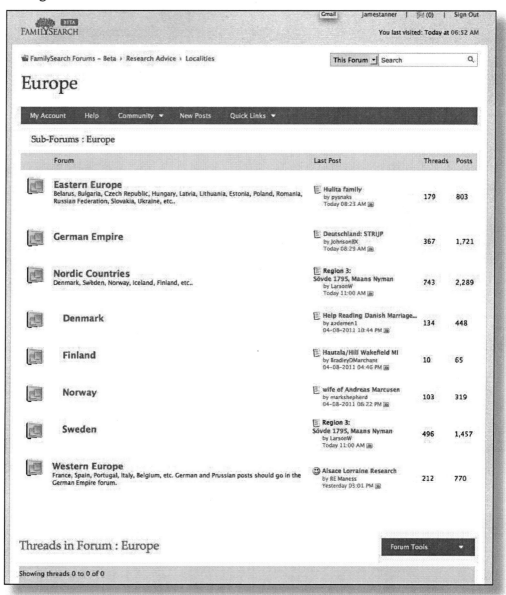

You can see that the next level still contains Sub-Forums. If you focus on the upper left-hand corner, you can also see that the path to this page has become longer. Here is what happens if I click on the Denmark Sub-Forum:

Figure 1.148

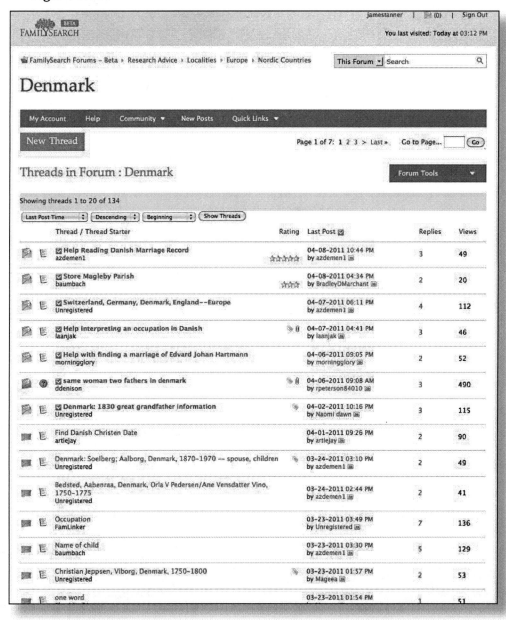

Now, we are finally down to the level of the individual threads. But we are still not at the level of the posts. In the case of the set of threads shown on Figure

1.148 some of the threads have well over a 100 views, others have fewer. Remember, this is an active website and the screens will change from minute to minute and from day to day. In addition, you can see that there are many more views than replies. Clicking yet again on a category takes up to one of the individual threads, this one was entitled, Occupation:

Figure 1.149

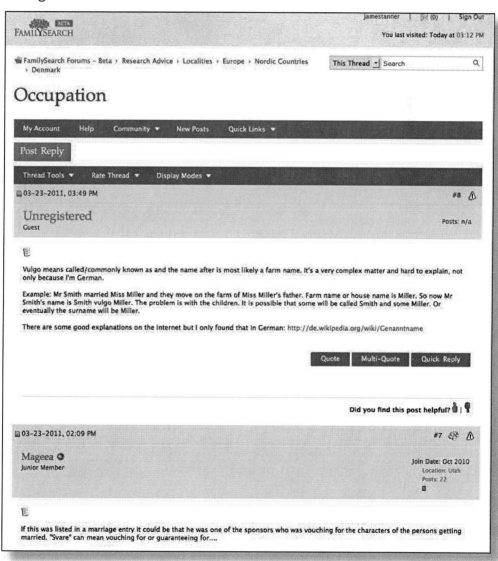

This is a thread about a specific question and the responders have tried to answer the question. I might note that the discussion was still going on at the time of this screen shot and there were a number of responses. Here is a screen shot at the bottom of the long list of posts:

Figure 1.150

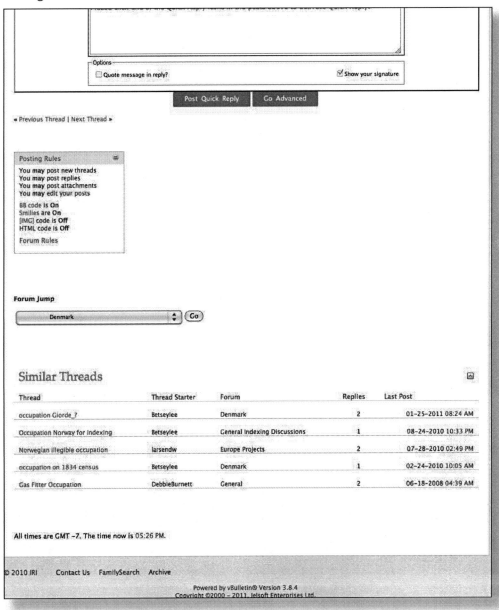

Those who use the Forum are automatically classified by the amount of their participation in the Forum. Those who do not sign in are labeled as "Guest." After signing in, the Forums will keep track of the number of threads you post and responses you make. You are classified as a Junior Member until you have posted 30 posts when you become a "Member." When you pass 100 posts, you become a senior member. Your reputation and therefore your credibility on the Forums depends entirely on the quality (and frequency) of your posts. There is no reason why you need to try to answer questions or respond. You can use the Forums site without participating in the discussions.

As you continue to investigate the site, you can see that the Forum offers more and more links. At the bottom of the page there are links to Similar Threads. These may lead you to additional information, as it is not impossible that the same topic is being discussed in more than one location in the Forums. Also included is a link to the Forum rules as shown in the following screen shot:

Figure 1.151

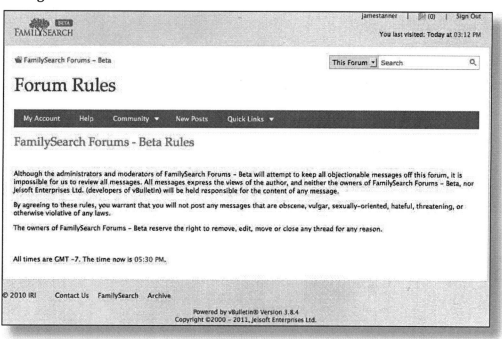

Each Sub-Forum has one or more Moderators. These are people who watch the Forums and enforce the rules of the Forum and try to respond to questions in a timely fashion. They are generally very experienced in the Forums as well as in genealogy. You can click on any individual name to see their Personal Page. The

Personal Page contains a brief description of the person, his or her qualifications, and some statistics concerning participation in the Wiki, any one who has registered as a "Friend" and contact information. The Personal Page also shows a list of recent visitors to that page. Less information is maintained on individual users who are not moderators.

If I jump back to the bottom of the startup page, you can find a list of all of the moderators, Family History Library Research Consultants and Super Moderators. Here is a screen shot showing the link to the list of Moderators referred to here as "Forum Leaders."

Figure 1.152

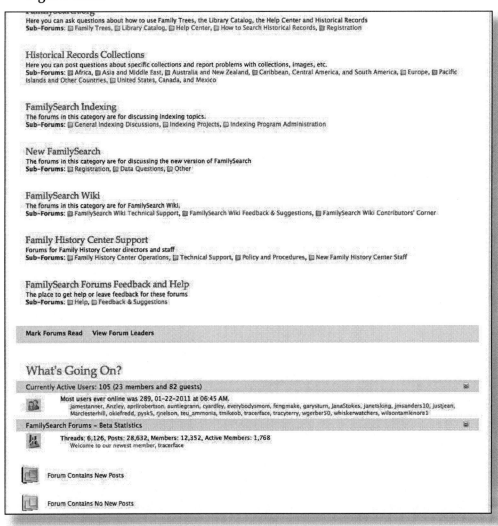

The Forum Leaders are listed according to Moderators, Family History Library Research Consultants and Super Moderators. You can send a private message to each one or an email message to some.

Figure 1.152.1

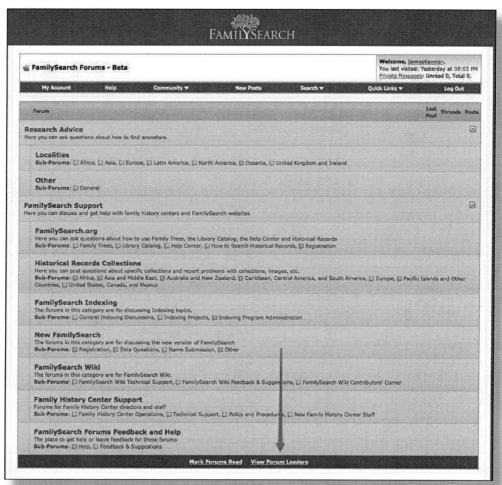

There are several interesting links at the bottom of the pages that are shown by the arrows in the following screen shot:

Figure 1.152.2

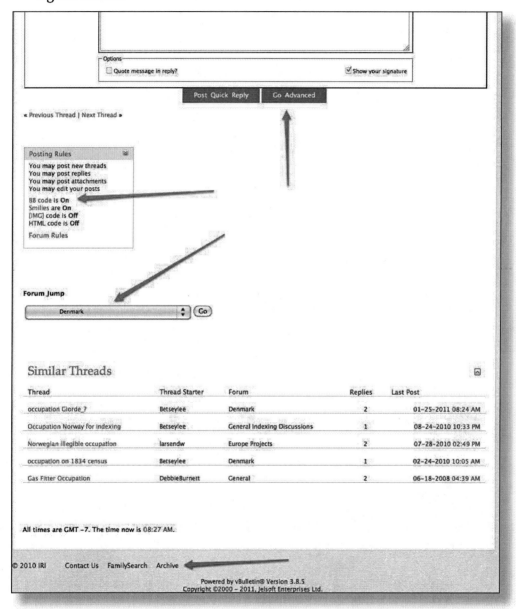

The topmost arrow points to a link entitled, "Go Advanced." If you choose to click on a Quick Reply to one of the posts, you can then click on this link to have some additional options, such as showing your signature, parsing the links in your text and disabling smilies. You can also manage your attachments and subscribe to the Thread. Here is a screen shot of the Advanced options:

Figure 1.153

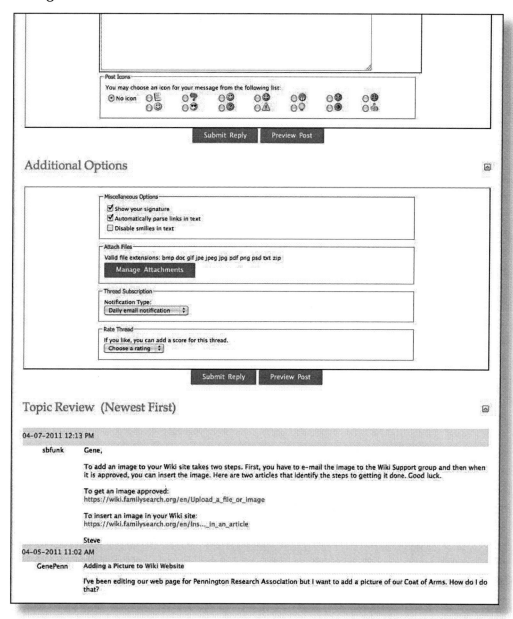

The next arrow down and to the left, points to a list of options that are not user choices, but merely notifying users which options have been enabled and which are disabled. The BB code (or Bulletin Board code) is a way of adding HTML formatting to your messages. If you are not familiar with HTML, then you will not need to refer to this link. This information is also part of the Help menu. Here is a screen shot of a part of the instructions you can see as a result of clicking on the BB code link:

Figure 1.154

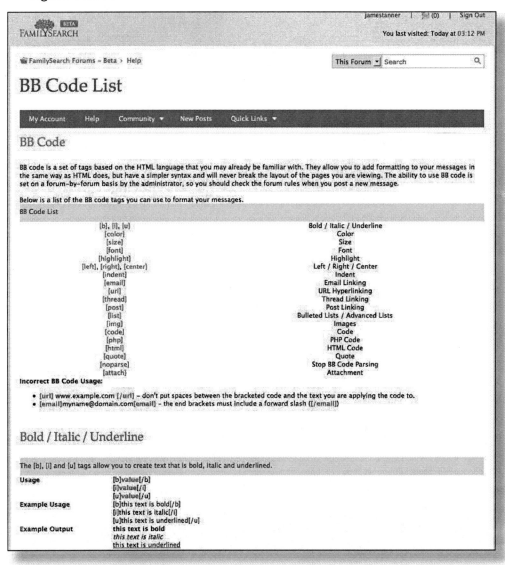

The rest of the page goes on to explain each of the different HTML tags and how they work. As I mentioned this page is part of the overall Help menu for the Forums. The Help pages are similar to those in the Research Wiki, that is, they are not part of the overall FamilySearch.org Help Center, but individual pages in the Forums or Wiki that explain the use of only the Forums and Wiki. There are two different links on this page entitled "Help." Here is another screen shot with arrows showing the two different links:

Figure 1.155

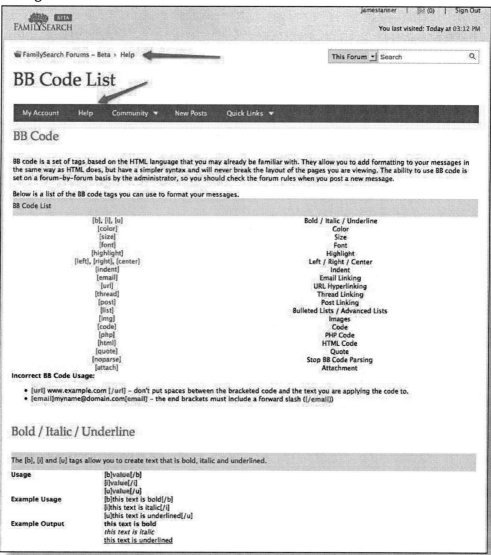

I anticipate that this issue will be resolved as the program is updated. But at the time of this Guide, there are two entirely different Help resources. Clicking on the Help link right at the top of the page takes you to a search page like the one shown in the following screen shot:

Figure 1.156

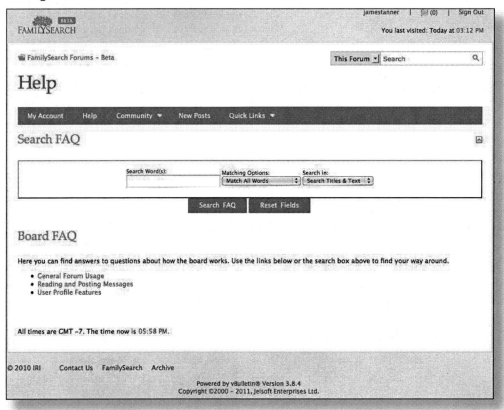

Clicking on the other Help link, in the menu bar, takes you to the Family-Search.org Help Center startup page as shown in the following screen shot:

Figure 1.157

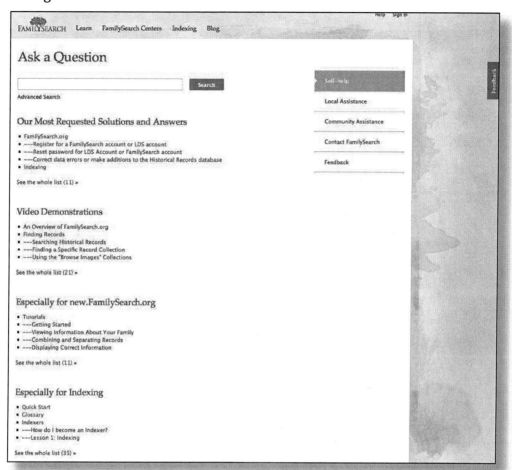

Referring back to Figure 1.156, clicking on the links at the bottom of the page will take you lists of help messages by topic rather than searching by words using the search field. For example, clicking on the General Forum Usage link gives you the following list of topics:

Figure 1.158

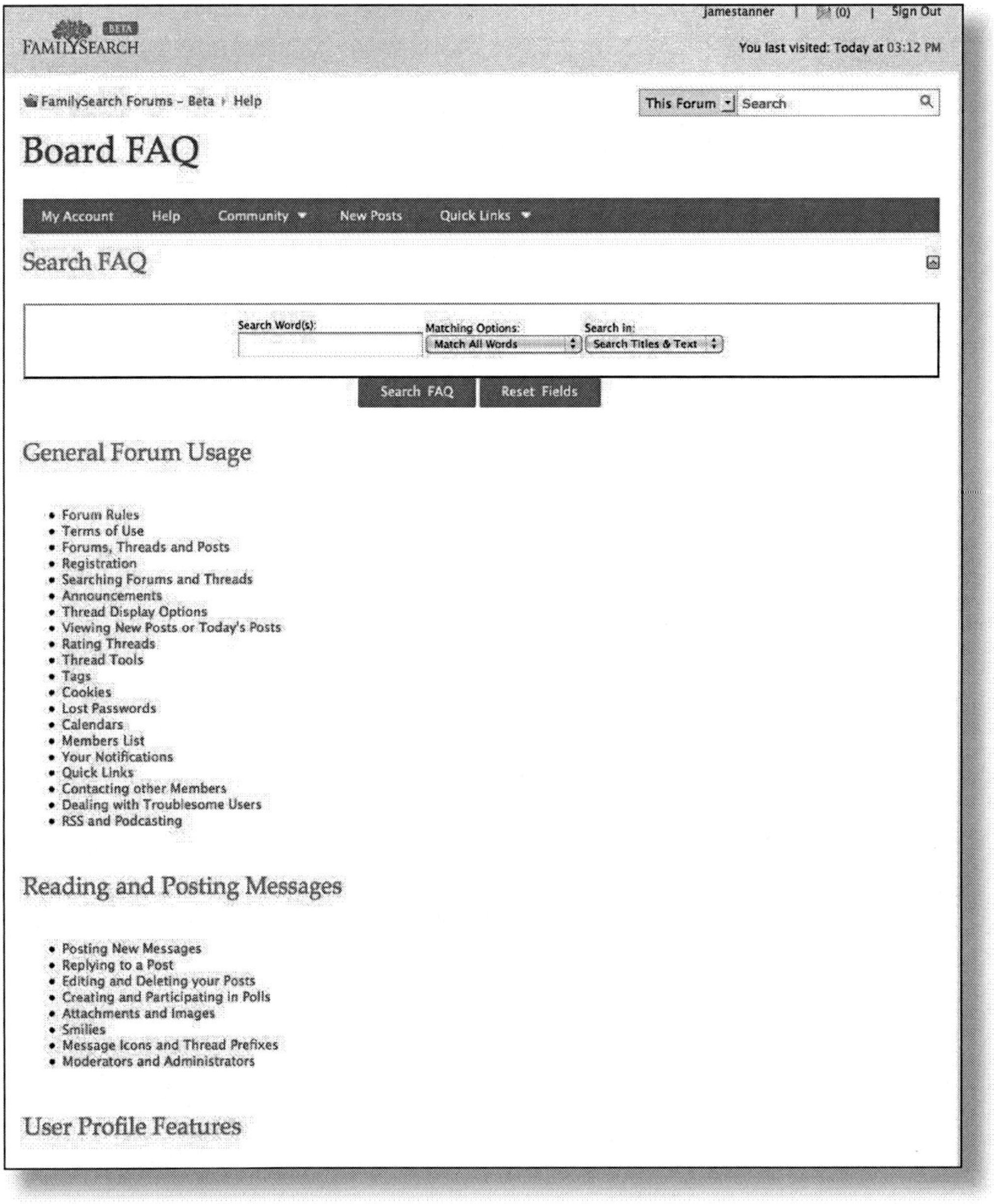

This difficulty with the Help menus illustrates the fact that all of these programs are works in progress and changes can be expected at any time.

Figure 1.152.2 has two more links as shown by the arrows. The Forum Jump is a pull-down menu of locations within the Forums and lets you move to the page directly. The bottom arrow points to three links: Contact Us, FamilySearch and Archive. The Contact Us link brings up an email box to send a question directly to Support@FamilySearch.org. The FamilySearch link jumps directly to the Forum startup page. The Archive link was not operational at the time this Guide was written.

Now it is time to go back a little and examine the search capabilities of the Forum website. Here is a screen shot of the Forums startup page with an arrow pointing to the Search drop-down menu.

Figure 1.159

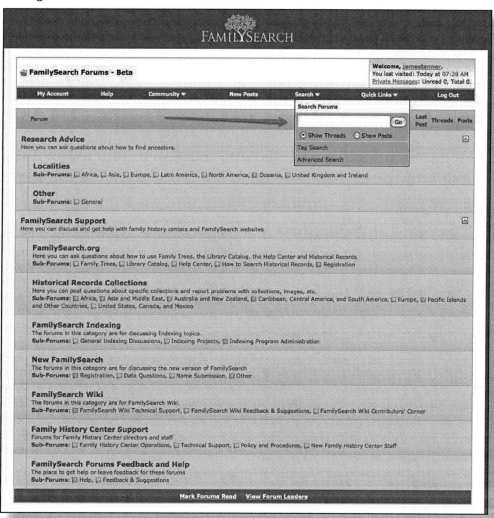

The Search Forums field will look for any word or combinations of words. However, if you wish to do a through search, you may wish to try the Advanced Search which is sort-of hidden in the menus. To get to the Advanced Search, click on the magnifying glass in the empty search field (showing the word "search"). When the results come up, click on the word "Search:" in the upper left hand corner of the results. Here is a screen shot of the Advanced Search page:

Figure 1.160

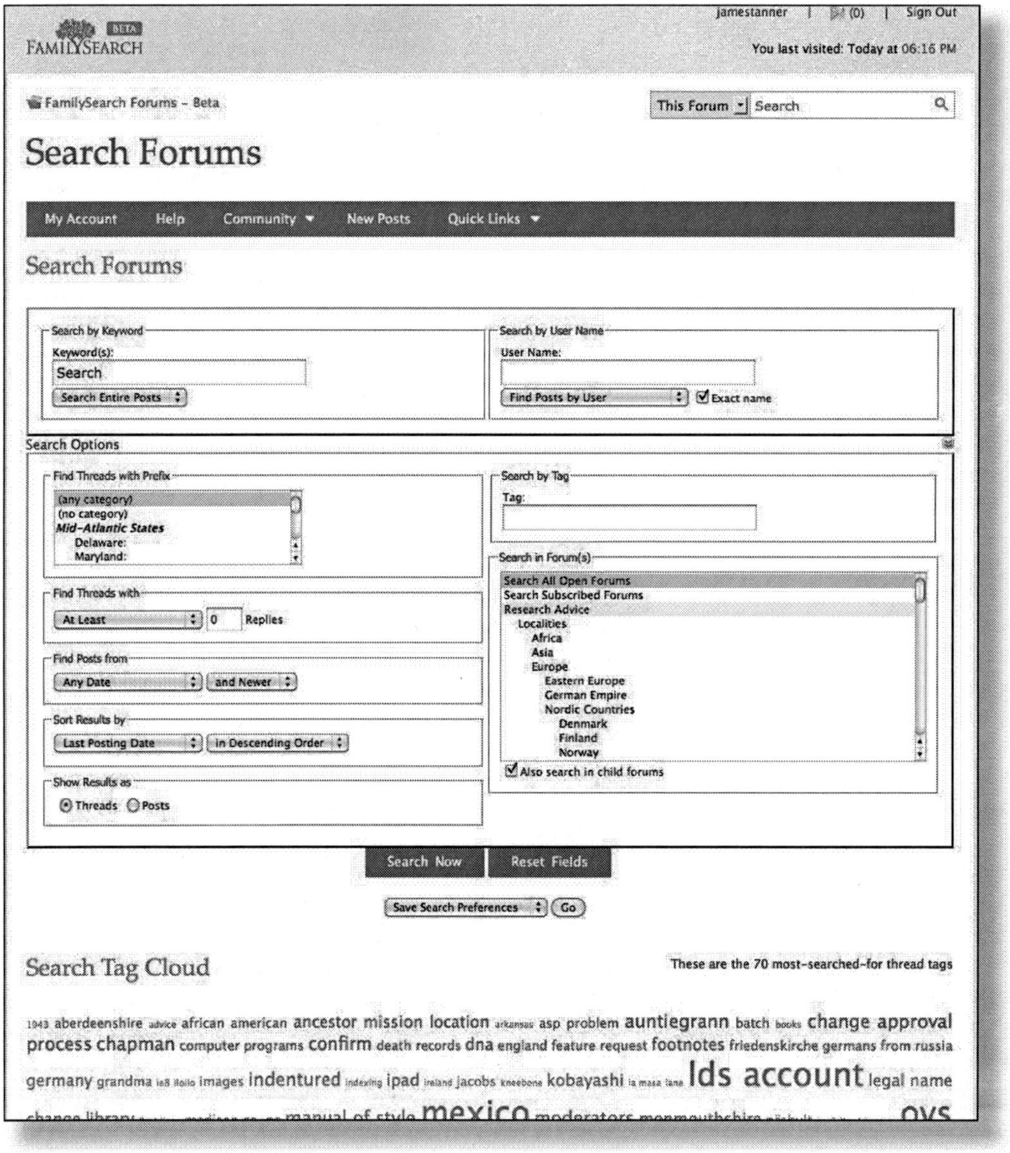

Starting at the top, you can see that the page showing is found at the highest level of structure of the Forums website, right under the startup page. You can search either the entire posts or only the titles by keyword or keywords. There is a second field where you can also search for posts by a specific User or only those threads started by a particular User. There are a number of other filters to limit your search to specific categories, threads with a certain number of replies, posts from a certain date or range of dates. In each case you can show either the threads (list of posts) or the posts themselves. In the box on the bottom right you can limit the sub-forums you search. Advanced searches are generally a way to limit the number of results either by specifying where you search or limiting your search to specific topics or words. But remember, you can get too specific and miss related topics.

The Forums website also allows you to tag individual posts or threads. At the bottom of the page, you can see the Tag Cloud, that is a graphic example of the topics that are most commonly discussed.

Forums Menus

There are several options across the tops of the Forum pages. They are visible in Figure 1.160 above. They are:

> My Account
> Help (already discussed)
> Community
> New Posts
> Quick Links

My Account

Each of these options available under the My Account selection, leads to even longer lists of links and options. Here is the screen shot for my own User Account page:

Figure 1.161

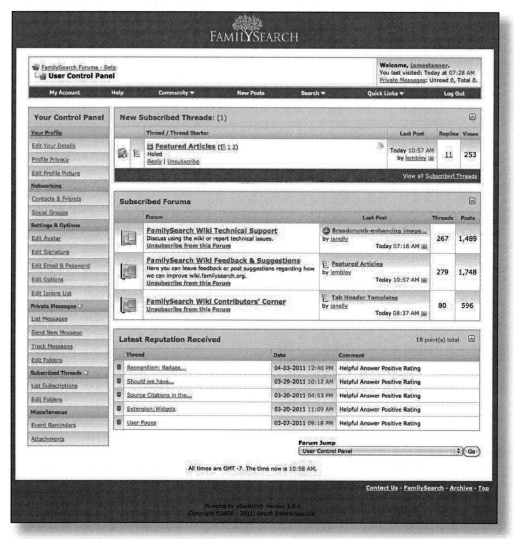

I will summarize the options down the left side of the page without inserting screen shots in every case, unless it appears that a screen shot is absolutely necessary.

Your Control Panel

The following are the categories of links and links in the "Your Control Panel" list.

Your Profile: This is the place to go to add in or edit your personal information shown on the Forums website. You can provide a brief description of who you are and see your statistics that is your total number of posts. You can also view your friends and contact information. This profile is public and anyone else using the Forums website can also view your information. As part of your profile, you can set individual privacy settings for contact information, your picture (if you have one uploaded), your about me information, your friends, your recent visitors and group memberships. In each case you can let everyone view the information or limit the viewing to either registered members, your contacts or only your friends. The last choice under the "Your Profile" link allows you to upload a profile picture and edit it.

Networking: Although this is not a social networking website, Forums allows you to establish friends in the community. If you have any friends in the Forums, they will be listed here. You can also join one or more social groups. These are generally special interest groups centered around an individual ancestor or a subject or location.

Here is a screen shot of the Social Groups page:

Figure 1.162

Down the right-hand side of the page, you can see the types of groups that have been created. You can subscribe to a group and receive email notification of any changes or posts and you can also create a new group. By the way, very few groups have more than one member although this may change as the Forums website becomes more popular and is easier to find.

Settings & Options: This section does exactly what is says it will do, it lets you edit your settings and options. You can edit your Avatar. This option concerning an Avatar is not an invitation to create one so much as it is an option to use an Avatar you already have designed. An Avatar is a graphical representation of the user or the user's alter ego or character. It is not necessary to have one. The second choice is a link to edit your signature. You can add emoticons or smileys and other things like links to your signature. Next, you can edit your email address and your password. There are a long list of options which you can edit from the next link. What you choose to allow and not allow is an entirely personal issue. Last, you can edit your Ignore List. This feature allows you to block receiving messages or posts from a specific member of the Forums.

Private Messages: Although the Forums website is not a substitute for having your own email address and messaging program, you can use the Forums to send a limited amount of email to specific members. You are only allowed to store the past 50 messages. Here is a screen shot of the screen where you can send messages. You can send messages to up to five people at a time.

Figure 1.163

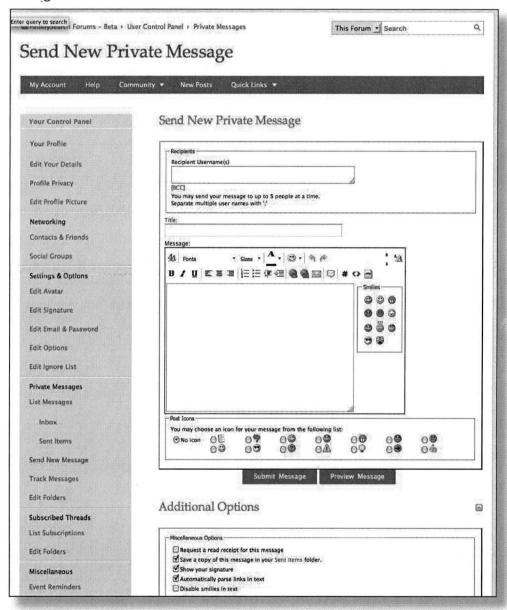

Again, note the list of options down the left-hand side of the page. You can also see the selection of smileys. In the form of text markers such as ": -)" smileys have been around for a long time. They are generally used to express a specific emotion that might not be well conveyed by the text. Emails can be ambiguous and sometimes unintentionally offensive and smileys have evolved to try and eliminate some of those issues. The next option, to Track Messages, is just that, a list of your messages and any responses. The last option allows you a limited ability to create folders for storing your email messages.

Subscribed Threads: There is no requirement that you subscribe to anything in the Forums. If you do subscribe, be sure and have some idea what you are getting into. As I have mentioned before, if you subscribe to very popular topics, you may have dozens, possibly hundreds, of email messages. The two links to List Subscriptions and Edit Folders take you to pages that, obviously, list your subscriptions and let you put the subscriptions into folders to organize them. Again, there is no requirement that you subscribe and so there is no reason to view the list or organize your subscriptions. But if you do subscribe to any sub-forums, you have a way to list and organize them.

Miscellaneous: There are two more links, one to Event Reminders that requires a higher level of access than a mere user and the other Attachments, that only has content if you have attached some document or page to a post.

I have already discussed the Help menu option, so next is Community.

Community

This drop-down menu has links to the Social Groups shown in Figure 1.162 and the Contacts and Friends discussed in Networking above. The last selection gives you a long list of everyone who is registered on the Forums, at the time of this Guide, over 10,000 people.

New Posts

The New Posts link gives you a page listing all of the new posts (what a coincidence).

The Search menu item was already discussed previously, so there are only two more left:

Quick Links

Here is a screen shot of the Quick Links menu:

Figure 1.164

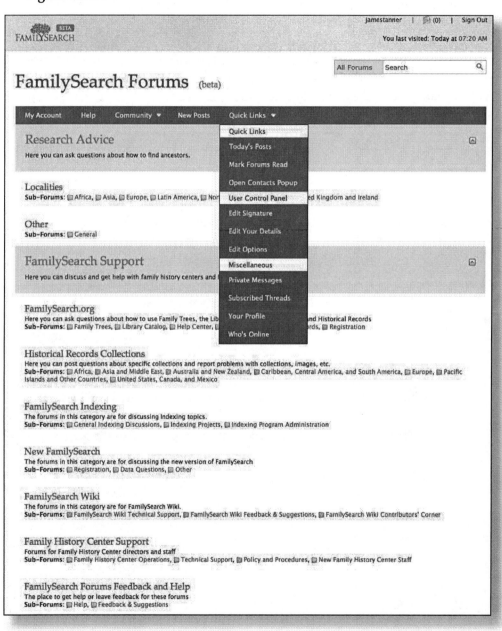

These are all links that duplicate ones in the more expanded lists and are provided as a convenience. The last menu item is Log Out, which is also self-explanatory.

* * * * * * * * * *

A Note on Participating in Forums

Like social networking, participating in a forum is voluntary and not necessarily suited to everyone's interest and/or needs. If you are not in a hurry for an answer to a question, using a forum is a great way to involve a much larger community of individuals to address any particular issue or question. Forums have their most useful function as a place for those participating in the FamilySearch Wiki or other programs to go and discuss recommendations for changes. The questions and responses can be as technical or a simple as those participating desire. Those who do not wish to participate civilly or who abuse the system are fairly quickly eliminated from participation. One comment made in a class on the Forums was appropriate however, the student in the class exclaimed, "You could spend your whole life doing this stuff." Yep, you could spend your whole life doing this stuff.

* * * * * * * * * *

FamilySearch TechTips

One of the more recent additions to the FamilySearch websites is Familysearch.org/TechTips/. TechTips is essentially a moderated blogging site with multiple authors. During its development, the site has been re-named several times, during the writing of this Guide. The current name is supposed to be permanent.

The site has a changeable marquee and so any screen shot of the startup page will be inaccurate almost instantly. In addition, the content changes daily as new posts are written, reviewed, approved and posted. The site is updated daily also. Here is a sample page:

Figure 1.165

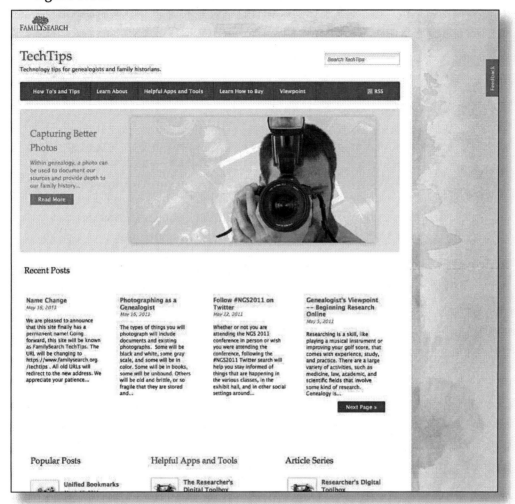

The site has a very simple organization and lacks the multitude of links in the other websites. The drop-down menu items are merely categories of topics for the posted articles. You can subscribe to all the post via an RSS Feed. See discussion above. To read an article or post, simply click on the article's title. TechTips is actively soliciting contributors. If you are interested in writing for the site, you can click on the Contribute menu to find an explanation of how to do so. The link to Family-Search TechTips is still buried in the FamilySearch.org website on the Learn link page at the very bottom. You can also get to the site by keying in the address, https://www.familysearch.org/techtips/.

FamilySearch Labs

FamilySearch Labs is the proving ground for new developments in Family-Search's online world. Included at the time of this Guide on the website are both the Forums and TechTips websites. Here is a screen shot of the top part of the startup page:

Figure 1.166

Welcome to FamilySearch Labs

FamilySearch Labs showcases new family history technologies that aren't ready for prime time. Your feedback will help us refine new ideas and bring them to market sooner. Have fun playing with these innovations and send your feedback directly to our development teams.

The FamilySearch Labs blog has the latest scoop on our current projects.

Current Projects

Family Tech

Discover technologies that will improve your family history research and knowledge. Try Family Tech, currently in alpha testing.

Forums

The Forums project is aimed at providing the most up to date information to anyone who uses FamilySearch products to work on their family history. Through the Forums anyone can ask questions about product features, research techniques, hints and tips, or even about specific families in specific locations. And anyone who knows the answer can reply. Instead of a limited number of support agents available to answer the questions there will be tens of thousands of users collaborating together. There will even be special forums for Family History Consultants, or leaders assigned to foster local family history participation. Come participate and give us your feedback. The more who use it the better the information.

Ahora hay foros en español.

England Jurisdictions 1851

The England Jurisdictions 1851 project simplifies research by consolidating data from many finding aids into a single searchable repository that can be accessed by clicking in a parish boundary. Features include contiguous parish and radius search lists and

FamilySearch Labs has several ongoing projects, some of which have been abandoned others have been incorporated into existing websites. The current projects include:

TechTips: Currently online as indicated above.

Forums: Currently online as discussed above.

English Jurisdictions 1851: This Labs project is an interactive map of the English counties, Parishes, Diocese, Rural Deanery, Civil Registration Districts, Poor Law Union, the Hundred, Provinces, Divisions and the Ordnance Survey as they existed in 1851. The base map can be either a Google Street Map or a Google Satellite Map. Here is a portion of the map in a screen shot showing the Parishes, Counties, Civil Registration Districts and Diocese:

Figure 1.167

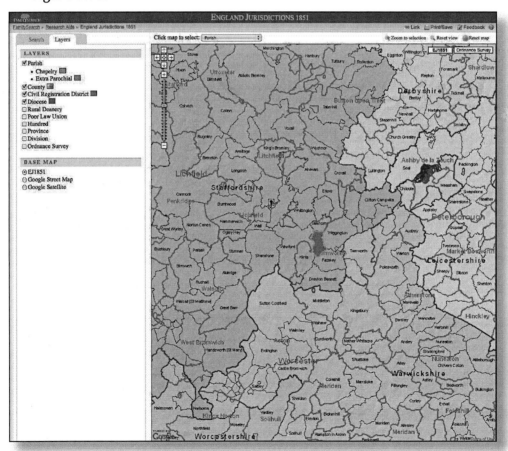

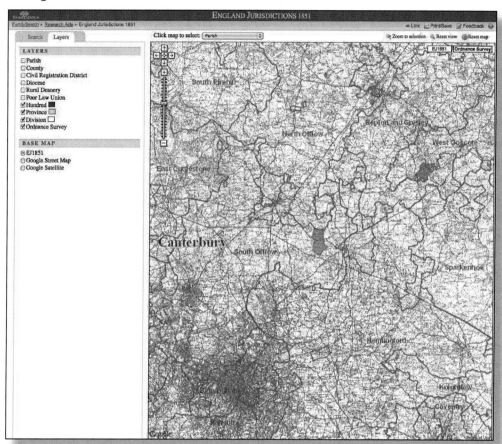

Selecting different map overlays will produce different information. Here is another example of the same area of England, but this time showing the Ordnance Survey and Provinces, Divisions and the Hundred:

Figure 1.168

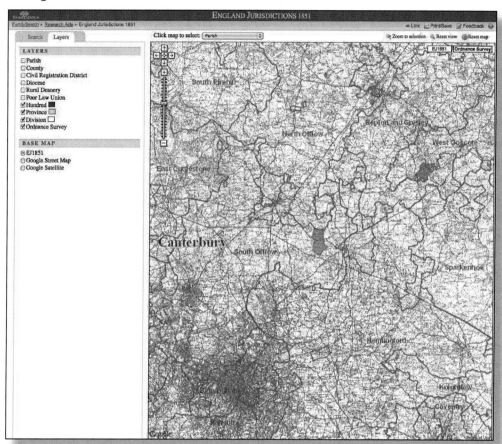

Here is yet another screen shot, this time showing the Ordnance Survey:

Figure 1.169

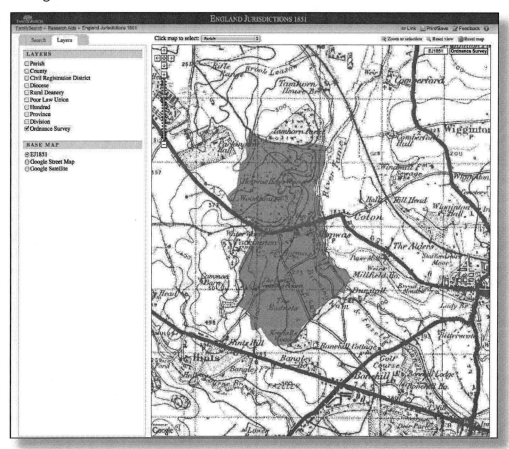

There is a lot of information contained on these maps and overlays in any of the possible combinations. The maps are particularly useful to establish the historical location of an item and see exactly where it is located on a modern satellite image.

Standard Finder: This is a database of names, locations and dates in a standardized format as used by FamilySearch applications to both enter the information into the programs and in searching for exact spellings. This database is a work in progress and subject to changes from FamilySearch as well as suggestions from the users. Although it is not readily apparent, the program can also be used to find variants of names.

• • • • • • • • • •

A Note on Standard Names

The idea of having a standard place name and date format is appealing but can be misleading. Place names frequently change over time. The genealogical standard is to use the name of the place and the jurisdiction at the time the event occurred. The town or city name may be the same as it is today, but the county may have changed once or more times over the years. It is also not unusual for place names to change over time due to a whole list of causes. Some areas of Eastern Europe, for example, have changed names every time a new country conquered the area: Polish names were changed to German, then to Russian and then back to Polish. Standardized names should be used with extreme caution so as to avoid losing valuable historical information.

• • • • • • • • • •

This is a screen shot of the Standard Finder application:

Figure 1.170

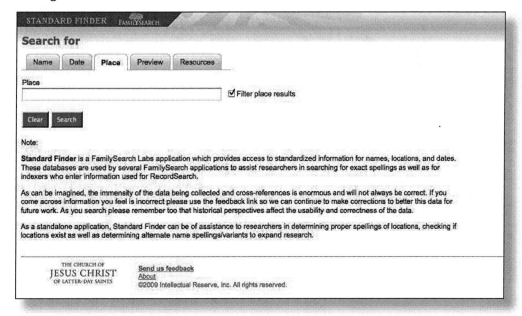

There are five tabs or links to the search areas. Clicking on the Name tab brings up search fields in two formats, one for direct entry, the other including prefixes and suffixes. If you enter in a name, you will get many possible variants as shown by this screen shot:

Figure 1.171

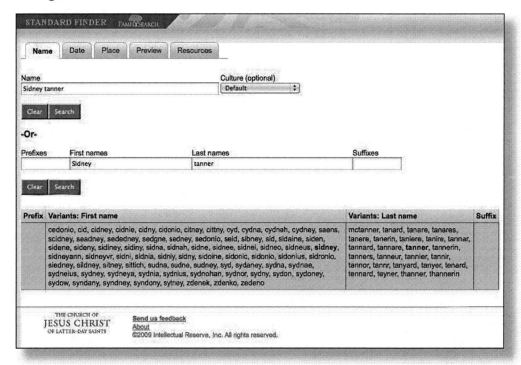

There is also a selection for culture that is marked optional. This is a pull down menu of cultural locations around the world. Selecting one of the cultures from the drop-down list will adapt the responses to that culture.

The Date selection is somewhat confusing since it seems to do little more than change the date to standard genealogical format: day, month, full year. But it does affect a change to dates falling within the time period of the change from the Julian to the Gregorian calendar.

The place search gives a wealth of information as shown by this screen shot:

Figure 1.172

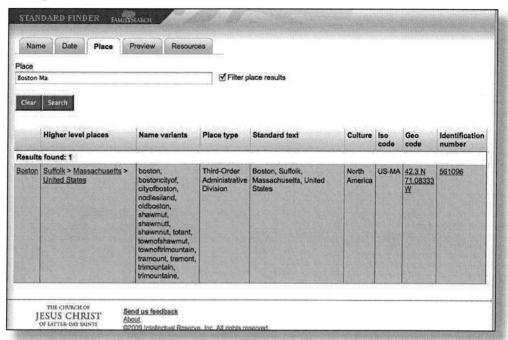

When I entered "Boston Ma" the Standard Finder returned the county, with a list of name variants, the type of place, a standardized name for the location, its cultural designation, its ISO code, its Geo code and Identification number. The ISO code is the International Organization for Standardization code for the names of the principal subdivisions of all countries. Subdivision names are listed as in the ISO 3166-2 standard published by the ISO 3166 Maintenance Agency (ISO 3166/MA).[29] The Geo code is essentially the place's latitude and longitude. Clicking on the Geo code takes you to a Google Map of the location. Last is the Identification number. Clicking on the Identification number is like hitting the jackpot. You get a listing of all of the associated place names.

The last link is to some additional resources from Google Earth, Google Maps and ArcReader from ESRL. The Tips and Instructions tell how to create a personalized map in Google Earth.

Community Trees:

Community Trees are lineage-linked genealogies from specific time periods and geographic localities around the world. It is a separate website located at

HistFam.FamilySearch.org and can be accessed directly by typing in the URL. The information also includes the supporting sources. Each Community Tree is a searchable database with views of individuals, families, ancestors and descendants, as well as printing options. This is a relatively unknown and little used resource. Here is a screen shot of the startup screen:

Figure 1.173

FAMILYSEARCH
Community Trees

Search

Last Name:

First Name:

Search

- Advanced Search
- Surnames
- Search Families

Community Trees are lineage-linked genealogies from specific time periods and geographic localities around the world. The information also includes the supporting sources. Each Community Tree is a searchable database with views of individuals, families, ancestors and descendants, as well as printing options.

See Community Trees

Read Search Strategies for Community Trees

See Oral Genealogies

Contrary to most of the FamilySearch websites, there are only a few options on the startup page. You can begin your search by entering a family name. Clicking on the Advanced Search really gives you a lot more options. Here is a screen shot showing the expanded search options:

Figure 1.174

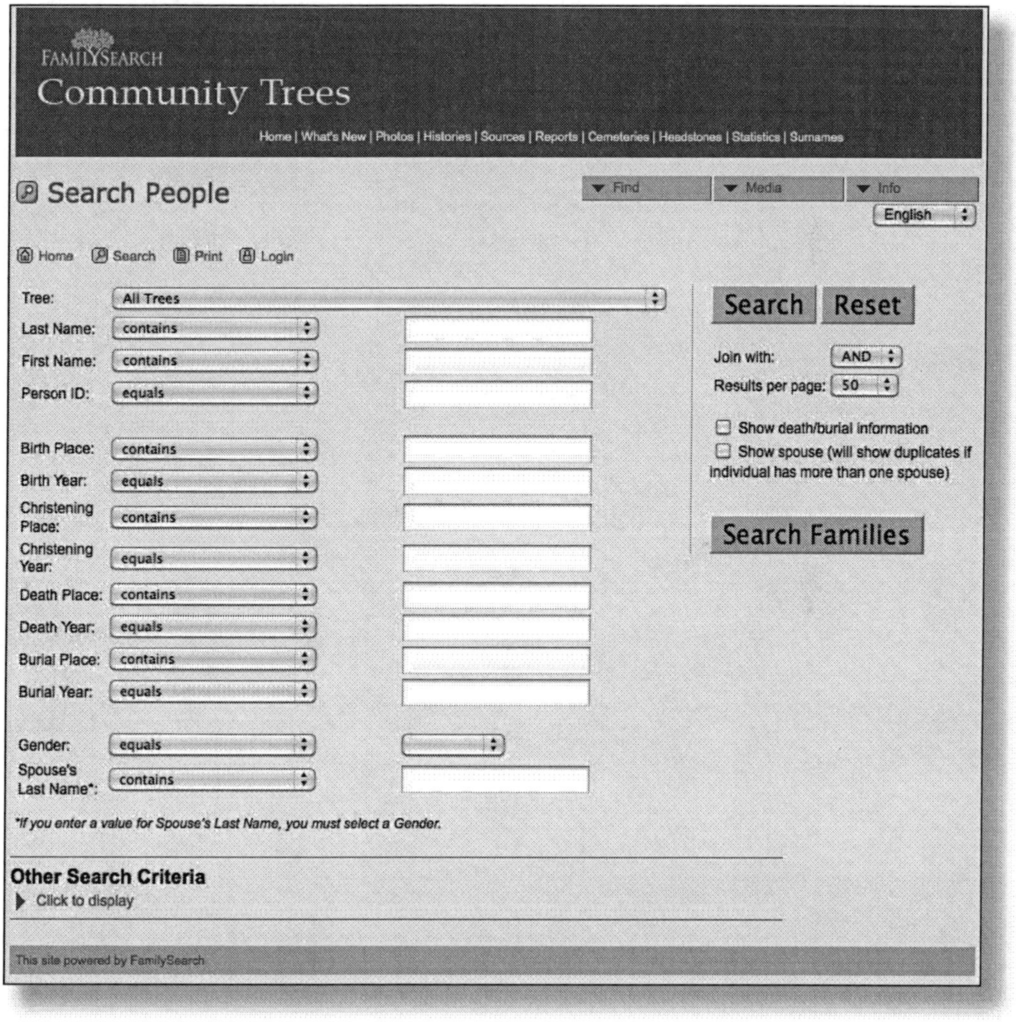

If you wonder what you are searching, you need to click on the See Community Trees link on the startup or home page. The list of Community Trees has grown relatively slowly but consistently since 2009. Here is a screen shot of just the top of the page showing a list of the Community Trees:

Figure 1.175

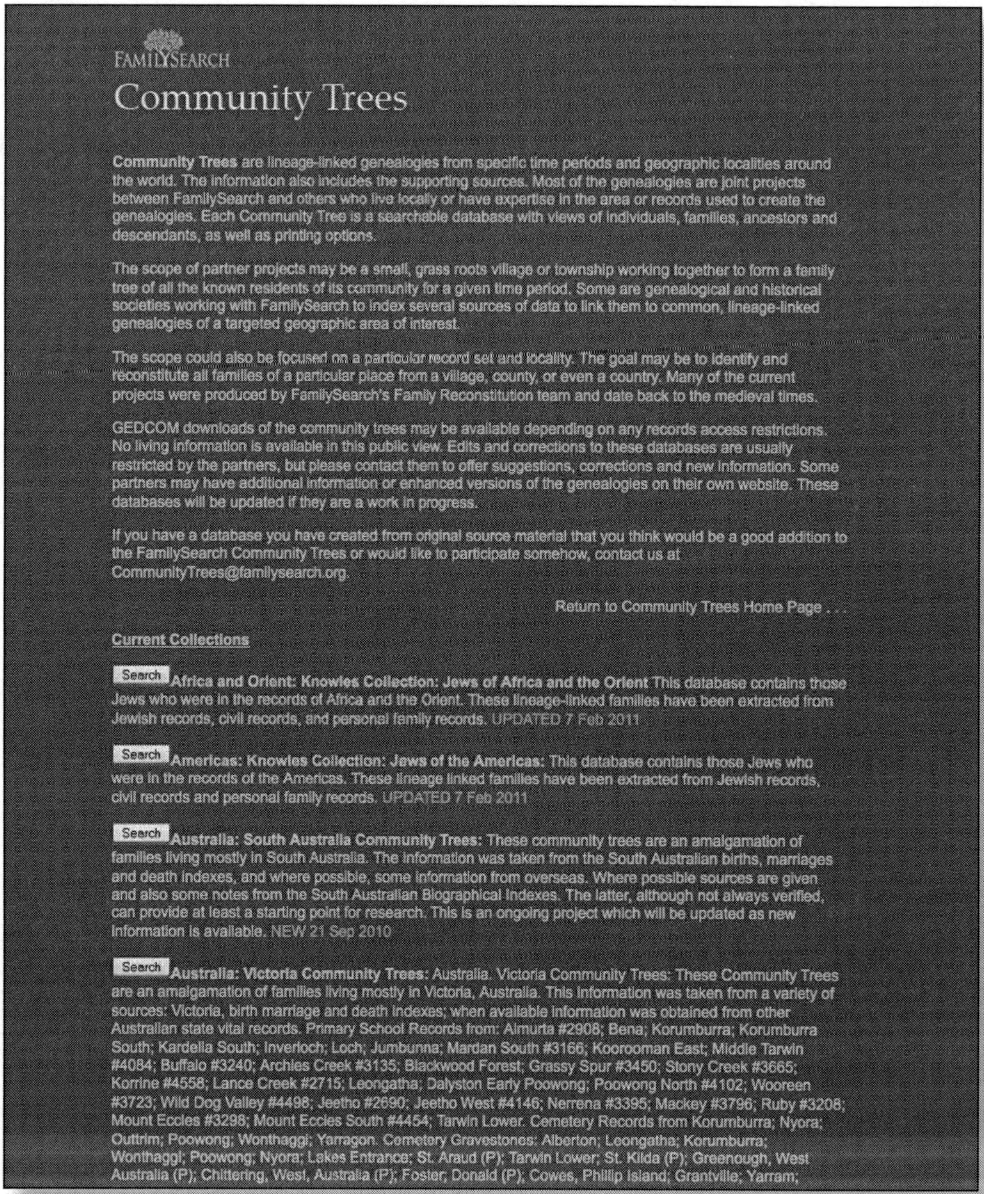

FAMILYSEARCH

Community Trees

Community Trees are lineage-linked genealogies from specific time periods and geographic localities around the world. The information also includes the supporting sources. Most of the genealogies are joint projects between FamilySearch and others who live locally or have expertise in the area or records used to create the genealogies. Each Community Tree is a searchable database with views of individuals, families, ancestors and descendants, as well as printing options.

The scope of partner projects may be a small, grass roots village or township working together to form a family tree of all the known residents of its community for a given time period. Some are genealogical and historical societies working with FamilySearch to index several sources of data to link them to common, lineage-linked genealogies of a targeted geographic area of interest.

The scope could also be focused on a particular record set and locality. The goal may be to identify and reconstitute all families of a particular place from a village, county, or even a country. Many of the current projects were produced by FamilySearch's Family Reconstitution team and date back to the medieval times.

GEDCOM downloads of the community trees may be available depending on any records access restrictions. No living information is available in this public view. Edits and corrections to these databases are usually restricted by the partners, but please contact them to offer suggestions, corrections and new information. Some partners may have additional information or enhanced versions of the genealogies on their own website. These databases will be updated if they are a work in progress.

If you have a database you have created from original source material that you think would be a good addition to the FamilySearch Community Trees or would like to participate somehow, contact us at CommunityTrees@familysearch.org.

Return to Community Trees Home Page . . .

Current Collections

Search **Africa and Orient: Knowles Collection: Jews of Africa and the Orient** This database contains those Jews who were in the records of Africa and the Orient. These lineage-linked families have been extracted from Jewish records, civil records, and personal family records. UPDATED 7 Feb 2011

Search **Americas: Knowles Collection: Jews of the Americas:** This database contains those Jews who were in the records of the Americas. These lineage linked families have been extracted from Jewish records, civil records and personal family records. UPDATED 7 Feb 2011

Search **Australia: South Australia Community Trees:** These community trees are an amalgamation of families living mostly in South Australia. The information was taken from the South Australian births, marriages and death indexes, and where possible, some information from overseas. Where possible sources are given and also some notes from the South Australian Biographical Indexes. The latter, although not always verified, can provide at least a starting point for research. This is an ongoing project which will be updated as new information is available. NEW 21 Sep 2010

Search **Australia: Victoria Community Trees:** Australia. Victoria Community Trees: These Community Trees are an amalgamation of families living mostly in Victoria, Australia. This information was taken from a variety of sources: Victoria, birth marriage and death indexes; when available information was obtained from other Australian state vital records. Primary School Records from: Almurta #2908; Bena; Korumburra; Korumburra South; Kardella South; Inverloch; Loch; Jumbunna; Mardan South #3166; Koorooman East; Middle Tarwin #4084; Buffalo #3240; Archies Creek #3135; Blackwood Forest; Grassy Spur #3450; Stony Creek #3665; Korrine #4558; Lance Creek #2715; Leongatha; Dalyston Early Poowong; Poowong North #4102; Wooreen #3723; Wild Dog Valley #4498; Jeetho #2690; Jeetho West #4146; Nerrena #3395; Mackey #3796; Ruby #3208; Mount Eccles #3298; Mount Eccles South #4454; Tarwin Lower. Cemetery Records from Korumburra; Nyora; Outtrim; Poowong; Wonthaggi; Yarragon. Cemetery Gravestones: Alberton; Leongatha; Korumburra; Wonthaggi; Poowong; Nyora; Lakes Entrance; St. Araud (P); Tarwin Lower; St. Kilda (P); Greenough, West Australia (P); Chittering, West, Australia (P); Foster; Donald (P); Cowes, Phillip Island; Grantville; Yarram;

By returning to the home page and clicking on the Advanced Search option, you can get another set of links. These include What's New, Photos, Histories, Sources, Reports, Cemeteries, Headstones, Statistics and Surnames. Here is a short discussion on each of the links. See Figure 1.174 above at the top of the screen. Clicking on these links shows the experimental nature of this site. Although the Trees information is extensive and useful, most of these secondary links are either empty or have very little data added.

What's New: You would assume that this would tell what's new in the database, but it was not particularly up to date at the time of the writing of this Guide.

Photos: Likewise, Photos seems to have been started and then abandoned. There were only 19 photos listed at the time of the search.

Histories: Also under development.

Sources: A searchable list of sources from the Trees. This list is rather extensive with almost 6000 sources.

Reports: This link is empty.

Cemeteries: There were three cemeteries in the database at the time of the Guide.

Headstones: There were only examples of three headstones in the database.

Statistics: This link shows how many names are in the database. Here is a screen shot showing the statistics page:

Figure 1.176

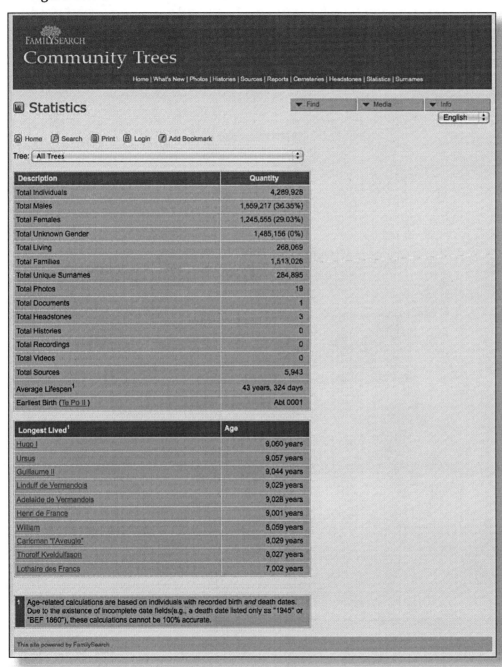

You can see that this is quite an extensive database but not large compared to the Historical Record Collections.

Surnames: This link shows some interesting statistics and numbers of names. Here is a screen shot of the link:

Figure 1.177

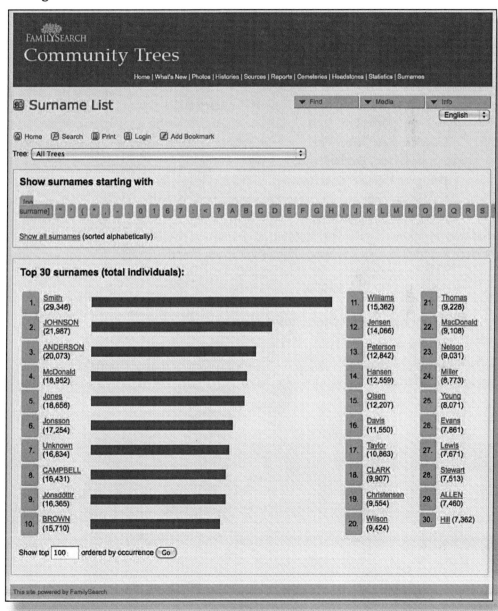

You can go to the list of Community Trees and search each of the individual databases.

Other FamilySearch Labs Projects:

FamilySearch Labs past and discontinued projects include:

FamilySearch Beta: Converted to the current FamilySearch.org website in December 2010.

Research Wiki: Currently incorporated into the FamilySearch.org website.

Record Search: Retired in September 2010 when the Historical Record Collections on FamilySearch.org replaced it.

Family Tree Prototype: Retired in February 2010. Parts of this program may have been incorporated into New.FamilySearch.org. This link no longer is active.

Life Browser Prototype: Last updated in 2007, this interesting program does not seem to have been implemented any place in the current FamilySearch lineup.

Pedigree Viewer: Last updated in 2007, this interesting viewer program had features that show up in the Pedigree View portion of New.FamilySearch.org.

I have not included screen shots or further explanations for these programs that were either incorporated in current programs and therefore discussed elsewhere or were abandoned. I suggest you might want to explore these older versions on your own if you have any interest. The links are still active and the programs still operate except for the Family Tree Prototype.

FamilySearch.org in other languages

The FamilySearch Research Wiki is available in Spanish and Swedish. The links to the other languages is located near the bottom of the startup page. Here is a screen shot with arrows pointing to the links:

Figure 1.178

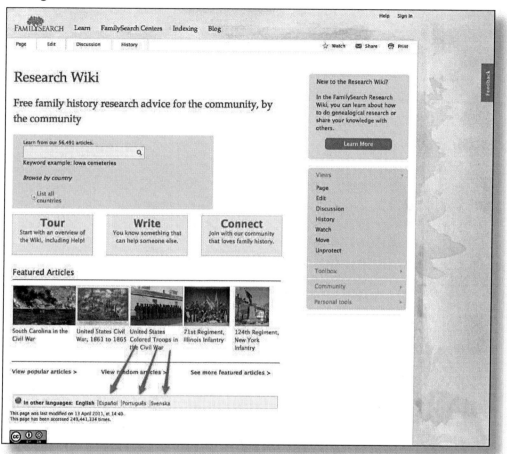

You might note that my screen shot shows a Wiki in Portuguese. This Wiki has since disappeared although it is possible that additional languages will be added in the future. Each of these different language Wikis are presently entirely separate from the English version. They each require their own separate login although you can use your LDS Account or FamilySearch Account to log in.

Section Two: FamilySearch Indexing

There was a brief introduction to the FamilySearch Indexing program earlier in the Guide, but now I will go a little deeper into the subject. There is a FamilySearch *Guide to Indexing* which is located in the Help Center in the section entitled Especially for Indexing. There is a short list of topics but if you click on "See the whole list (35)," the list expands and you will see an entry for the User Guide. Here is a screen shot of the Help Center with an arrow pointing to the Especially for Indexing section:

Figure 2.1

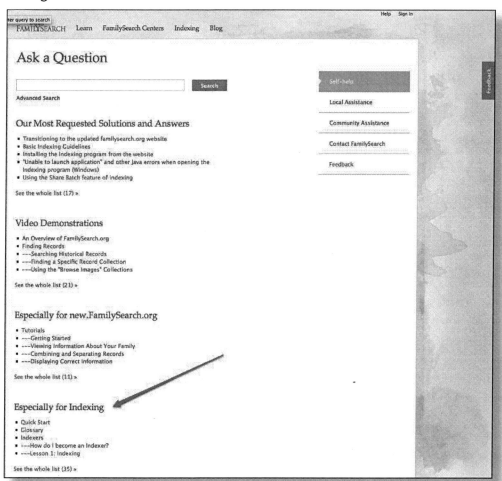

Clicking on the link to show the whole list brings up the following screen:

Figure 2.2

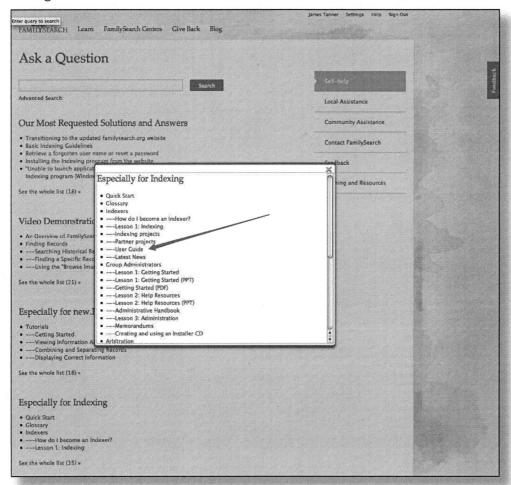

Clicking again, this time on the link to the Users Guides, begins download-ing a copy of the User Guide to your computer in PDF format, either for members or for those who are not members. It is a small file, only 2.3 Megabytes and even with a slow connection should not take long to download. Here is a screen shot of the cover:

Figure 2.3

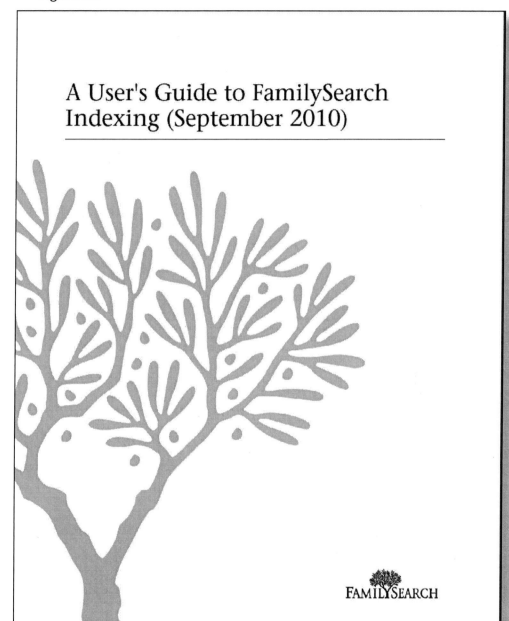

As I have mentioned before, it is not my intention in writing the present Guide, to reproduce the information that is already in the 90 page User's Guide to FamilySearch Indexing in a different format. This Users' Guide will give you an overall introduction to Indexing and tell you exactly how to get started.

What is the FamilySearch Indexing program?

You will recall that FamilySearch is in the process of digitizing millions of records stored on microfilm in the Granite Vault outside of Salt Lake City, Utah. The FamilySearch Indexing program coordinates tens of thousands of volunteers across the world who are indexing the scanned images.

Earlier in this Guide, at Figure 1.35, I talked about the Historical Record Collections. To review a little, there are three types of records in the Historical Record Collections; those with images only, those with images and an index to the images, and those with indexes only and no images. Those indexes come primarily from the efforts of the volunteers in the FamilySearch Indexing program.

Making digital images of the microfilms in the Granite Vault proceeds much faster than indexing those same records since one film may contain hundreds or even thousands of names and other information. As each microfilm is digitized, the digitized records are separated into batches containing from 20 to 50 names. The Indexing volunteers, view the records online and record selected information from each record, including names, dates and places, onto digital online forms provided by FamilySearch. Two different people acting independently index each set of microfilmed records. If the two indexers do not agree, the record is sent to a third volunteer for arbitration. The Arbitrator compares the two interpretations to the original record and makes any needed changes. Recent changes to the Indexing program give the users feedback and more information on the arbitration process. These changes allow the users to see how well they are doing in the indexing process.

Once the extracted information is corrected, the separate Indexing batches are consolidated into a complete database corresponding to the images or records from the original microfilm. The consolidated indexes are then prepared for online publication and the indexes eventually appear in the Historical Record Collections.

By providing indexes to these historical records, the Indexing program is opening up the vast world of records previously available only through the microfilms from the Granite Vault. Participating in Indexing helps move this valuable work forward.

Access to FamilySearch Indexing

FamilySearch Indexing has multiple startup pages depending on how you access the program. Primary access to the program is through its URL address, http://indexing.familysearch.org that will take you to the following startup page:

Figure 2.4

I will come back to the various sections. But, first, I want to illustrate the various entry points for the program. If you go to FamilySearch.org, you will see a link at the top of the page to "Indexing." Here is a screen shot of the startup page with an arrow pointing to the Indexing link:

Figure 2.5

If you click on the Indexing link, before signing in, you are taken to a different startup page for the site as shown in the screen shot of the top portion of the page:

Figure 2.6

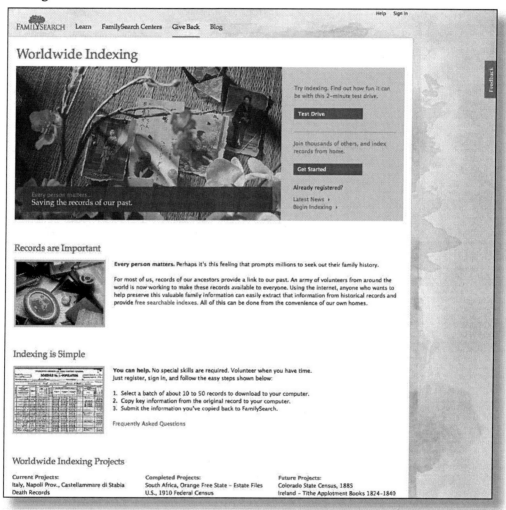

It is very likely, that as the websites evolve, that these separate startup pages will be consolidated.

After you sign in to the FamilySearch.org website, you can access a link to the Indexing program through the "Give Back" link at the bottom of the page. Clicking on the "Giving Back" takes you to a page as shown in this screen shot:

Figure 2.7

From this page, you can click on the link for FamilySearch Indexing that will take you to the page shown in Figure 2.6.

Having several entry points seems complicated to explain, but in practice you will find which entry point you choose will depend on where you begin. If you are already registered, you will need to primarily access the program from the icon on your desktop or other local link to the program on your computer, but it is helpful to know the other entry points for the program.

Getting started with FamilySearch Indexing

Indexing is an ongoing volunteer program. You can spend a few minutes a week or hours a day, depending on your interest and dedication. The Indexing program installs on your computer. You can down load the program for free by clicking on the indexing tab or clicking on a "Get Started" button. When you click you will be given the following instructions:

Figure 2.8

To begin using the FamilySearch Indexing program, you click to download the program and then run the Indexing program from your desktop. Once you click the download button, there are screen instructions for you to follow to download the program. You will also need to sign into your LDS or FamilySearch Account. If you haven't signed up for an account, then you will have to do so. Once you sign into the Indexing program, you are ready to begin indexing. An email message will be sent to you with instructions for new indexers.

Remember to check out the Help Center for more information about the Indexing program. The Users Guides also give a lot of helpful information about getting started with the program. Note that there are two manuals, one for members of the Church and the other for those who are not members. At the time of the writing of this Guide, the online Indexing Users' Guide had not been updated with information about the updated FamilySearch.org website but most of the information was current and applicable.

There are some additional requirements for participating in the Indexing program. Most importantly, is that the program is intensively graphic and FamilySearch recommends a high speed Internet connection and a minimal computer configuration. In order to adequately participate in the Indexing program, your computer must not only be able to download information quickly from the Internet, it must also be fast enough and have enough memory to run graphic intensive and video applications. Most of the training and instruction for Indexing is in the form of downloaded video presentations and if your computer cannot handle these video files, you will be very frustrated. Most computers purchased in the last few years are perfectly adequate, but if you have an older system, you might need to upgrade to a newer computer.

* * * * * * * * * *

A Note about Email and Security

As I mentioned near the beginning of this Guide, many of the FamilySearch programs depend, to some extent, on email. If you become involved with FamilySearch websites, you will receive email both from FamilySearch in response to your questions, or providing updates, or from other users of the programs. This is most evident if you participate on the Administrator or Arbitrator level in FamilySearch Indexing or if you contact other users of the New FamilySearch program. A word of caution is advised. Always look carefully at the address of any email message you receive from an unknown person or entity. Email messages can contain dangerous, self-executing programs that can harm your computer. These programs rely on your ignorance and expect that you will not examine the message before opening it. FamilySearch will never send you a message that is not clearly marked and identified as being from FamilySearch. There is no reason to be overly concerned with problem, but do not routinely open every message you receive.

* * * * * * * * * *

Skills needed for Indexing

The skills needed for Indexing go to the heart of the some of the more difficult issues with genealogical research, reading old handwritten records and correctly transcribing your findings. In order to help newcomers to the program, there are a series of lessons and explanations in a variety of languages in the Indexing Resource

Guide. In Figure 2.8 above, you can see the tabs at the top of the screen. The tabs are as follows:

- Indexing
- News
- Projects
- Help

The last tab is Help. Clicking on that tab, by default, brings up the following screen showing the Indexing Resource Guide:

Figure 2.9

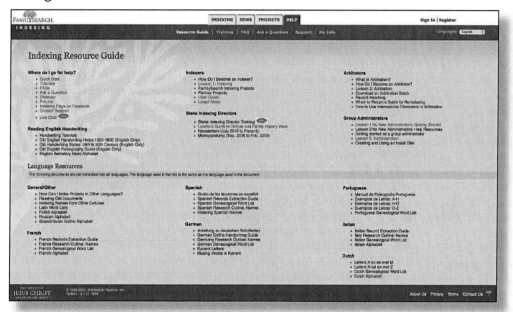

Currently, the options include the following languages:

- French
- Spanish
- German
- Portuguese
- Italian
- Dutch

The topics covered include:

- Where do I go for help?
- Reading English Handwriting

- Indexers
- Stake Extraction Directors
- Arbitrators
- Group Administrators

I will take some time to explore the many resources available for training and support of the Indexing program.

Initially, you will want to focus on the links available under the heading "Where do I go for help?" Those links are as follows:

- Quick Start
- Tutorials
- FAQs
- Ask a Question
- Glossary
- Forums
- Indexing Page on Facebook
- Contact Support
- Live Chat

The initial training can be as simple as going through the Quick Start and beginning Indexing or studying the Tutorials and participating in the Forums and Live Chat.

FamilySearch Indexing Quick Start

Many of the resources available to teach you how to do Indexing are in the form of video presentations. These videos require that your computer have both audio and video capabilities. If you haven't previously done so, start with the short video entitled "Quick Start." Please be aware that this is not all that you need to get started but you have to start somewhere.

Figure 2.10

FamilySearch Indexing Tutorials

The wealth of resources available to introduce you to FamilySearch Indexing continues with a set of online Tutorials. These presentations, unlike the Quick Start, are not videos, but do have some animation.

Figure 2.11

You can see that the Tutorials are divided into three sections corresponding to the way that FamilySearch Indexing operates. The vast number of volunteers are at the Indexing level. Some of the more experienced indexers who are detail-oriented, act as arbitrators. FamilySearch indexing involves a stake extraction director, who oversees the indexing program within a stake or district of The Church of Jesus Christ of Latter-day Saints, or a local group administrator, who oversees the indexing program for a genealogical society or organization. Although the Indexing program involves Church officers, the indexing is not in any way limited to Church members. Any interested person can participate in the program either individually or as part of a society or other interested group. Both Directors and Group Administrators may provide training and support to the individual indexers.

Even if you do not plan on participating in FamilySearch Indexing as a Director or Group Administrator, you may find the Tutorials interesting and helpful to understand how the overall program is organized and works.

FamilySearch Indexing FAQs – Frequently Asked Questions

Although some of this information is repetitious and cumulative, this is a good resource to gain an overall understanding of the Indexing project in a short time. Here is a screen shot of the top of the page showing some of the questions, but the answers are lower on the page and not showing:

Figure 2.12

FamilySearch Indexing Ask a Question

Although the program provides a number of help menu items as I am outlining, there is still the need to ask specific questions. FamilySearch Indexing has its own email question screen. Here is a screen shot of the Ask a Question screen:

Figure 2.13

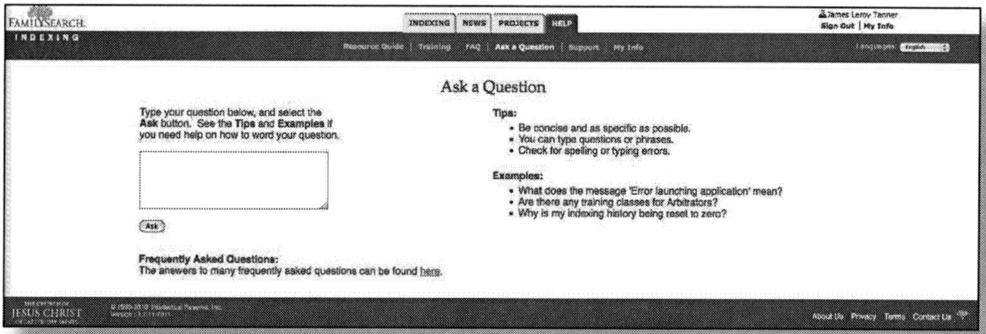

There is also a link back to the Frequently Asked Questions shown in Figure 2.12.

FamilySearch Indexing Glossary

Earlier in this Guide, I mentioned that you can always look for the meaning of a word or term by doing an online search. However, it is convenient to have a glossary of terms used in a specific context. The Indexing link to a Glossary, downloads a small PDF file to your computer. You need to be aware where these files download. The file may open automatically when the download is complete, but once you close the file, you may have to search for it on your computer. I suggest that all downloaded files go to the same designated folder or onto your operating system's desktop, so that you can find the files without difficulty.

The Glossary is not exhaustive but does have a number of pages of useful terms in a straightforward text based file. Here is a screen shot of the beginning of the file:

Figure 2.13.1

Glossary

A key and B key or double-blind indexing process	A process where two indexers work independently to type genealogical information from the same digital images of historical documents into the FamilySearch indexing computer program.
application	A computer program (such as a word processor or a spreadsheet) that performs one of the major tasks for which a computer is used.
	The indexing computer program is sometimes referred to as the indexing application.
arbitration	The process of choosing between the entries typed by the A key and B key indexers when they differ. Arbitration is done after an entire batch of records has been indexed using the A key and B key process.
arbitration batch	A batch (see Batch) with the associated information typed by the A and B key indexers. An arbitrator downloads this type of batch in order to compare and resolve discrepancies between the A and B key information.
arbitrator	The person who compares the A key and B key discrepancies that are identified by the initial computer check. This person either selects the correct entry or overrides both versions and types his or her interpretation of the information recorded on the document.
background color	An indicator in a field meant to remind the indexer or arbitrator to double-check what was typed against what is on the document. The background color does not mean a mistake was made. It only indicates that the flagged name or word is not included in the associated lookup list.
	An indexer can choose whether the program flags information with a background color or a red wavy underline.
basic indexing guidelines	Basic instructions for indexing that apply to all projects.

I have provided a limited Glossary at the end of this Guide but it does not contain all of the terms listed in this Indexing Help file.

FamilySearch Indexing Forums Support

There is a three-tiered level of support for the Indexing program. At the first level, indexers are encouraged to use the abundance of self-help resources available online as I have already reviewed. However, there are more help areas that are not covered from links in the website itself. At the time of the writing of this Guide, it appears that the links to the newer resources have not been included. For example, the Help Center has a whole section of 35 items linking to help for the Indexing program.

Here is a screen shot of the Help Center topics and links:

Figure 2.14

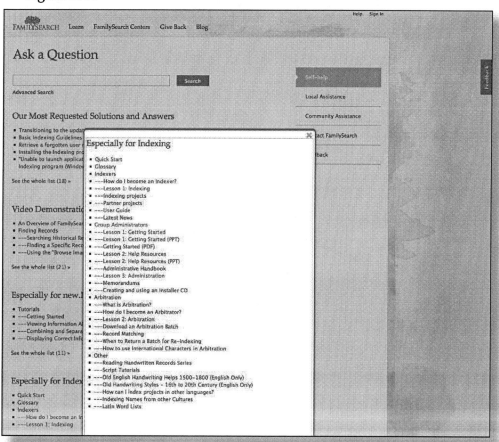

These links are, for the most part, duplicative of links that you can access through the Indexing Resource Guide, see Figure 2.9 above.

The second major resource, not mentioned in the materials linked on the Indexing Resource Guide is the FamilySearch Indexing Forum available at https://www.familysearch.org/learn/forums/en/ Here is a screen shot with an arrow pointing to the FamilySearch Indexing Forum:

Figure 2.15

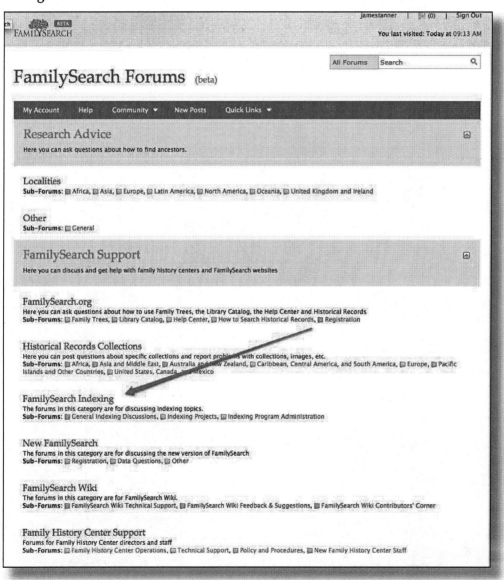

I will refer you back to the discussion on the Forums, but you need to note that this resource is also available for help with questions about Indexing.

FamilySearch Indexing Page on Facebook

The popular social networking site Facebook has several FamilySearch oriented pages including one for FamilySearch Indexing. I have not included a screen shot of the page because of the personal pictures and comments on the page, but you can visit the page for comments and discussion of topics of interest to indexers. If you read the comments you can see that you can also brag a little about your indexing accomplishments.

FamilySearch Contact Support

The levels of support are outlined in this page linked to the Contact Support selection of the "Where do I go for help?" links. There are at least two links to the Contact Support page, as shown in the following screen shot as indicated by the arrows:

Figure 2.15.1

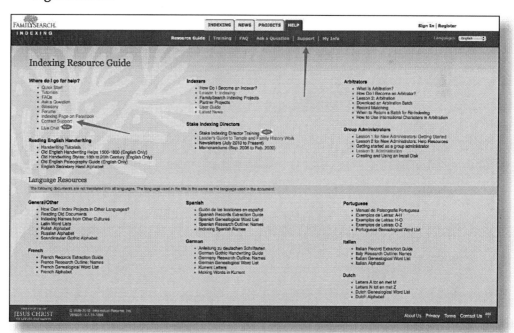

Clicking on either option will show the following screen:

Figure 2.15.2

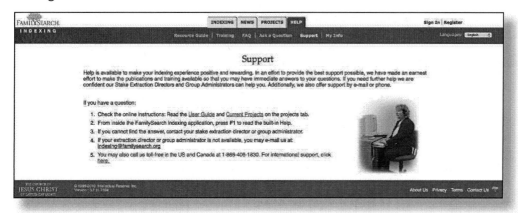

FamilySearch Live Chat

Live Chat is an online real-time written conversation with whomever is online at the time. You will be asked to enter your name, email address and a telephone number. You will then likely get a call from a FamilySearch Representative. Once again, this is not an area that I can show with a screen shot. I suggest you try out the chat and see if you can get specific questions answered.

Please take advantage of the other extensive resources.

Now back to the remaining menu items in the Help tab. Here is another screen shot with the tabs and menu selections marked with arrows.

Figure 2.15.3

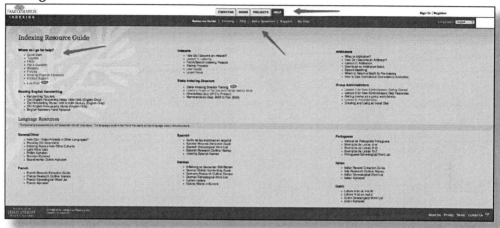

Any confusion that might occur is as a result of the items being redundant. Redundancy is good because it gives different options to accomplish the same goal. When the goal is providing support, it is especially needful to have different options for obtaining help.

In the text above, I started with the Help Tab and then went to a discussion of the Menu Items under the Help Tab and the Resource Guide Menu, which included a detailed discussion of the "Where do I go for Help?" links. I am now returning to the Menu Items.

The Menu Items include the Resource Guide, which I have already discussed, and the following menu items:

- Resource Guide
- Training
- FAQ
- Ask a Question
- Support
- My Info

For the most part these options duplicate the choices in the "Where do I go for Help?" list. The Training Menu Item is the same as the "Tutorials" link in the list. See Figure 2.11. The FAQ Menu Item is the same as the "FAQs" link in the list. See Figure 2.12. You can probably guess that the Ask a Question option is also the same as the same item in the list. See Figure 2.13. Finally, the Support Menu Item is the same as Figure 2.15C.

The next and last item of the Menu Items is the My Info link.

My Info

The My Info link under the Help tab gives a minimal amount of information about you and your involvement with the Indexing program including you name, email address, your Indexing Group, your role as either an indexer, arbitrator or administrator and the date your account was created. You can also get an idea of your Indexing statistics and your membership status. The last area of Preferences includes information about your email Preferences, Level of Difficulty, and Project Languages you would like to support.

Family Search Indexing Projects

At any given time, FamilySearch Indexing volunteers are working on dozens of different projects. The Projects tab links to a page with a long list of current projects. Here is a screen shot of some of the projects current at the time of the shot:

Figure 2.16

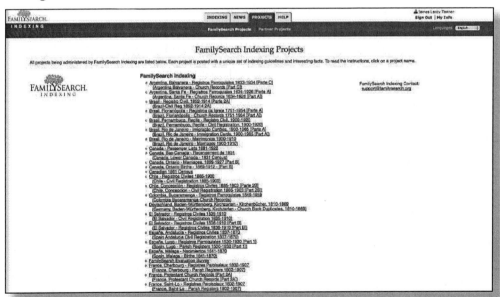

If you want information about any one of the projects, you click on the project and get a link to the Project Home Page. Here is a screen shot of the top part of the Project Home Page for Canada, Ontario – Marriages, 1869-1927 [Part B] from the list:

Figure 2.17

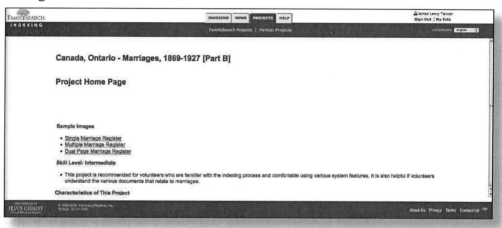

Besides linking to sample images, indicating the skill level and characteristics of the project, the rest of the page lists a Description of the Records, Additional Information about the Project, Access Restrictions, and finally, How to Help With This Project.

Each project has its own Project-specific indexing instructions, Basic indexing guidelines, Field-by-field helps and Project updates.

Section Three: New.FamilySearch.org

With this section, I move to the New.FamilySearch.org website. It is an extremely large unified family tree website. The site allows users to collaborate with others in their family and to build, share, manage and preserve their family history online. It also helps members of the Church to perform temple ordinances on behalf of their deceased family members.

PLEASE NOTE:

New.FamilySearch.org (NFS) has a highly developed manual of over 200 pages plus thousands of pages of detailed help in the Help Center. For these reasons, I have chosen to provide an overview and commentary to the NFS program with less depth than the other FamilySearch websites. Where it is appropriate, I will refer you to the Help Center or other resources rather than provide a duplicate set of instructions on how to use the program.

A Brief History of New FamilySearch

NFS is the latest in a long history of methods of submitting and verifying names of deceased ancestors in order to perform the required temple ordinances.

* * * * * * * * * *

A Note on Temple Proxy Ordinance Submission

The driving forces of the present New.FamilySearch.org website include the need to approve names for submission to the Church for proxy temple ordinances and at the same time, avoid duplication. Historically, prior to 1927, members of the Church brought their ancestors' names directly to the temples but research was restricted to only four ancestral lines. In 1927, the Church established the Temple Records Index Bureau (TIB), a manual 3x5 card system, to track temple ordinances and attempt to avoid duplication. In 1969, the Church began listing proxy ordinances in the Computer File Index that later became the International Genealogical Index. In 1998, the ordinances from the International Genealogical Index were transferred to the Ordinance Index and became part of FamilySearch.org.[30] Depending on the nature of the records and whether or not the individuals recorded are still living, some or all of these records can have restricted access.

In 1942, submissions for proxy ordinances were done on paper by Family Group Record sheets. As a result, in addition to the Ordinance Index, the Family History Library has approximately five million family group record forms submitted for proxy temple work from 1942 to 1969. In addition, the TIB cards were filmed from 1973 to 1991. This information is included in what is called the Endowment Index covering the years from 1842 to 1969.[31] The index was compiled from 1922-1971 and is available only on microfilm at the Family History Library. Access to the Index is limited. Some of the information in the Endowment Index was included in the International Genealogical Index (IGI). The IGI was made available to Church members on microfiche and later on a set of Compact Discs (CDs). Until the IGI was computerized, it was necessary to make a manual search of the records. In 1993, the Church introduced the TemplyReady program. Checking names for prior ordinances became a complicated multistep process using both the IGI and the newer TempleReady program. Church members used TempleReady until it was completely replaced by the multi-year introduction of New.Family-Search.org.[32]

• • • • • • • • • •

NFS was officially introduced in the St. Louis, Missouri Temple District on May 9, 2007 and activated on June 26, 2007. The program was slowly introduced in various temple districts across the U.S. and into Canada and Mexico during 2007 and into 2008. The last temple districts to be activated were in Utah in 2009 and in the Far East in Taiwan, Korea and China in 2010.[33] In 2011, FamilySearch began the introduction of the program to those who are not members of the Church.

New.FamilySearch.org was designed to become a complete replacement for all of the previous systems for approving names for temple ordinances and specifically to replace TempleReady. Through this entire multi-year introduction, NFS continued to evolve with updates and changes.

At the time of the writing of this Guide, the website continues to change. Here is a screen shot of the New.FamilySearch.org startup page at the time of the writing of this book.

Figure 3.1

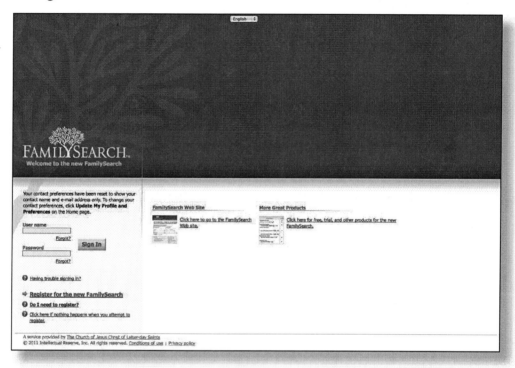

New.FamilySearch.org in multiple languages

New.FamilySearch.org comes in multiple languages. The different versions are available from the startup page in a pull-down menu. Currently, there are versions in English, Spanish, German, French, Italian, Portuguese, Russian, Chinese, Japanese and Korean. You can see the selections in this screen shot showing the pull down menu:

Figure 3.2

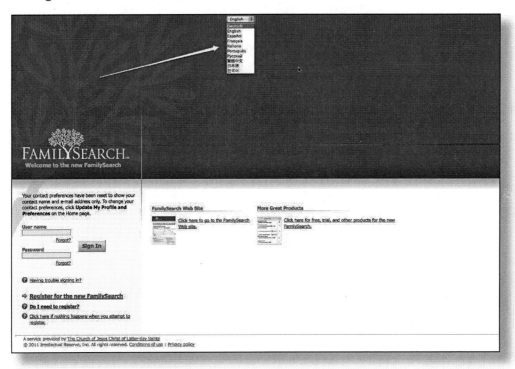

● ● ● ● ● ● ● ● ●

A Note about the word "New" in New FamilySearch

At various times since its introduction, the new.familysearch.org website has had different names. It is sometimes referred to as the FamilySearch Family Trees programs with several variations. There is some confusion with the present designation as "new FamilySearch" or with the "new" capitalized as in "New FamilySearch." Since the Family-Search.org website was updated in December, 2010, there is even more confusion because as long as the "old" FamilySearch.org website is online, the "new" FamilySearch.org website can refer to either the FamilySearch.org website as updated or to the entirely different New FamilySearch.org website. Eventually all of this will be sorted out as the sites are all combined into the "FamilySearch.org" website and the older Family-Search.org site goes away.

•   •   •   •   •   •   •   •   •

Registration for New FamilySearch

When New FamilySearch was introduced, all of the FamilySearch websites registration for the various FamilySearch websites was fairly complicated. Each site required its own login and password, although you could, if you thought about it, use the same ones for each site. In addition, the NFS registration process was complicated by members needing to supply both a membership record number and a confirmation date. Some members could produce a membership number but few knew their confirmation date. During 2010, the process was streamlined with the new LDS Account and FamilySearch Account consolidated registration. The main issue with registration then focused on the need to have a working email account. Most of those problems have been solved and there are only occasional problems now with registration, usually having to do with people's lack of understanding of computers rather than the process of registration itself.

If you need to register for an LDS or FamilySearch Account, there is a prominent link on the NFS startup page to do that. There are four links, actually as follows:

- Having trouble signing in?
- Register for the new FamilySearch
- Do I need to register
- Click here if nothing happens when you attempt to register

Clicking on the first selection, loads an extensive PDF file entitled, "Registering and Signing into the New FamilySearch Website." The second option takes you to the registration process. The last two options take you to the Help Center with suggestions about how to solve the login problem.

Because of security reasons, any time you close the NFS program you will be required to login again. This is not a bug in the program, but a security feature.

Links on the NFS Startup or Home Page

There are several links on the NFS startup page, although some of them are fairly obscure. Here is a screen shot with arrows pointing to the links:

Figure 3.3

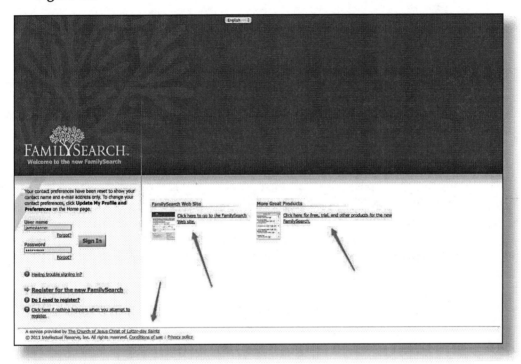

One arrow points at a link to the FamilySearch.org website. That is self-explanatory. The next link over takes you to a list of the Certified Products for new. FamilySearch.org (Family Tree). Incidentally, this reference points out the confusion with the name of the program. The links at the bottom of the page are to the Church's main website and the ever present Conditions of Use and Privacy Policy. As I have noted previously in this Guide, these links appear throughout the entire FamilySearch websites.

Here is a screen shot of the top of the Certified Products page:

Figure 3.4

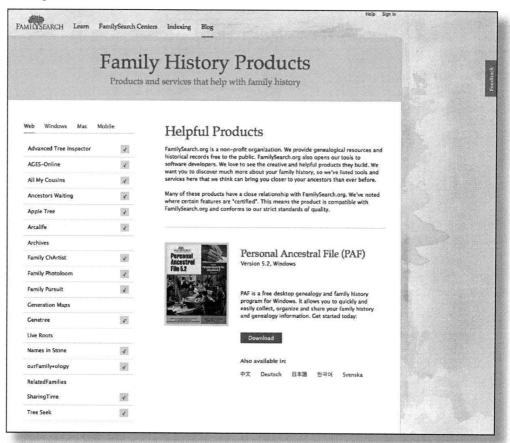

There are four different lists of choices, Web, Windows, Mac and Mobile. You will need to click on each choice to see a more complete description. The list includes New FamilySearch Certified Products and also other helpful products.

New FamilySearch Certified Products

FamilySearch has made agreements with many third-party software companies to provide access to the NFS program files so that the third-party products will work in concert with NFS. The link on the NFS startup page goes to a list of the third-party products. None of those products are supported or endorsed by NFS in any way, but the products are listed and their functions briefly defined. Each of the products has a link to its own website.

Although the Personal Ancestral File program appears on this page, FamilySearch has made it clear on a number of occasions that it will not be upgrading the PAF program and since there are no announced plans to upgrade the old PAF program, many developers have taken advantage of the opportunity to supply programs that are add-ons or supplement the features of NFS. Some of the programs utilize the database to exchange information between the local program and NFS. I suggest carefully evaluating these and any other software products that claim to have features beneficial to the use of NFS. Some of the programs have clear and obvious advantages, others are not so clearly advantageous.

.   .   .   .

A Note About Website Architecture

If you were to look at a schematic of a website like those of Family-Search, you would not see an orderly construction of rooms, but a series of boxes surrounded by spaghetti. Websites are not linear. Going through a website is not like touring a house, it is more like untangling string. Good website design allows a user to link to any other location within the site that may be related to the original location. This is the fundamental reason why nearly every page of the FamilySearch websites (or any website for that matter) is loaded with links to other pages within the site. Good website design also tries to avoid having dead ends or links that cannot return to the starting point. Even though browsers have a link back button or back arrow, good design should not make the user click on the browser's buttons to negotiate the site. For the most part and almost always, FamilySearch has followed these guidelines.

If you are navigating through a website such as NFS, you need only look around on the page for other links. Sometimes the links are not as obvious as they might be, but usually there is some way to continue searching the website. In the event you cannot find any way to get back to the beginning, remember to click on the logo or in extreme cases use the back button on your browser.

.   .   .   .

After you have signed into NFS, you are taken automatically to the Introductory Page.

The Introductory Page or Home Page of NFS

Similar to many pages in all websites including FamilySearch's other sites, this page is mostly a series of links to other pages. Here is a screen shot of the Introductory Page or Home Page:

Figure 3.5

In the upper left hand corner of the screen, there is a FamilySearch logo. Since NFS is not completely integrated into the FamilySearch.org website, clicking on this logo will do nothing. In the future, if you click on the logo and you are taken to another of the FamilySearch web sites, you can assume that NFS has been completely integrated into the other websites. At the time of writing this Guide, there is no announced timetable for that to happen.

The links on this page are somewhat redundant and duplicative. Here is a list of the links with the duplications indicated:

- What's New in FamilySearch
- Learn How to Use FamilySearch
- See Temple Information (Schedules, Driving Directions, etc.)
- See Me and My Ancestors the same as the tab Me and My Ancestors
- Search for Ancestors the same as the tab Search
- Add information the same as the tab Add Information
- Temple Ordinance the same as the tab Temple Ordinances
- Sign in to Help Someone Else
- Update My Profile and Preferences
- Help Center essentially the same as Help with This Page

• • • • • • • • • •

A Note on Homepage vs. Introductory Page vs. Startup Page

Earlier in the Guide, I explained the usage of the term "startup" page versus the use of the term "Home" page. I think it is time to explain that concept again. In the past, website design has worked off of a homepage. That page was where the user went to start all of their explorations and was like the switchboard for the website. More recently, website design has drifted away from a definite home page to a more de-centralized format for website design. In the case of the FamilySearch websites, you may only infrequently go to the main or home page of the site. For this reason, I have called the initial contact page of the site a "startup" or "introductory" page. In the case of NFS, once you leave the introductory or homepage, you likely will not return to it for any reason unless you restart the program. However, if you get lost, you may wish to return to the beginning of the program and start over again.

• • • • • • • • • •

Now, I will take an initial look at each link or sets of links.

What's New in FamilySearch

From time to time, FamilySearch makes changes to the operation and functions of the website. These changes are explained and listed in a series of PDF documents. All of the changes are also available in the Help Center by making a time sensitive advanced search.

I just mentioned the Help Center again. If you need help with any of the Family-Search programs or websites, you need to remember this valuable resource. In the case of NFS, there is a more than extensive help structure in the form of an online 201page manual. As I have noted previously, I am not attempting to restate or replace the already existent manuals. There are huge sections of the programs where there is no manual, but in those areas where manuals are present, such as FamilySearch Indexing and the present NFS, if you need further help, please refer to the manual.

Learn How to Use FamilySearch

Clicking on the Learn How to Use FamilySearch brings up separate small page listing a number of tutorials and guides. Here is a screen shot of the list:

Figure 3.6

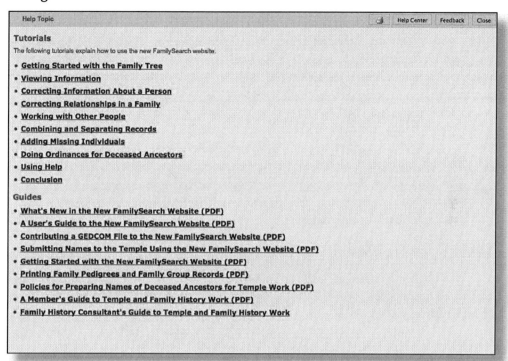

 As you can see from the list, the help topics are very comprehensive. In my experience, providing support for users of the NFS program, I have found that nearly all of the questions I have been asked are adequately covered by either the Help Center or the other resources such as the manual and the list of help topics.

See Temple Information

This selection is a link to the LDS.org website's Temples section with information about all of the Church's Temples' schedules and locations.

NFS Operational Links

The next four links in the list from See Me and My Ancestors to Temple Ordinances are the links to the operation of the program and appear in the tabs at the top of each page. I will discuss these links a little further on in the Guide.

Sign in to Help Someone Else

An innovative function of the NFS program is the ability to sign on to help others with their data entry and management. When you set up your preferences, you are given a Helper access number that is usually, by default, the last five numbers of your membership number if you are a member of the Church. Otherwise the number can be any combination of 5 numbers or letters. Anyone with number can help you work with the program and can remotely view your screen. If someone signs on as a helper, you still own the data entered.

 If you need help in signing in to help someone else, there are complete instructions in the Help Center, the tutorials and guides to the NFS program. Before getting into a difficult situation in trying to help others, I suggest that you may wish to review what has already been written in the extensive documentation.

Update My Profile and Preferences

When you obtain an LDS or FamilySearch Account, you provide some information about how you would like to be viewed online and other issues. The categories of information you supply is as follows:

- What information do you want other people to see about you when you contribute information?
- When you search for an individual, how do you want to enter the name?
- In what language do you want to use FamilySearch?

You can change your selections and update your personal information at any time by clicking on the Update link.

Data Ownership in NFS

If you enter information into the NFS program you "own" that information. No one else can change or delete owned information unless they have entered the program with your login and password or unless you give them your Helper Number for access. This is one of those features that is both good news and bad news. You are the only person that can make any changes to data or information you enter into the program, but at the same time, you cannot change anything anyone else has entered. One of the issues with the program is the inability of users to make changes, even when the information contained in NFS is obviously inaccurate or incomplete. Another issue is the unavailability of the contributor. Some of the information in NFS comes from people who have died or are no longer online and available to contact. In those cases, NFS has provided a path to obtain "ownership" of abandoned data in some limited cases.

NFS refers to "legacy" data as data submitted to FamilySearch through the Ancestral File, Pedigree Resource File or other source before NFS came online. In those cases, users have the option to "Declare This Legacy Contributor as Yourself." The present rules are that you may claim legacy for the these types of records:[34]

- Patrons may claim a legacy of their own prior submissions. The request will be evaluated and matched against the original contact name to ensure that the patron and the submitter are the same person.
- Patrons may claim a legacy of a submission made by a deceased ancestor only if they are a direct descendant.
- Patrons may claim legacy for a deceased spouse.
- If couples made a joint submission, only one may claim the legacy (usually the first person to claim it will be granted it). However, if there is a dispute, the legacy reverts back to no one as the legacy recipient.

If you consider trying to claim legacy ownership of some records, check the Help Center for the latest policy and instructions.

You may have noticed that I just suggested you use the Help Center yet once again. In my years of teaching genealogy, I have found that repetition is one of the best ways to remind people of a resource. This is especially true because NFS is a program where you can literally say, it is all in the manual or the Help Center. Anything you want to know about the program is readily available and searchable online. This is the main reason that my coverage of NFS is more of a commentary than a how-to manual.

● ● ● ● ● ● ● ● ● ●

An Important Note on Live People and Dead People in NFS

NFS is a program for viewing and recording information about dead people. It is designed specifically so that only your own personal information will be shown and very limited information about any other living individuals including spouses and children. Many people when they view the program for the first time assume that information about their immediate family members is missing. That is not usually the case. For members of the Church, all of the membership information and Temple information has already been included in the program. If you find that any of this information is missing or inaccurate, you must contact your local Ward or Branch Clerk to make any additions or changes. Adding information for and about live members will result in more duplication. If you are **not** a member of the Church, then you will probably need to add your personal information into the program. However, do not assume that your ancestors' information is not already been recorded in NFS. Take time to check to see if any ancestor's personal information is already in the database before entering the information again. If you use a third-party program to synchronize your information or add information to NFS, those programs will usually check for duplicate information before allowing you to add more. However, when you are working with the program directly, you need to remember not to add anyone to the database before checking to see whether or not someone else has already entered the information. This is especially true as you work back to remote ancestors. It is always possible that one of the ancestor's descendants already submitted information to NFS or one of the predecessor databases.

●　●　●　●　●　●　●　●　●　●

Viewing and Recording Family Information in NFS

Clicking on the link from the Homepage for "See Me and My Ancestors" will take you to the main working page for NFS called the Family Pedigree with Details. Here is an example showing some of my ancestors. In this Guide I will try to avoid showing anyone in a pedigree or family group who has not been dead for some time. Here is the screen shot:

Figure 3.7

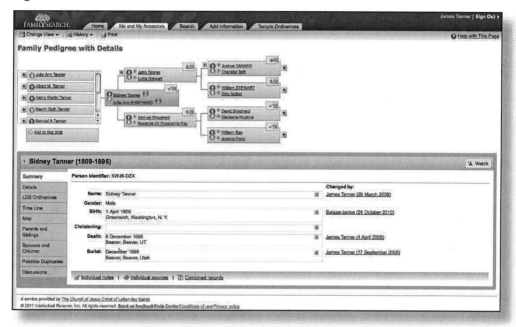

This screen looks familiar to anyone who has, at least, some background in genealogy. The top portion of the screen is a modified pedigree chart and the bottom portion of the screen contains individual information about the person selected in the pedigree chart. The tab showing in the individual information section is the Summary. The Summary view lets individuals choose which of the various versions of the individual information to show on the screen.

Conflicting and Duplicate Information in NFS

FamilySearch had several large databases of information already online before introducing NFS. These databases included:

- Ancestral File (AF)
- International Genealogical Index (IGI)
- Pedigree Resource File (PRF)
- Church Membership Records
- Temple Records

Some of these databases already had duplicate and inaccurate information. Unfortunately, no attempt was made to eliminate either the inaccuracies or the duplicate information before it was included in NFS. As a result, even some of the very early adaptors of the program found that their pedigrees were full of inaccurate, duplicative and contradictory information. At the time of the writing of this book, most of that information has yet to be corrected. FamilySearch has yet to provide a way to correct inaccurate or incomplete information, in every case, the solution is to add yet another entry with the "correct" information. Since its release to the Church membership across the world and now to those who are not members, there is sometimes even more duplicative inaccurate information.

If you find that your family is one of those with a lot of contradictory information in NFS, until the program changes and users are allowed to make corrections to that information, there is really no adequate strategy for correcting the information.

However, some types of inaccurate information can be corrected by FamilySearch. For example, if the gender of an individual is misidentified the incorrect information can be sent to FamilySearch and they will make the change. As of yet, however, there is no adequate way to change the entries that are merely wrong or incomplete. You can show your preferred selection on the Summary tab of the individual's details section. This has to be done one-by-one as there is no way to process a batch of individuals.

Personal Detail Screens

There are a nine different personal data views, including the Discussions. They are as follows:

- Summary
- Details
- LDS Ordinances
- Time Line
- Map
- Parents and Siblings
- Spouses and Children
- Possible Duplicates
- Discussions

Each of these views has different information. Although the Pedigree view does not include a way to view any children, the detail screens have views for both parents and siblings and for spouses and children. Here is a screen shot with arrows to show the various navigational links built into NFS.

Figure 3.8

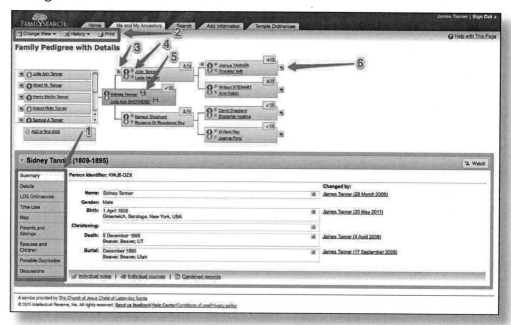

Here is the explanation for each of the numbered areas:

#1 Personal Details Screens

These are the links to the Personal Details Screens as listed above. I will show a screen shot of each of the screens below.

#2 Change View/History/Print Links

This arrow points to three different links. If you click on the Change View tab, you get a choice of whether to view the information in NFS in the present view or to go to an entirely different sort of Family Tree type of view which will be shown below. The History link shows a drop-down menu that will give a list of individuals previously selected. By clicking on an individual's name, the program will move directly back to that individual. The last selection gives you an option of printing what you see on the screen.

#3 Multiple Parents Marker

This little asterisk indicates that there are more than one set of parents for the selected person. If you click on the asterisk symbol you will get a screen allowing you to choose which set of parents you want to show on your screen. This in no way affects the duplication in the program, it is merely a way to hide any offensive or inaccurate information when you use the program. In this case for Sidney Tanner the resultant screen looks like this:

Figure 3.9

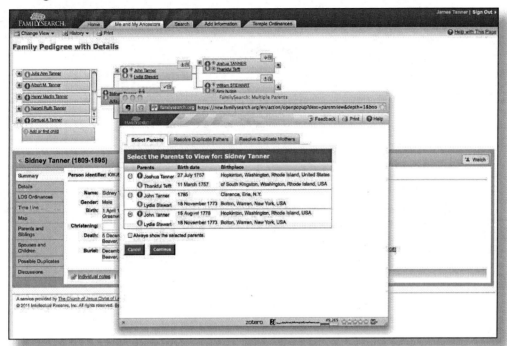

There are several choices for this particular entry, however, depending on the number of individuals in your own line and the number of duplicates, you may never see this kind of choice. If you make a choice of which parents to view, you make that choice the default choice by clicking in the check box next to "Always show the selected parents."

• • • • • • • • •

A Note About the NFS Dilemmas

As it is presently constituted, NFS does not allow users to make any edits or changes to information submitted by other users. In the case of complicated and duplicative pedigrees, it may be impossible to display the correct information consistently. For example, in the above screen, Figure 3.9, you can choose one of four different parent combinations to display. However, each pair of parents has their own pedigree and there is no way to tell which of the four pedigrees may be the most accurate, especially here, where there are two choices with very similar data. In each of the choices presented, you may also have a problem determining which of the choices is correct. The greater dilemma comes if none of the choices is acceptable, what if they are all wrong? At the present time, there is no practical solution for these dilemmas.

• • • • • • • • • •

#4 Move Individual to Primary Position Arrow

By clicking on the small triangle arrow next to each individual you navigate through the pedigree by moving the individual to the primary position. It is a shortcut method to move rather than use the arrows indicated by #6.

#5 Multiple Marriages Marker

The little square with a plus sign surrounded by two figures indicates multiple marriages for that individual. Clicking on the marker shows a list of the marriages:

Figure 3.10

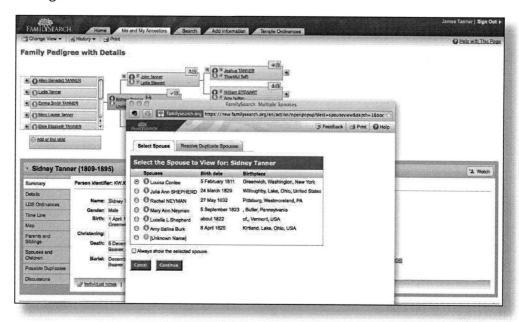

You can make a choice of which of the marriages you wish to show. As I indicated previously, you may never see this many choices in your data, depending on how many people have submitted information about your family. You may also be faced with the problem of determining for yourself which of all of these choices, if any, are correct. I have chosen to show this particular line for the reason that all of the options and features of the program are illustrated in abundance.

#6 Navigation Arrows

At either end of the pedigree chart there are little arrows pointing either to the left or right. Clicking on these arrows allows you to navigate through the pedigree one generation at a time.

Since it is possible that you may become lost in the pedigree, there are a couple of options. First, you may wish to change the view to the Family Tree View. Second, you may wish to backtrack using the History drop down menu as described above. The Family Tree View is selected by using the drop down menu from #2 above. Here is a screen shot of the same individuals in Family Tree View:

Figure 3.11

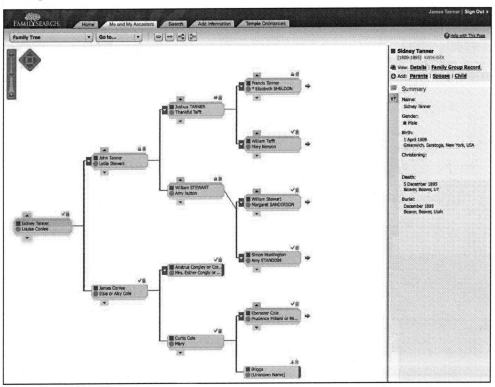

This view is dramatically different from the default view but ultimately has most of the same information. Clicking on the left and right arrows opens up more of the pedigree. You also have the option of viewing the ancestor's descendants by clicking on the selection buttons at the top of the screen. There is also one more option for viewing the information under the drop-down menu for Family Tree, the Individual List. Here is a screen shot of the Individual List view for Sidney Tanner:

Figure 3.12

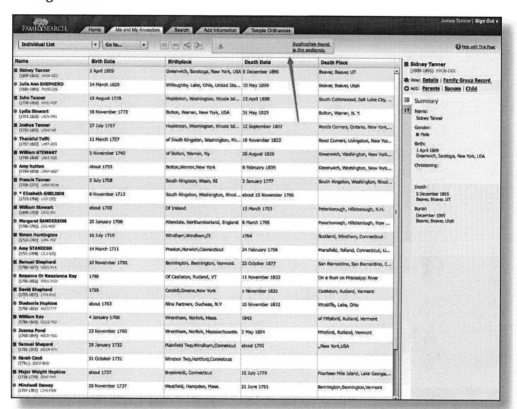

Note the error message (which is an understatement in this case) "Duplication found in the pedigree." Clicking on the names in the list produces their individual information in the box on the right. You can view details, a Family Group Record, the individual's parents, spouse and children from the box also. If you select an individual in the Individual List, that individual will remain highlighted in the Family Tree view. Likewise, if you select an individual in the Family Tree view, that selection will carry over into the Individual List view.

Clicking on the Duplication Found message will give you further information about the problem with the pedigree. Here is an example of the type of message you might get from clicking:

Figure 3.13

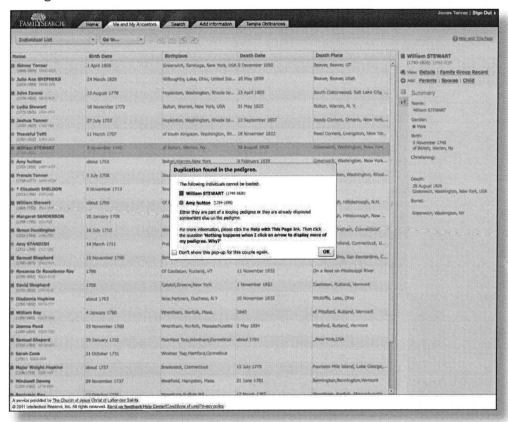

In this case, I cannot do anything about the error message, since I cannot make changes to information that I did not enter.

If you double click on any individual in either the Family Tree view or the Individual List view, you will return to the information in the Family Tree with Details view for the individual. Here is an example after double clicking on William Stewart:

Figure 3.14

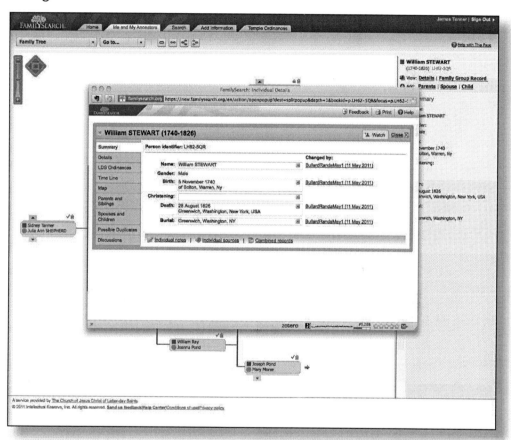

If you click on the little left facing arrow next to the name, the program will take you back to the Family Pedigree with Details view as seen in the following screen shot:

Figure 3.15

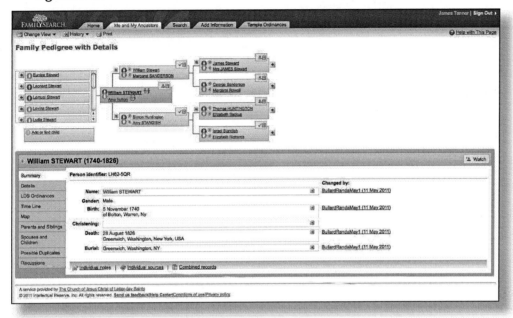

Now, except for the change in individual, you are right back where you started.

Watch Individuals

In the upper right-hand corner of the Individual description there is a button allowing you to "Watch" that individual. If you have an email address in your registration, the program will send you an email notification each time changes or additions are made to the individuals you are watching.

Personal Detail Screens

To repeat the list of Personal Detail Screens, on the left side of each individual's personal information:

- Summary
- Details
- LDS Ordinances
- Time Line
- Map
- Parents and Siblings

- Spouses and Children
- Possible Duplicates
- Discussions

I will discuss each of these individually.

Summary

The main purpose of the Summary screen is to show the user's preferred selection of information or default information. This screen assumes that there are multiple choices of information for each category for the individual; Name, Gender, Birth, Christening, Death, and Burial. If the information in the Detail section is the same as the summary, that is there is no more information than that contained in the summary, there is no real choice. But as you will see with William Stewart, there can be a huge selection of choices due to differing submissions about the same individual.

* * * * * * * * * *

A Note About Not Giving Up on NFS

NFS is designed as a tool for recording information about individuals and families and submitting that information for proxy ordinances in the Church's Temples. It is not presently designed as a complete solution for the general online storage of genealogical files. In short, it is not a substitute for keeping your information in a dedicated local genealogical database program. There are now several individual programs that will share and synchronize data with NFS. The value of using one of these programs should not be overlooked. Many of the limitations and problems evident from the data I have cited in this Guide, cease to be an issue if you use one of the database programs presently available. I hesitate to name names, there are quite a few good programs available for both PCs and Apple Macintosh computers.

* * * * * * * * * *

Details

Here is a view of the Details selection for William Stewart. As you can see, the information goes on for more than a complete screen. In fact, the list is very, very long. You may never see anything like this list if you family has little or no duplication in NFS.

Figure 3.16

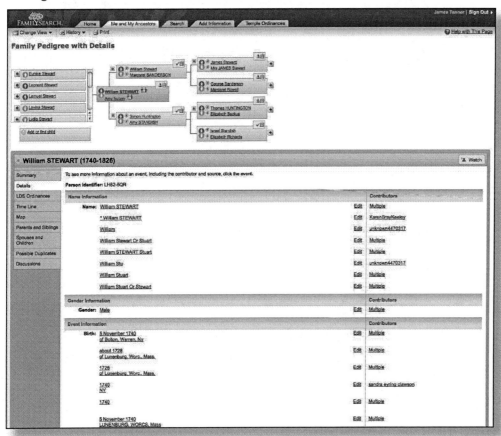

There are actually 27 different birth entries. The birth dates vary from 1728 to 1758 and the places include cities and towns in Rhode Island, New York, Massachusetts and Connecticut.

Obviously, not all of the information can be correct. But to remind you, none of the information that you do not contribute yourself, can be deleted or changed. NFS archives all of the entries equally, whether right or wrong.

LDS Ordinances

Now, let's look at each of the different Personal Detail Screens. We have already seen views of the both the Summary and Detail screens in Figures 3.15 and 3.16. Clicking on the link to the Screen for LDS Ordinances will give you a list of Baptism, Confirmation, Intiatory, Endowment, Sealing to Parents and Sealing to Spouse. Just as with many genealogical database programs that allow you to show or hide Church ordinances, if you are not a member of the Church, you will not be able to view this information and it will just not be an option. For members, the fields in the list tell them which ordinances have been completed and which are still left undone. I will have more to say about ordinances later on in this Guide. I have also skipped showing a screen shot.

Time Line

The Time Line option shows you a list of the events in the individual's life with list of icons set against a time line of the years. Here is a screen shot showing the top part of the long Time Line for William Stewart:

Figure 3.17

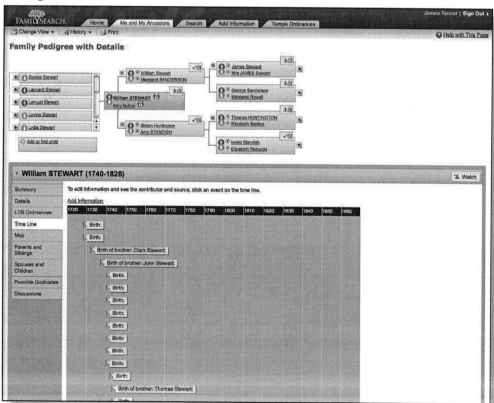

As you can see, the Time Line reflects the duplicate and contradictory information in the Detail link. You can click on any one of the events to see the full information about that particular entry. Clicking on the event for "Birth of brother: John Stewart" shows the following pop-up screen:

Figure 3.18

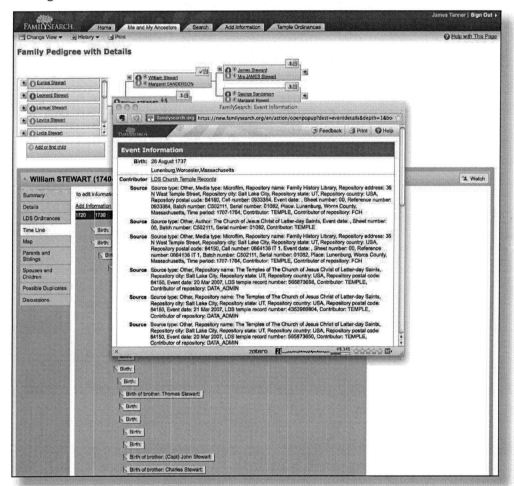

The pop-up window shows you a view of the source list for the birth of John Stewart broken down into contributor and Source. If you look carefully at the first entry, you will see where this information came from originally. This is the source listed:

ContributorLDS Church Temple Records

Source Source type: Other, Media type: Microfilm, Repository name:

Family History Library, Repository address: 35 N West Temple Street, Repository city: Salt Lake City, Repository state: UT, Repository country: USA, Repository postal code: 84150, Call number: 0933384, Event date: , Sheet number: 00, Reference number: 0933384, Batch number: C502111, Serial number: 01082, Place: Lunenburg, Worcs County, Massachusetts, Time period: 1707-1764, Contributor: TEMPLE, Contributor of repository: FCH

Looking at this Source, you can see that the information came from a microfilm in the FamilySearch Family History Library. If I were to take the "Call number" which is really the film number, I can search for that film in the Family History Library catalog. Here are some screen shots showing the process. First, the search in the Catalog:

Figure 3.19

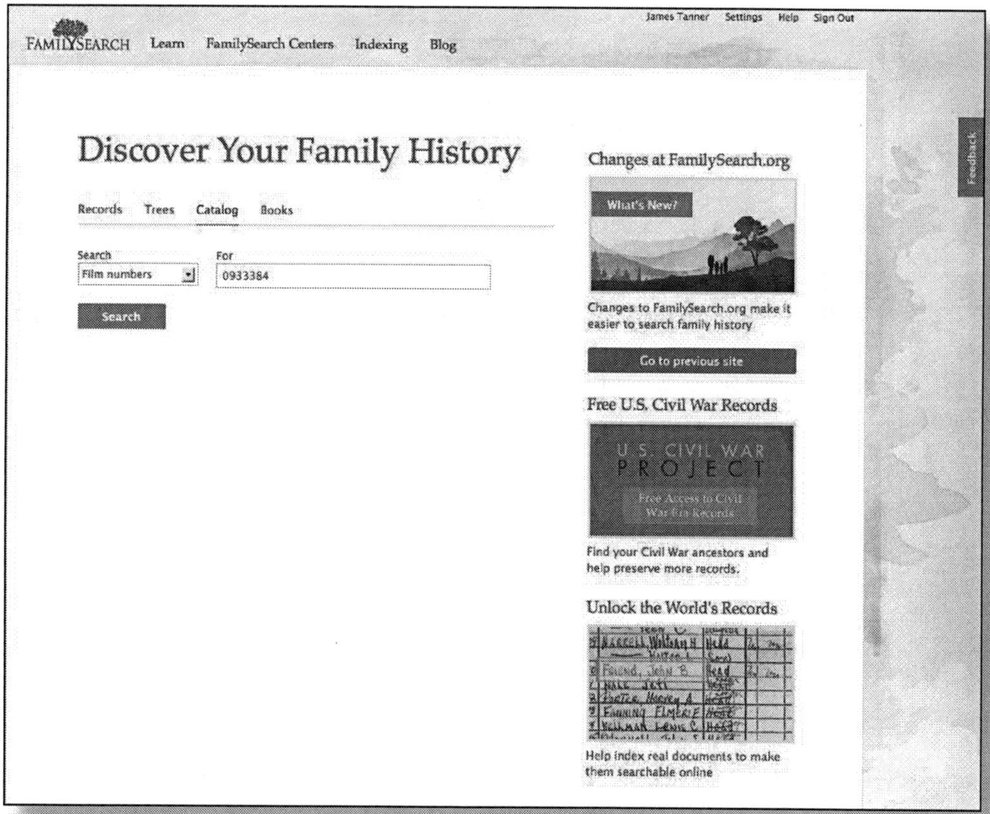

I chose to search by a Film number and put the number from the Source list into the search field. When I clicked on Search, I got the following listing.

Figure 3.20

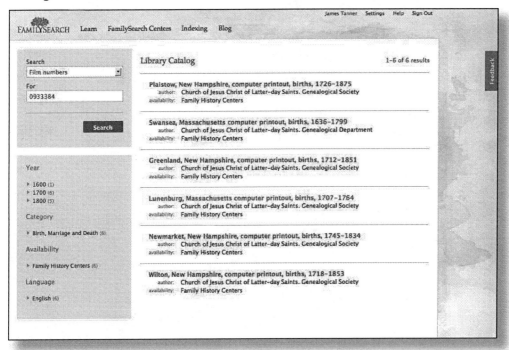

Comparing this information to the Source listing, I see that the particular record I am looking for is for Lunenburg, Massachusetts. Further, by clicking on the title of the record, I can get the screen showing all of the information about that particular record. Here is a screen shot of the information on the entire record:

Figure 3.21

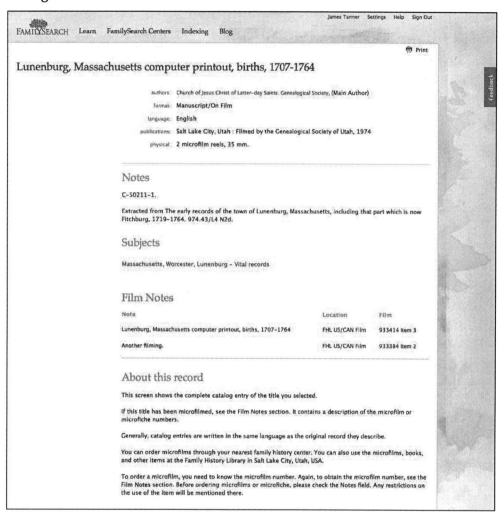

• • • • • • • • • •

A Note About Extracted Records

In order to provide names to do ordinances in the Temples, members of the Church have "extracted" names from some types of records. These names are sent to the Temples for use by patrons who do not have family names of their own to take to the Temple. Because the extracted records are a copy of the original and not the original, you should take the time to search for and look at the original record. In the case shown here, the microfilm is a copy of a computer print-out and not an original record. Records have been extracted from original sources all over the world, but the original sources are usually still available for research.

• • • • • • • • • •

If you examine this record, you will see that the information came from records that were extracted from the "The early records of the town of Lunenburg, Massachusetts, including that part which is now Fitchburg, 1719-1764." There is also a catalog subject classification number for the document from which the records were obtained. The number is 974.43/L4 N2d. I can now use that number to do another search in the Family History Library Catalog. Here are the results of that search:

Figure 3.22

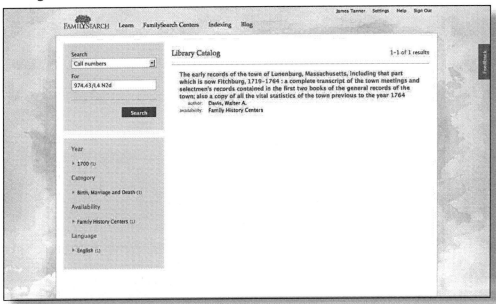

Clicking on the name of the document gives you the following screen:

Figure 3.23

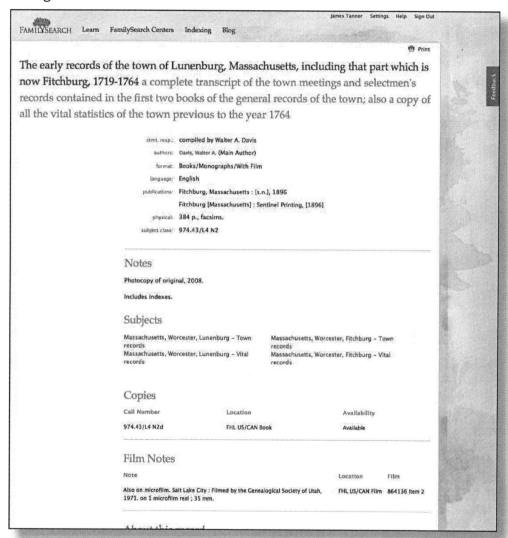

This source is also derivative. It is a transcript of the original records. It may be that the original records are no longer available and this is all the further you can go to find the originals. But if the original records are, by chance, still available, there will be at least one more step before you see the original documents. It is very important for you to go through this process so that you can see exactly what you are looking at and not take the information in NFS at face value. You might note that there is a microfilm copy of this particular book available should you wish to see it.

All this came from clicking on the entry in the Time Line. As you can see there are multiple layers of information about any of the entries in NFS.

Map

Now, I will move on to the Map. Here is a screen shot of William Stewart's Map. Even if you have a fast Internet connection, you will need some patience: NFS may be slowed by excessing use.

Figure 3.24

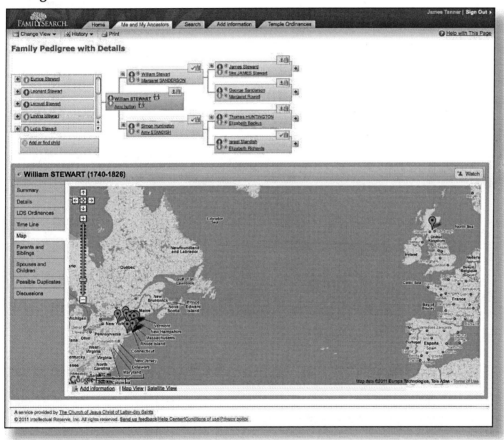

You can choose a Map view, a Satellite view or Add Information. I will talk about adding information a little later on in the Guide. The Map view plots the events listed in all of the screens for each individual. Clicking on any one of the markers will bring up a balloon box with the specific information about the event. You use the slider on the left side of the box to zoom in or out of the geographic area.

Parents and Siblings

The next selection is Parents and Siblings. Here is a screen showing the parents and siblings of William Stewart:

Figure 3.25

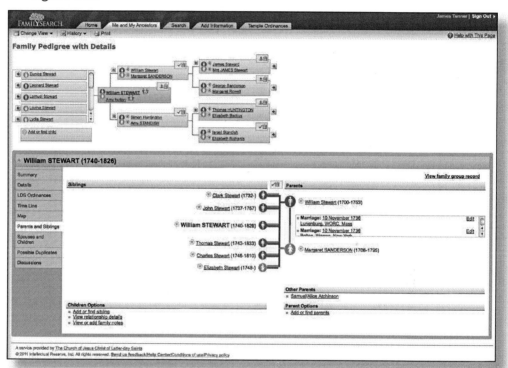

Next to each individual, there is a small down pointing arrow or triangle. These arrows open a drop-down menu of editing choices for each individual to either delete the individual (only possible if you are the contributor) or to combine the individual with another. At this point, I will take some time to explain combining individuals and then come back to the process when I get to the Possible Duplicates link.

Combining Individuals in NFS

As I mentioned earlier, NFS can have multiple copies of any individual or event. The process of combining individuals is compared to putting the various copies of the individual into one master folder. Each individual in NFS automatically receives a Person Identifier Number when added to the database. Combining individuals creates a new combined person number. You can see this from the Combined Records link from in the Detail and Summary Screens. Here is a screen shot showing the Combined Records for William Stewart:

Figure 3.26

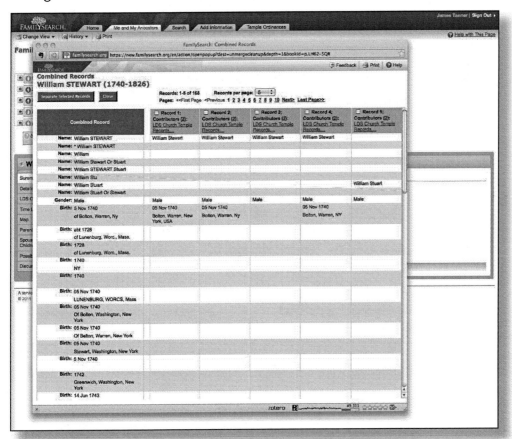

You can see from this screen shot that William Stewart has 168 combined records. If your ancestors are new to the FamilySearch system, you could possibly have no duplicates at all, but in some geographic areas, such as New England, duplicate entries are common. This screen shot is the top portion of the list for William Stewart, here is another shot showing some of the combined Person Identifier Numbers marked by arrows:

Figure 3.27

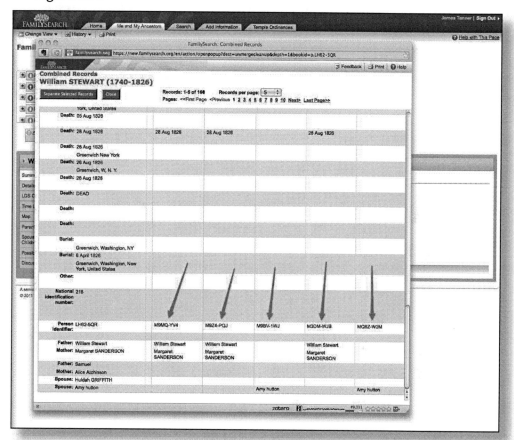

You will note that there is a Person Identifier listed in the left most column. This is the Person Identifier that shows on the program as the main number. The record for this individual then shows all of the combined information summarized from each of the individual entries. I will get into the mechanics of combining individuals below in the Possible Duplicates link. Now back to Parents and Siblings.

Look again at Figure 3.25. In between the parents shown for William Stewart, there is a scrollable menu listing all of the variations in marriage dates. In this case there are eight different dates. Below, there is also a listing for Other Parents. Any variations in parents for the target individual will also be listed. If any of the individuals listed as siblings or parents happen to be duplicated, you can use the drop-down menu from the little arrows or triangles by each person to combine the duplicates.

This screen also allows you to Add or find additional siblings, View relationship details and View or add family notes. Here are screens for each of those functions. First the Search for Deceased Ancestors screen:

Figure 3.28

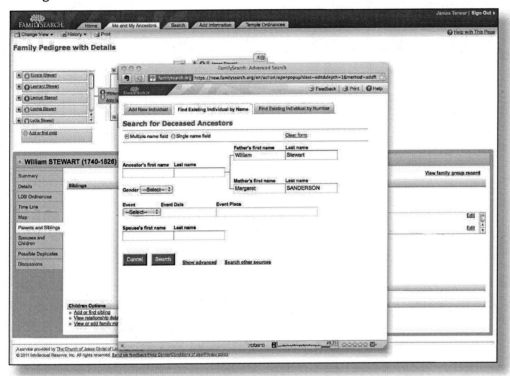

You can see from the tabs at the top of the screen, that this pop-up screen will also let you Add New Individual and Find Existing Individual by Number (meaning the Person Identifier Number). Here is the variation of the screen for adding a new individual:

Figure 3.29

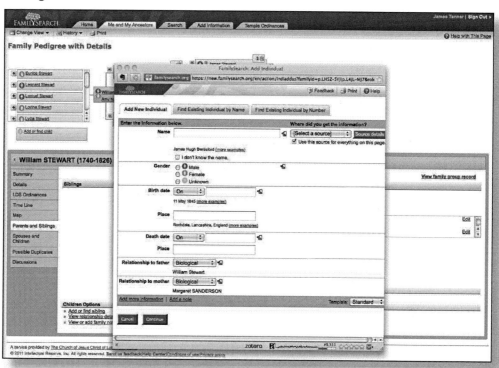

And here is the screen for Find Existing Individual by Number:

Figure 3.30

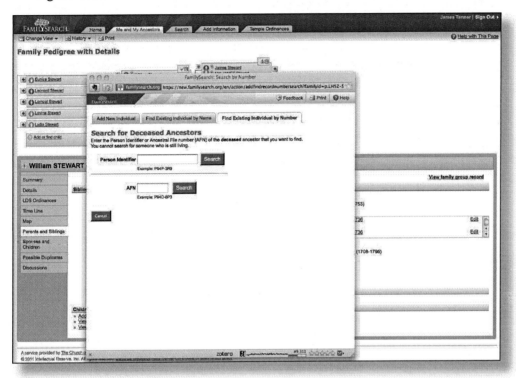

These three screens illustrate the basic functions of the NFS program; searching to see if the information is already in the database and then adding individuals and event information. You can see this repeated again and again throughout the program.

The next options in the Parents and Siblings screen are to View relationship details and to View or add family notes. Here is the screen from View Relationships:

Figure 3.31

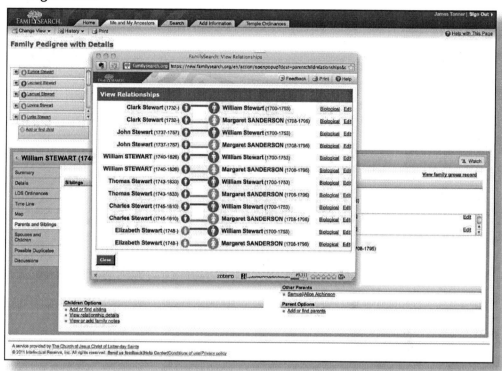

In this example, you can see that each child appears twice, once as a child of the father and again as a child of the mother.

The next screen shows the notes in the file for this individual and his or her spouse. In the case of the following example, there were more notes than would fit on one screen. I am not certain how helpful most of the existing notes are for this individual.

Figure 3.32

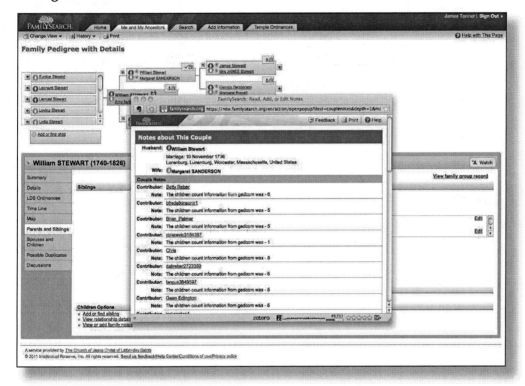

One advantage of the list is that there are a number of contributors listed who may have further information about this family.

Spouses and Children

Now, back to the Personal Information links. The next item on the list is Spouses and Children. Here is a screen shot for William Stewart:

Figure 3.33

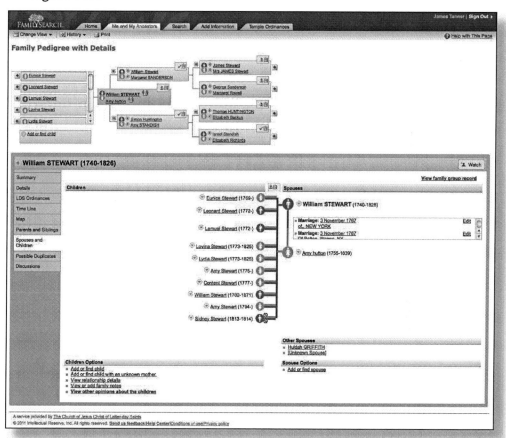

You can see additional information on this screen. There is a place to list other spouses. Clicking on the alternative spouse moves that individual to the primary position. You can add or find a spouse and there are similar options for the children. One additional screen lets you View other opinions about the children. Here is a screen shot of the top portion of that screen:

Figure 3.34

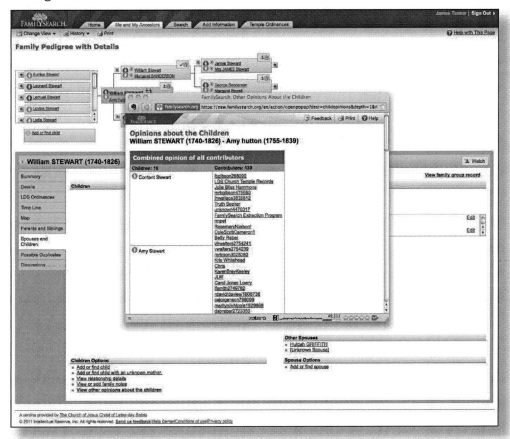

This option can give you an idea where the information in the main screen is coming from. It may also give you some insight about possible relatives working on the same lines.

Remember to use the online manual or Help Center for more information. If you look at each of the pages closely, you will see that there is always a "Help with This Page" link in the upper right corner. In addition, there is a link to the Help Center at the bottom of the page with copyright information. You can also ask questions in the New FamilySearch Forum at Forums.FamilySearch.org. If you need more detailed instructions on any of the functions or concepts of the program, enter the main words of you question into the search box in the Help Center.

Possible Duplicates

Possible Duplicates is the next link in the Personal Information list. Clicking on this link will automatically do a search for possible duplicates based on the information that is presently available in the Detail link.

* * * * * * * * * *

A Further Note About Duplicates and Combining Individuals

If you are new to genealogy and you know of no work that has been done to identify your family members, it is easy to assume that NFS will not have any information about your family. You should never make this assumption, no matter how sure you are that your information is unique. You may well have unique information, but it is also very likely that by going back a couple of generations that one of your distant cousins has already submitted information to the database. To be safe and sure and to avoid duplicates, you should always check for duplicates every time you add information to the program. If you find duplicate individuals then you can combine the duplicates and essentially, as I indicated previously, put the duplicates in the same virtual "folder" with one umbrella Person Identifier Number. For a very detailed account of the need and benefits of combining duplicate individuals, you can click on the link at the bottom of the Select the records screen that says "Overview: How Combining an Individual's Information Affects Your Family Line."

* * * * * * * * * *

 For more information on combining individuals please search in the Help Center. There are also detailed instructions about how to separate (uncombine?) individuals if they have been improperly combined.

Discussions

The last option in the Personal Information links is the Discussions link. Previously, NFS had a system whereby you could dispute what you felt was inaccurate or incorrect information. You could also dispute a person who was improperly combined such as a child who did not belong in a family. Some of these disputes are still evident in the program in the form of a circle with a diagonal line. You can see a disputed child in Figure 3.33. This system of allowing disputes was replaced with the Discussion link. All of the Disputes will eventually be removed and disputes will no longer be allowed. Clicking on the Discussion link allows you to enter a topic or title for your discussion and then enter the information you want to convey. On the right-hand side of the screen there is a button allowing you to "Watch" the information in the Discussion so that an email message will be sent to you automatically if anyone comments on your discussion topic or enters another topic.

The Search Function Tab

You can and should search for your ancestors before entering new information into NFS. The duplicate entries you may have noticed in the screens I have used for examples, indicates that not everyone who enters information into the program bothers to search before adding the information. The Search tab is prominently displayed before the Add Information tab in the menu bar. Here is the screen from clicking on the tab:

Figure 3.35

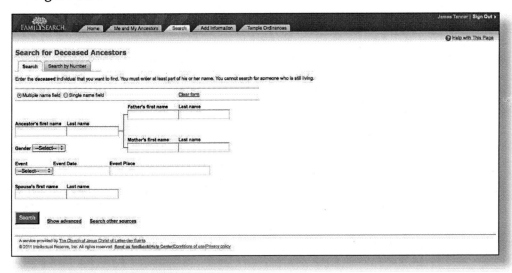

You can see, if you look closely, that you can search by name or by Person Identifier Number. Obviously, if you are entering information into the program for the first time you will not know any of the numbers. This option is more for navigation, to return to individuals you may have difficulty finding by moving level by level through the Pedigree view. Here is a view of the advanced search:

Figure 3.36

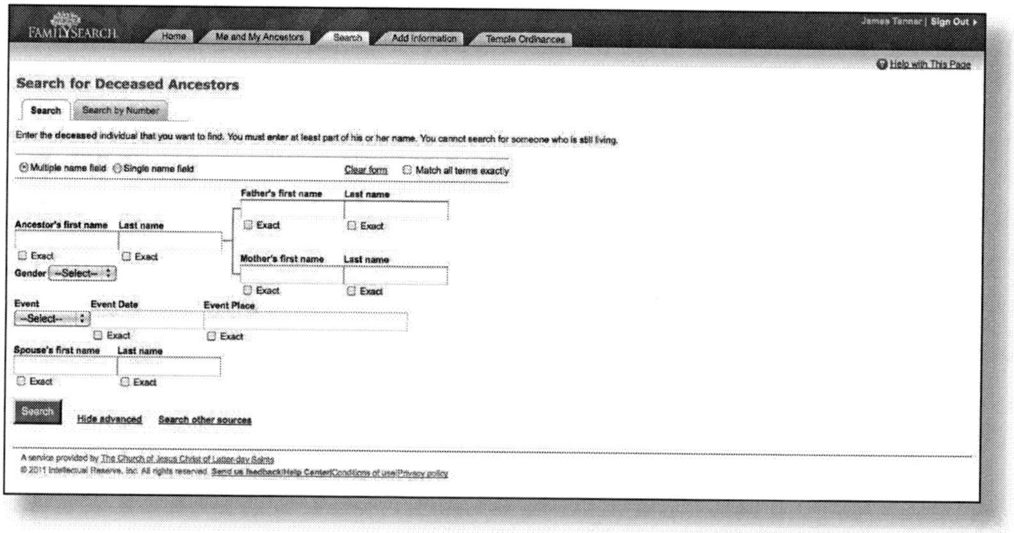

As you can see, the advanced search allows you to specify an exact entry in any of the fields. There is one more option on this screen, Search other sources. This link takes you to the old FamilySearch.org program for a search of the Ancestral File, Census, International Genealogical Index, Pedigree Resource File, U.S. Social Security Death Index and the Vital Records Index. If you find your individual in any of these resources, you can assume that the individuals was included in the NFS database and you should look further for duplicate information.

Add Information Tab

The Add Information tab gives you four options as shown in the following screen shot:

Figure 3.37

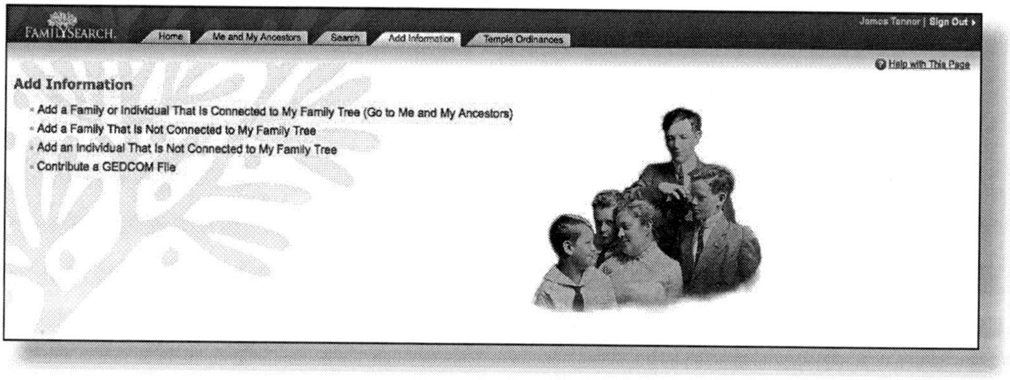

I have already shown the Add Family or Individual screen which is accessed from the Parents and Siblings or Spouses and Children screens. You have to go to the location on your pedigree where the new individual is going to be located in order to enter the information. If you try to add a family that is not connected to your family tree, you can do so, but you must first Add or find the husband, wife or child. Here is a screen showing the entry screen for adding a family not connected to your family tree:

Figure 3.38

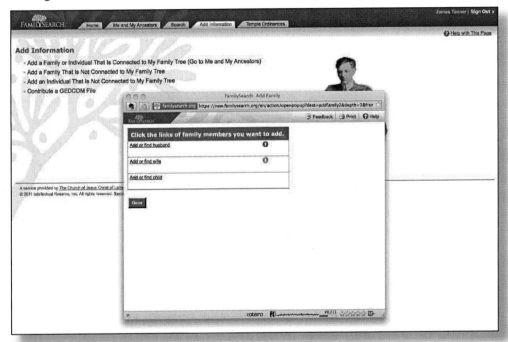

If you want to add one individual who is not connected to your family tree, you can select that option and you will get the following screen:

Figure 3.39

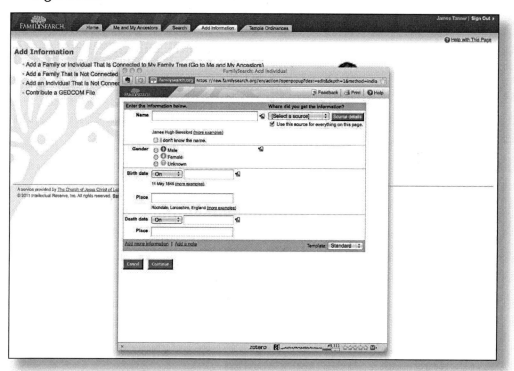

If you have any questions about how to add information, remember the extensive Help Center and Help Screens available as well as the Users Guides. If you look in the upper right-hand corner of each entry screen you will see another link to a help menu. I suggest clicking on the Help links just to get an idea of the types of questions you might ask about entering individual or family information into the database. In addition the Users Guides have specific instructions about adding names in different languages and cultures.

You can add more information by clicking on the Add more information link. Clicking the link brings up even more options for adding information;

Figure 3.40

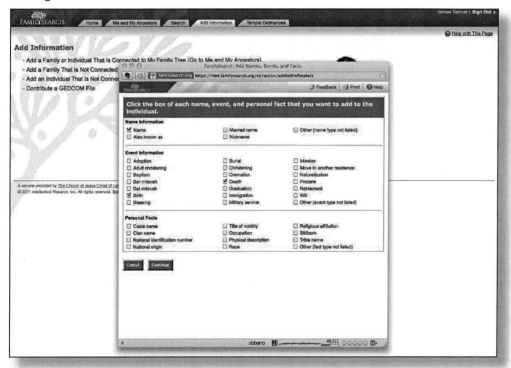

These options are available from all of the add information screens.

• • • • • • • • • •

A Note About All of the NFS Options

If you make it this far in the Guide, you probably have realized what I said at the onset, FamilySearch has a hugely complex set of websites. There are literally thousands of options and choices. You will probably never get around to using even a small percentage of the many features. As you get more experience using the programs, you will see that there is even more complexity than you originally appreciated. All of the links and sub-links in the Search and Add Information tabs are an example of the complexity of the programs. If you didn't notice, the links took you right back to the old version of FamilySearch.org. Incredibly, even the old program is still integrated into the NFS program. One thing you can count on, however, is that the program will change.

· · · · · · · · ·

The last option in the link list is to Contribute a GEDCOM file. Guess what? This is not a good idea although it is possible. If you click on the link, you will get a strongly worded warning screen as shown below:

Figure 3.41

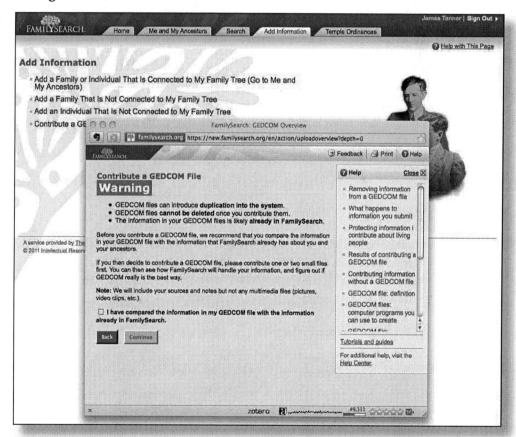

You can also see that the Help menu automatically appears with a lot of information about GEDCOM and contributing GEDCOM files. I suggest you read all of it before trying to submit information in this fashion. Simply put, do not go any further before following the instructions in the Warning and following my suggestion. Read ALL of the information about GEDCOM files, even if you think you are an expert.

Temple Ordinances

I have intentionally said very little about Temple Ordinances. For members of the Church, submitting names for Temple work is one of the main functions of the program. Those who are not members are not involved in this process. I debated long and hard about whether to include any information at all in this Guide about Temple ordinances, given the huge amount of information in the manual and Help Center. In the end I decided I would simply point the reader who needs that information to the resources available. All of that information is contained in the Help Center, online manual and other Church related materials. For those who are members and need help, they should talk to their local Family History Consultant or seek out a Family History Center. See Performing Temple Ordinances for Your Ancestors, Chapter 8 to A User's Guide to the New FamilySearch Website in the Help Center.

If you wish to qualify individuals for Temple work, I strongly suggest that you use a third-party database program rather than submitting names directly through NFS. This is especially true if you come from a family with ancestors in the Church. You can avoid a lot of frustration and duplication if you use one of those programs rather than trying to do your work directly in NFS. Using any one of those programs or others that may be designed to serve as an interface between your work and NFS will ultimately make your efforts a lot more productive and easier. Some of the programs have a free version which you can try in order to decide which one you like best. There are other options as well, such as an add-on program for Personal Ancestral File. All of these programs are available on the Internet for download and/or purchase. Remember to look in the list of Third Party developers listed on the sign-in page for the whole NFS program.

Working with Other Users of NFS

NFS offers a number of ways to collaborate with other members of your family working on the same ancestral lines. At the basic level, everyone who contributes to NFS is identified as a contributor. If you find information in the database that is new to you or if you want to work with someone who is interested in the same lines you are researching, you can click on the links to contributing individuals and try to make contact either through email or otherwise. Unfortunately, many of the contributors are missing either because of email or address changes or because the information was contributed from a source other than an identified individual. In the Detail screen, you can see a list of contributors for each event. Here is an example from the Detail screen for William Stewart showing part of the list of contributors. This screen comes up when you click on a name or the word "Multiple" in the column on the right.

Figure 3.42

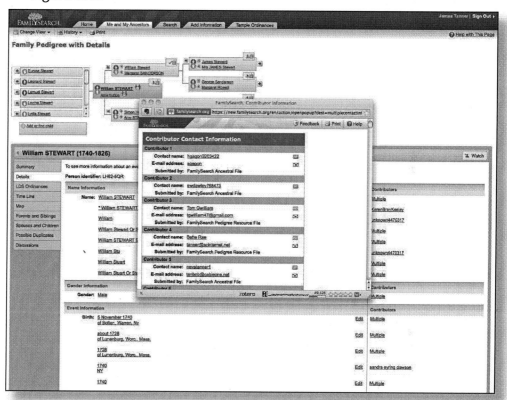

Each entry lists the Contact name, email address (if there is one) and Submitted by. As noted before, you may not see this much information in your own file depending on how many people have contributed. If you were to look at the small pedigree shown at the top of the screen (covered by the Contributor Contact Information) you would immediately see that the information cannot be correct. The names of the parents do not even match or come close to those of the children. The information that is shown in NFS is not a consensus of the Contributors, it is compilation with no editorial oversight at all.

Additional methods of finding relatives and collaborating can come through the Discussions link and by watching the pages.

* * * * * * * * * *

A Note on the Complexity of NFS

As a program, NFS is not particularly complex or difficult to under-stand. What is difficult is the data. Normally, if you were starting to use a new program, the program wouldn't already come loaded with not only your information but what everyone else in the world thought about your information. Most people who start out using NFS are surprised at the amount of information already in the program's database. They are also usually concerned about the accuracy of the information. As I have said before in this Guide and it is worth repeating, it is important to recognize that NFS is not presently designed to be a place to store your genealogical information. It is a tool for identifying, reserving and preparing ChurchTemple ordinances and a platform for collaboration between family members. It can incidentally be used to store genealogical information. If you and your family lines are new to genealogy, you will find the database adequate but no substitute for having your own infor-mation on your own computer and using a good genealogical database program. Future editions of the NFS program may include the ability to edit data, remove inaccurate data and other useful functions which will add to the utility of the program. Right now, it does its basic function, to prepare names for Temple ordinances, very well.

* * * * * * * * * *

Section Four Other FamilySearch Websites

FamilySearch is not limited to the sites I have already covered. There are many more online connections to their vast resources. Among those are some narrow technically oriented sites, social networking sites and online utilities for ordering microfilm.

FamilySearch.org on Facebook and Twitter

It was inevitable that FamilySearch would be integrated into the popular online social networking sites. Facebook, one of the largest websites online anywhere has several FamilySearch connections. Here are the links to some of the sites:

- http://www.facebook.com/familysearch
- http://www.facebook.com/pages/Family-Search/115402318514696
- http://www.facebook.com/familysearchwiki
- http://www.facebook.com/pages/Family-History-Library/169173515997
- http://www.facebook.com/familysearchindexing
- http://www.facebook.com/pages/FamilySearch-Indexing-Espa%C3%B1ol/113336168717255
- http://www.facebook.com/RootsTech

As stated by the FamilySearch Group on Facebook.com, FamilySearch is "a place to discuss all things related to FamilySearch with other users and patrons of FamilySearch as well as the people that make it work." I am not going to include any screen shots from Facebook, for the simple reason that they contain personal and copyrighted information. You will have to go to the sites yourself, if you have a Facebook account, and check out the information offered. Browsing through the posts shows that there is a lot of discussion about research and quite a few questions answered and asked.

Film.FamilySearch.org – Ordering Microfilm Online

FamilySearch's Microfilm Ordering service is your gateway to a vast collection of genealogical and historical records. The service allows you to reserve and loan films to family history centers and affiliates. The loan is free, but there is a small shipping and handling charge for each film ordered. The service is not yet available in all areas of the world, but FamilySearch is adding areas and you should check with the site to see if online ordering is available in your area. As of July, 2011, Online Film Ordering was in place in Australia, New Zealand, the British Isles, Ireland, Germany,

France, Portugal, Canada, parts of Utah and Idaho and other parts of the United States. During 2011, FamilySearch indicates that it will gradually be introduced throughout the United States.

Here is a screen shot of the startup page:

Figure 4.1

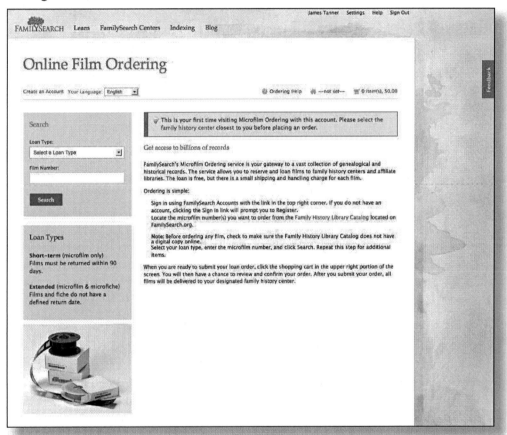

There are several prerequisites to ordering microfilm online. First, you need to understand that the film will be shipped to a Family History Center near your location, so you must select a Family History Center before placing an order. Also, you cannot receive the films at home: the films are shipped to the Family History Center you selected for viewing at the center. You also need to select a loan type: short term, long term or renewal. You must also provide a billing address and other contact information. If your geographic area is not served, then the ordering system will not find a Family History Center. There is a short downloadable User's Guide to Film Ordering.

Here is a screen shot of the first Film Ordering screen:

Figure 4.2

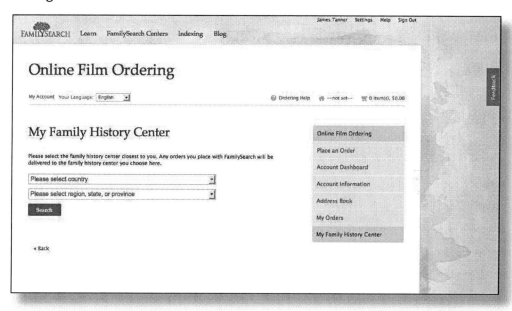

The Family History Center Portal

This website is not a page for general public consumption. Here is the address: http://www.fhc.familysearch.org/. This site is designed to act as a portal page for Family History Centers. There are links to specific resources for Center directors and personnel, but little for use by the general public. Here is a screen shot of the page which does not appear to be linked to any other part of the FamilySearch websites:

Figure 4.3

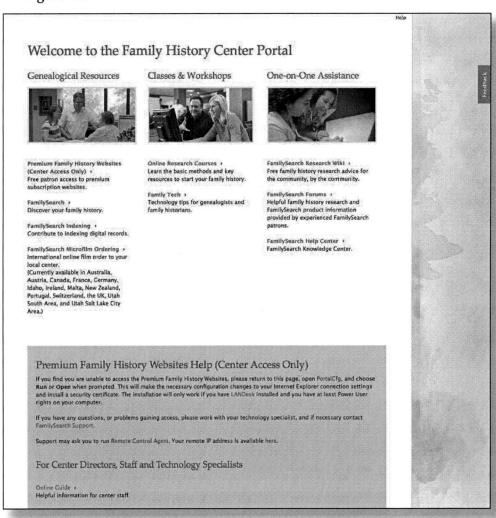

FamilySearch Developer Network

Devnet.FamilySearch.org is the FamilySearch Developer Network. It provides information and resources for software programmers who support the FamilySearch Platform. Although this is a public website, it is of very narrow interest and scope. It is designed to allow third party program developers a path to gain access to the FamilySearch codes necessary to function within the umbrella of Certified Programs. Registration is limited to software programmers and software companies only.

FamilySearch Consultants' Page

This page is for those who serve as Family History Consultants for the Church. There is a wide selection of training materials. At the time of the writing of this Guide, the page was not further integrated into the FamilySearch websites. The link to the page from FamilySearch.org is under the Training and Resources link from the Help Center. The present link is FamilySearch.org/serve. In addition to the training screen, there is also a screen for registering as a consultant to receive emails from FamilySearch. Here is a screen shot showing the expanded list of training materials available online:

Figure 4.4

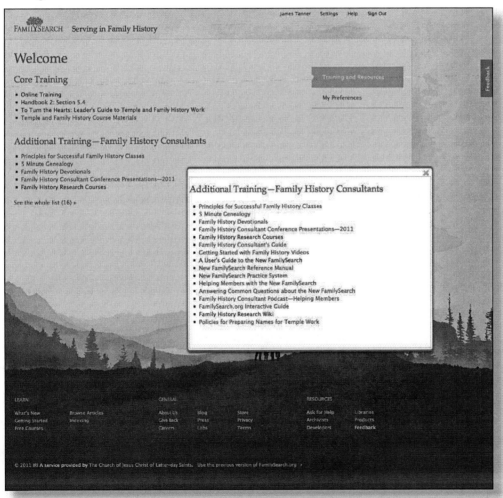

Some of the links go directly to the websites, such as the one for the Family-Search Research Wiki. Others go to training materials and other locations. Such as this link to Family History Consultant Devotionals:

Figure 4.5

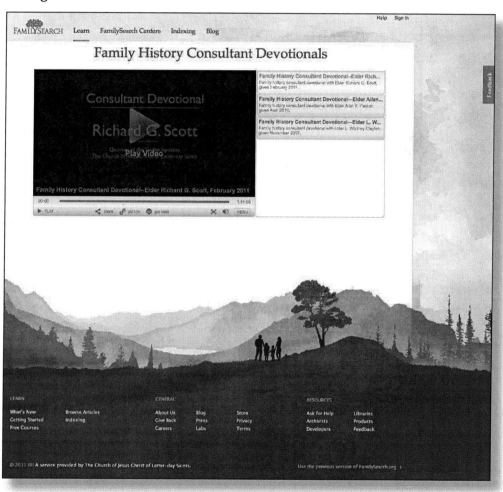

FamilySearch Remote Control Agent

Remote.FamilySearch.org is a closed website and available only to those in direct support positions at FamilySearch or through Family History Centers. There is not much on the startup page and I have omitted a screen shot.

Epilogue

Online, FamilySearch is a vibrant and growing community of websites. Each of those websites add a significant number of resources to the genealogical community. This book, like the websites I write about, is only a snapshot in time. The programs and websites from FamilySearch will continue to evolve and grow on a daily basis, especially now that millions of users around the world are contributing information. As I was writing this book, I kept hearing of changes coming to FamilySearch. As I mentioned earlier in the book, one significant change was the online addresses (URLs) of all of the sites. The old addresses look like this, for example,

http://wiki.familysearch.org

The new website addresses will look like this for the same website:

http://familysearch.org/learn/wiki

As FamilySearch phases in the new addresses, ultimately the older addresses will stop functioning. When will that happen? Estimates put the time frame in terms of years. What will be the effect? Everyone will, over time, change the links they have to FamilySearch websites to conform to the new standard URLs.

This is one small example of the way that a living, growing system of websites like FamilySearch continue to change. What will it be like in five years? Five years ago, I couldn't imagine any of the current features of the FamilySearch websites, I would guess the same thing will happen in the next five years. What will FamilySearch.org be like with over a million collections of records and hundreds of thousands of digitized books? Your guess is as good as mine. Stay tuned for change.

Glossary

Note: Although there may be other meanings of these terms in common usage, the definitions below are those used in the context of this Guide.

Access (noun actually a gerund): The state of having permission to use a file, a program or a database, as in, "He has access to New.FamilySearch.org."

Access (verb): The act of obtaining information from a file, a program or a database.

Ancestral File (AF): The Ancestral File contains user submitted lineage-linked names, dates and place names for the births, marriages, and deaths of millions of individuals. Access to the original file was through the old or classic Family-Search.org program. The information in the AF is now available both to the updated FamilySearch.org program and incorporated into New.Family-Search.org.

Ancestral File Number (AFN): An accession number assigned to individuals added to the Ancestral File. If an individual's information is downloaded from the file, then the AFN is embedded in the file information.

Application: A term used to refer to a computer program as in "running a word processing application."

Arbitration: A FamilySearch Indexing term for the process of reviewing entries made by the two separate indexers' entries to determine the most correct entry into the index.

Archive (noun): An organized repository for any kind of information. Usually, the term refers to places where documents are preserved for historical and genea-logical purposes.

Archive (verb): The process of protecting original documents from loss or destruction. In computer terms, making a backup copy that will not be used for daily access.

Article: A single topic or page in the FamilySearch Research Wiki program.

Backup (noun): An extra copy of a file or document stored in a location different from the original.

Backup (verb): The act of making an extra copy of a document or file as insurance against loss.

Batch: In FamilySearch Indexing, a group of related records separated for convenience in working with the indexing process and sent to the indexer at one time. In general, a group of related files.

Beta Test: A trial or review of a computer program by parties unrelated to the developer.

Beta: A designation of a computer program in the development stage before final release.

Browser: A program running on an individual computer designed to read web pages on the Internet.

Catalog: An organized listing of the contents of a library or database.

Classic FamilySearch.org: The original FamilySearch online program which is still available online.

Data (see Information): Information in a form suitable for use with a computer.

Database: A computerized and organized collection of data in a format that can be accessed by a computer program.

Digitized Images: A numeric representation of a real world object, document or scene that has been transformed into a set of instructions to a computer for visualization.

Disk: Usually a physical storage device. Historically, computer data was stored on external media such as floppy disks, however the current use of the term usually refers to hard disk drives or to other storage media such as CDs or DVDs.

Document (see also page and article): The word "document" has a contextual meaning depending on the program and the way data is stored. In genealogy, a document is usually an original source in some physical form. The word can be applied to a single page or entire book or ledger.

Download (verb): In computers, the act of obtaining a file from a remote source, i.e. the file is stored on the remote source and then downloaded to the local computer or hard drive.

Drive: In computers, a drive is a mechanism for storing data. Drives can be both physical and virtual. For example, an internal or external hard drive may be partitioned into two or more virtual "drives."

Electronic Database: Information stored in a specific type of program that can be accessed by a computer.

Extraction (noun): Records of individuals that have been copied from original sources without primary regard for relationships.

Extraction (verb): The act of copying individual records from original sources in bulk without primary regard to relationships.

Family Group Record: A physical or electronic form for entering genealogical information about a single family unit, usually patrilineal.

Family History Center (see FamilySearch Center)

Family History Library Catalog: An online catalog on FamilySearch.org to the more than 2.4 million microfilms in the Library's collection.

Family History (see genealogy): The activity of compiling historical information about families, usually related through lineage. The term is used to expand the concept of lineage searches to include historical information about the families being examined.

FamilySearch Center: A world-wide network of volunteers organized by FamilySearch and The Church of Jesus Christ of Latter-day Saints to provide resources and support for genealogical research.

FamilySearch: The tradename, trademark and corporate entity for genealogy sponsored by The Church of Jesus Christ of Latter-day Saints.

Feedback: An online resource for sending messages to FamilySearch to make suggestions or to ask questions.

Field: A designated place in a database for entering information. Usually a field will hold only one type of information although the length of the field may vary with the nature of the entry.

File (noun): A virtual representation of a document stored on a computer. For example, a word processing document when saved becomes a file in the computer's memory or on a storage device.

File (verb): To save information in a specific location i.e. file the document in a folder.

Filter (verb): A selection from a search menu that narrows the results in a specific way. For example, clicking on a filter for results before 1800 will limit the results list to only those records before 1800.

Filter (noun): In searching for records, a filter is a selection that allows you to limit the search to a specific topic or area.

Flash Drive: An electronic device that uses solid-state memory components and no moving parts, to store computer data and files.

Folder: A virtual storage location created by the computer's operating system. All current operating systems allow folders within folders for file organization purposes.

Format (noun): A method used by computer operating systems and file management systems to differentiate between files created by different programs. The format of a file is usually indicated by its file extension such as .ged for a GEDCOM file.

Format (verb): To prepare a storage medium for storage as in to format a hard drive. Formatting a disk will erase all of the information stored on the disk.

Forum: An online discussion group in which participants with common interests can exchange open messages. Forums are sometimes called newsgroups (in the Internet world) or conferences.

GEDCOM: An acronym for Genealogical Data Communication. A text based markup language developed by the Church to facilitate the transfer of data between genealogical lineage-linked database programs.

Genealogical Department: A division of The Church of Jesus Christ of Latter-day Saints that handles issues and programs dealing with genealogy.

Genealogical Society of Utah: Founded in 1894 this is an incorporated, nonprofit educational institution for the advancement of genealogy.

Genealogy (see also Family History): The activity of discovering one's ancestors through research.

Google: A popular search engine on the Internet.

Granite Vault: A huge storage facility in a tunnel carved into the rock of Little Cottonwood Canyon outside of Salt Lake City, Utah. It houses over 2.4 million rolls of microfilmed genealogical records.

Hard Disk: A mechanical/electronic device that uses a spinning disk of metal or other substances with a magnetic coating to record information from a computer. Hard disks may be either mounted inside the main box of the computer or in a separate box connected to the computer with a cable.

Help Center: The FamilySearch resource for answering questions about all of its products.

High-resolution: A relative term that indicates that visually the image or screen has a high enough count of image units such as pixel, to be easier to read.

Historical Archives Collection: A collection of digitized family history related books online through FamilySearch.org.

Historical Record Collections: An online database of documents that can be used to identify one's ancestors from scanned images of the vast library of microfilms in the Family History Library Catalog.

Home Page: The main page of a website to which the user can return to gain access to all other pages within the site.

HTML (Hypertext Markup Language): A form of programming that uses commands in text format to give instructions to a web browser program for displaying web pages.

Index (verb): In FamilySearch Indexing, the volunteers examine the original source documents scanned from microfilm and record certain chosen information to form an online index of the information in each batch.

Indexer: A person who participates in the FamilySearch Indexing program.

Indexing: Creating an online index for the FamilySearch Indexing program.

Information: Facts provided or learned about something or someone.

International Genealogical Index (IGI): A large database of names of individuals with information about birth dates, death dates and marriage dates either extracted from other source records or contributed from the Church's Temple records.

Internet: The Internet is a global system of interconnected computer networks that use the standard Internet Protocol Suite (TCP/IP) to serve billions of users worldwide.

Learn Link: The tab link on the startup page of FamilySearch.org that goes to the FamilySearch Research Wiki and other resources.

Lineage: A person's ancestry or pedigree usually spoken of collectively.

Link (noun): A connection between two parts of a website activated by clicking.

Link (verb): In genealogy, the act of finding a relationship between two or more individuals.

Little Cottonwood Canyon: The site of the Granite Mountain Vault located south and east of Salt Lake City, Utah.

Logo: A graphic symbol for a company or organization. In current Internet protocol, clicking on the site's logo takes you to the startup or home page.

Microfilm: A method of photographically preserving genealogical and historical source documents by taking a picture of each document or page. The photos are printed to a roll of file, either 16mm or usually, 35mm and read by special microfilm projector/readers.

Millennium: The thousand years of peace coming after the return of Jesus Christ in which the faithful hope to do a lot of genealogical work.

New FamilySearch: A huge online database of names and relationships which incorporates a number of previously compiled databases.

Ordinances: Special and sacred religious practices such as baptism.

Page (See article): In the FamilySearch Research Wiki, a separate article on a specific topic.

Pedigree Chart: A stylized representation of a person's ancestors showing parent/child relationships.

Pedigree Resource File (PRF): A large FamilySearch database of user submitted family trees, originally produced to allow users to backup their genealogy files online through uploading a GEDCOM file.

Periodicals: Any publication that comes out serially, i.e. weekly, monthly, bi-monthly etc.

Person Identifier Number: A unique accession number given to each individual added to the New FamilySearch database. Any individual may have several or more combined individual Person Identifier Numbers, however, only one number is used in the database to identify the individual.

Preferences: In computer programs, preferences are the individual choices the user can make to personalize the program's settings.

Preservation: Used in reference to documents and historical artifacts, preservation involves making copies of the original or otherwise preventing the object from being lost, damaged or deteriorating over time.

Program (noun): A set of instructions to a computer for a specific function and usually either sold or provided free as an entity, for example, Personal Ancestral File is a program.

Program (verb): The act of writing some kind of computer code.

Pull-down menu: A programming convention used frequently in websites to provide links to related functions or areas of the program through clicking on a single topic allowing a list to appear below the topic.

Record (noun) (see article and page): In genealogy, the term "record" has a variety of meanings and uses. The term is used to refer to an individual document or a whole collection of documents. It is also used to refer to historical narrations.

Record (verb): The act of making an entry or inserting information. Also, the act of preserving information in a specific format, such as recording an oral history.

Record Search Pilot: The predecessor program to the Historical Record Collections. When the FamilySearch.org website was updated, this particular collection was frozen and all of the records merged into the Historical Record Collections.

Repository: A location dedicated to preserving original historical and/or genealogical source records.

Research Courses: A selection of online courses compiled and made available through FamilySearch.org.

Research Wiki: A huge resource of genealogical reference material online through FamilySearch.org.

Results (see also Return): Used interchangeably with the term Return, this is the list of items produced when you do a search.

Return (see also Results): Used interchangeably with the term Results, this is the list of items produced when you do a search.

RootsTech: An annual genealogical conference held in Salt Lake City, Utah for technology providers and technology users in the area of genealogy.

Salt Lake City, Utah: The Capitol of the State of Utah and home to FamilySearch, the Family History Library, the Granite Mountain Vault and many other genealogical resources.

Salvation for the dead: 1 Corinthians 15:29: Else what shall they do which are baptized for the dead, if the dead rise not at all? Why are they then baptized for the dead? A basic doctrine of the Church concerning the efficacy of proxy baptisms and other ordinances.

Save: The act of preserving work done on a computer, i.e. saving a file after working on it.

Scanner: An electronic device for making digitized copies of physical documents and other objects.

Screen shot: A way of taking an image of a computer display monitor's screen at any given moment showing what is then on the screen.

Server: A computer used to administer a network.

Settings: Choices the user can make to personalize a computer program.

Spam: Unwanted and unsolicited postings to email or to a forum that contain offensive or commercial messages.

Startup Page: The first page encountered when entering a website. Sometimes referred to as the home page, however, the startup page may simply function as an entry into the site and not as a homepage.

Tab menu: A list of links to various functions of a program usually displayed as choices across the top of a computer screen.

TechTips: A specialized FamilySearch.org website to provide articles on technical subjects.

Temples: Special building sacred to the members of the Church where ordinances are performed for deceased relatives.

The Church of Jesus Christ of Latter-day Saints: The parent organization to Family-Search headquartered in Salt Lake City, Utah.

Trees: Usually refers to a collection of genealogical information about a related family unit, often, represented in a graphic fashion.

Universal Resource Locator (URL): The address of a website on the Internet, usually in the format of http://siteaddress.com.

Variable Links: Clickable links within a computer program or online website that change depending on previous choices.

Vital Records: Usually birth, marriage and death records.

Vital Records Index (VRI): Previously, in the classic FamilySearch.org website, this was an index to records from Mexico and Scandinavia only.

Waypoint: Distinctive features or events in a program or database that enable the user to find additional information.

Wiki: wiki is a type of website that allows the easy creation and editing of any number of interlinked web pages via a web browser using a simplified markup language or a WYSIWYG text editor.

World Wide Web (WWW): A system of Internet servers that support documents written in HTML usually viewed by means of program called a web browser.

WYSIWYG: Pronounced wizzywig, literally "What you see is what you get." A visual graphic interface for computer programs.

Zion: An idealized concept of a location where the Saints of God can have refuge.

Footnotes

1 Genealogical Society of Utah, minutes, Nov. 13, 1894, Genealogical Department of the Church.

2 "Genealogy's Place in the Plan Salvation," Utah Genealogical and Historical Quarterly, January 1912, pp. 21-22. Quoted in Lloyd, R. Scott, *A century of progress in family history work*, Church News, The Church of Jesus Christ of Latter-day Saints, June 26, 1999. https://new.familysearch.org/help/viewdocument?documentId=109104&sliceId=SAL_Member&userQuery=releases+new.familysearch.org. Accessed 19 April 2011.

3 Lloyd, R. Scott, *'Historic step' as Web site promises great boon to family history research*, Church News, The Church of Jesus Christ of Latter-day Saints, Saturday, May 29, 1999. https://new.familysearch.org/help/viewdocument?documentId=109104&sliceId=SAL_Member&userQuery=releases+new.familysearch.org. Accessed 19 April 2011.

4 *Wide publicity given to new family history Web site*, Church News, The Church of Jesus Christ of Latter-day Saints, Saturday, June 5, 1999. https://new.familysearch.org/help/viewdocument?documentId=109104&sliceId=SAL_Member&userQuery=releases+new.familysearch.org. Accessed 19 April 2011.

5 http://www.quantcast.com/familysearch.org viewed on 28 February 2011.

6 Information for this section was obtained, in part, from James B. Allen, et. al., *Hearts Turned to the Father*, a special issue of *BYU Studies* 34:2 (1994-95), pp. 303-337.

7 Lloyd, R. Scott, *A century of progress in family history work*, Church News, The Church of Jesus Christ of Latter-day Saints, June 26, 1999. https://new.familysearch.org/help/viewdocument?documentId=109104&sliceId=SAL_Member&userQuery=releases+new.familysearch.org. Accessed 19 April 2011.

8 https://wiki.familysearch.org/en/Powerful_Tips_and_Tricks_for_Searching_Historical_Documents_in_FamilySearch accessed 25 February 2011.

9 https://wiki.familysearch.org/en/Digitizing_the_Records_in_the_Granite_Mountain#Brief_Timeline_of_the_Granite_Mountain_Records_Vault accessed 25 February 2011.

10 https://wiki.familysearch.org/en/Digitizing_the_Records_in_the_Granite_Mountain#Brief_Timeline_of_the_Granite_Mountain_Records_Vault accessed on 25 February 2011.

11 See https://wiki.familysearch.org/en/Family_History_Library_Catalog_Place_Search. Accessed on 6 March 2011.

12 https://help.familysearch.org/help/viewdocument?documentId=tfsiviewingfamilysearchstatushtml&sliceId=&userQuery=premier+membership Accessed on 11 March 2011.

13 http://www.gensocietyofutah.org/ accessed 15 March 2011.

14 http://www.trademarkia.com/company-intellectual-reserve-inc-613675-page-1-2 . Accessed on 15 March 2011.

[15] http://en.wikipedia.org/wiki/Wiki. Accessed on 17 March 2011.

[16] http://en.wikipedia.org/wiki/Wikipedia. Accessed on 17 March 2011.

[17] http://www.alexa.com/ Accessed on 17 March 2011.

[18] http://www.hpl.hp.com/research/idl/papers/wikipedia/index.html. Accessed 19 April 2011.

[19] http://www.mediawiki.org/wiki/Manual:Namespace. Accessed 28 March 2011.

[20] https://wiki.familysearch.org/en/FamilySearch_Wiki:Guiding_Principles#Neutral_Point_of_View. Accessed 18 March 2011.

[21] http://en.wikipedia.org/wiki/Creative_Commons. Accessed 18 March 2011.

[22] http://creativecommons.org/licenses/by-sa/3.0/us/. Accessed 18 March 2011.

[23] http://creativecommons.org/licenses/by-sa/3.0/us/. Accessed 18 March 2011.

[24] http://en.wikipedia.org/wiki/Wiki_markup. Accessed 21 March 2011.

[25] http://en.wikipedia.org/wiki/Markup_language. Accessed 21 March 2011

[26] http://en.wikipedia.org/wiki/Web_conferencing. Accessed on 23 March 2011.

[27] https://wiki.familysearch.org/en/FamilySearch_Wiki:Policies. Accessed 28 March 2011.

[28] http://www.webopedia.com/DidYouKnow/Internet/2008/forum_etiquette.asp. Accessed 30 March 2011.

[29] http://en.wikipedia.org/wiki/ISO_3166-2:US. Accessed 7 April 2011

[30] *Tracing LDS Families*, Research Outline, FamilySearch Research Guidance, June 9, 2001, http://www.familysearch.org/eng/search/rg/guide/LDSRec20.asp. Accessed 19 April 2011.

[31] *Tracing LDS Families*, Research Outline, FamilySearch Research Guidance, June 9, 2001, http://www.familysearch.org/eng/search/rg/guide/LDSRec20.asp. Accessed 19 April 2011

[32] Lloyd, R. Scott, *A century of progress in family history work*, Church News, The Church of Jesus Christ of Latter-day Saints, June 26, 1999. https://new.familysearch.org/help/viewdocument?documentId=109104&sliceId=SAL_Member&userQuery=releases+new.familysearch.org. Accessed 19 April 2011.

[33] http://ancestryinsider.blogspot.com/2009_11_01_archive.html. Accessed 19 April 2011.

[34] FamilySearch Help Center Document ID: 102884

[35] http://en.wikipedia.org/wiki/Internet accessed on 28 February 2011

[36] http://en.wikipedia.org/wiki/Wiki accessed on 10 March 2011

Index